Children of Hollywood

ALSO BY MICHELLE VOGEL

Gene Tierney: A Biography
(McFarland, 2005)

Majorie Main:
The Life and Films of Hollywood's "Ma Kettle"
(McFarland, 2005)

Children of Hollywood

Accounts of Growing Up as the Sons and Daughters of Stars

MICHELLE VOGEL

McFarland & Company, Inc., Publishers
Jefferson, North Carolina, and London

On the cover: *Background* ©2005 Photospin. *Clockwise from top:* Tyrone Power with daughters Romina and Taryn; Chris Costello on the back of her father Lou, with Bud Abbott *(courtesy Chris Costello)*; Damon Lanza in the arms of his father Mario *(courtesy Damon Lanza and Bob Dolfi)*; Joan Benny with her dad Jack *(courtesy Joan Benny)*

LIBRARY OF CONGRESS CATALOGUING-IN-PUBLICATION DATA

Vogel, Michelle, 1972–
    Children of Hollywood : accounts of growing up as the sons and daughters of stars / Michelle Vogel.
      p.   cm.
    Includes bibliographical references and index.

    ISBN-13: 0-7864-2046-9
    (softcover : 50# alkaline paper) ∞

    1. Motion picture actors and actresses—United States—Family relationships. 2. Children of motion picture actors and actresses—United States—Biography. I. Title.
PN1998.2.V6   2005
791.4302'8'092273—dc22   2005004749

British Library cataloguing data are available

©2005 Michelle Vogel. All rights reserved

No part of this book may be reproduced or transmitted in any form or by any means, electronic or mechanical, including photocopying or recording, or by any information storage and retrieval system, without permission in writing from the publisher.

Manufactured in the United States of America

McFarland & Company, Inc., Publishers
  Box 611, Jefferson, North Carolina 28640
    www.mcfarlandpub.com

For the perfect parents ... mine

Acknowledgments

I'd like to thank the following people for their help and support in putting this book together. In no particular order of importance, special thanks go to:

Bob Dolfi; Raphael Tennenbaum; C3 Entertainment; the Harold Lloyd Trust; Robert Bader; the Law Offices of Lawrence Turner; Bruce Lawton and Sheryl Stinchcum; Stefan Timphus; Laura Leff; Lou and Mary Jo Mari; Elizabeth Nocera; Kathy Anderson; Ron Palumbo; John Larrabee; Ted Wioncek; Michelle Malik; and the rest of those wonderful fan sites on the Internet that continue to promote the memory of those long forgotten stars of yesteryear.

The late Samuel Perkins for his candid snapshots of Arthur and Groucho Marx.

My family and friends—too many to mention, but you know who you are.

My husband, Matt, for your ability to make me laugh and see what's good, even when things are bad!

Last but not least, a big thank you to "the children of Hollywood," literally: Arthur Marx; Bill Marx; Maxine Marx; Joan Benny; Gary Lewis; Damon Lanza; Romina Power; Janet Cantor Gari; Brian Gari; Peter Ford; Douglas Fairbanks, Jr.; Harry Langdon, Jr.; Leatrice Gilbert Fountain; Chris Costello; Vickie Abbott Wheeler; Ron Fields; Gary Crosby (dec); Sara Karloff; Suzanne Lloyd; Eric Lamond; and John Longenecker.

TABLE OF CONTENTS

Acknowledgments   vii
Preface   1
Introduction   5

1 ★ Arthur Marx   23
2 ★ Billy, Alex, Jimmy and Minnie Marx   37
3 ★ Maxine Marx   44
4 ★ Joan Benny   50
5 ★ Gary Lewis   60
6 ★ Damon Lanza   65
7 ★ Romina Power   71
8 ★ Janet Cantor Gari and Brian Gari   78
9 ★ Peter Ford   88
10 ★ Sir Douglas Fairbanks, Jr.   99
11 ★ Harry Langdon, Jr.   108
12 ★ Leatrice Gilbert Fountain   115
13 ★ Chris Costello and Vickie Abbott Wheeler   131
14 ★ Ron Fields   148
15 ★ Gary Crosby   157

16 ★ Sara Karloff		172
17 ★ Suzanne Lloyd		178
18 ★ Eric Lamond		185
19 ★ John Longenecker		194
Motherhood Missed		206
Bibliography		213
Index		215

PREFACE

We've heard the phrase many times before, "poor little rich kids." Over the years we've all seen and read countless "tell all" books written by the children of famous celebrities. Some of it is truth, some of it is fiction, and most of it is to gain some much-needed cash after being left out of the family will.

Mommie Dearest, written by Christina Crawford, adopted daughter of Joan Crawford, would still be the most widely known "tell all" ever to be released by the child of a celebrity. No other book has come close to revealing such horrific accounts of child abuse at the hands of a celebrity parent. Was it true? Who knows! It was written *after* the death of Joan Crawford, so it is just one side to a very complex family story that will never be challenged. True or false, whatever the case may be, Christina Crawford got the last word. She won the battle.

The so-called "children of Hollywood" are the second generation—the children of those actors that we the public have put on such high pedestals that they seem almost larger than life. As in any family environment, the children are the innocent souls, looking to the adults of the house to love them, guide them and shape them into well-adjusted adults. Hollywood's children were no different, but the one thing that separated them from the "normality" of the general public's concept of family life was that they were the children of someone famous. They had a famous mother or a famous father or, in several instances, they were the product of a family environment where both parents were actors. As most of them say in their own stories, they knew no other way of life. Didn't every kid have this much fun all the time?

The lavish birthday parties, the celebrity friends, the expensive presents and the constant barrage of "star treatment" was normal for

Preface

them. Not until they grew up did they find out that not every little thing would be handed to them on a silver tray. These are the personal stories of the children of Hollywood—their (until now) well-guarded childhood memories, struggles and triumphs of growing up in the shadow of a famous parent, all of it told in their own words.

For every one story that is told in this book, there is at least another ten that were not. I've had many wonderful experiences over the course of my research and I've met and befriended some very special people who will continue to be in my life beyond this book. Still, there has been a dark side and I'd be lying if I didn't admit to that. I've also had many rejections, no response to multiple requests to participate, and abuse about writing the book in the first place. There were also the few who would share their stories happily if only I paid them a few thousand dollars to do so! All of the people involved in this book have offered me their stories, their time and their personal memories without wanting a single penny, only the chance to tell their story their way.

They've also allowed me to take a peek into their family albums and choose a snapshot that best represents them in two different phases of life—past and present. Each photo tells a story, and most of the photos chosen have never been seen before now. Keeping the memories of their parents alive through the publication of this book was enough of a reward for these Hollywood children and for that I am forever grateful. With that said, there are stories in these pages that were emotionally hard to tell. Their childhoods certainly were not all cotton candy, cute ponies and birthday clowns. There's more personal tragedy here than can be found in most Hollywood scripts.

Many of these children (although they're not so little anymore) lost a parent far too young. Some even lost both parents within months of each other. If it wasn't death that took their parents, it was divorce that split them apart. Not all stories are tragic; many are heartwarming and some are a combination of the two. All in all, this is a fascinating account of the lives of the children of Hollywood. More importantly, it's the truth!

In a slight twist on the original idea of getting the stories of the children of the stars, in a few instances I have the stories of the grandchildren. The grandsons of W. C. Fields and Eddie Cantor talk about their famous grandfathers as does Suzanne Lloyd, the granddaughter of silent comic Harold Lloyd. The grandson of Larry Fine, Eric Lamond, shares his memories of growing up in the zany world of *The Three Stooges*.

I simply can't end here without telling a mysterious family story that I uncovered along the way in researching this book. The Barrymores are considered Hollywood royalty. For generations they've all entertained us on stage and screen, and even today Drew Barrymore carries on the family name in the family business. However, the famous three in the golden era of Hollywood were, of course, siblings Ethel, John and Lionel.

Here's the mystery: Lionel Barrymore was married to Doris Rankin, a vaudeville entertainer and sometimes actress. There are conflicting stories about the exact happenings, but it is said that Lionel Barrymore and Doris Rankin had their first child, a daughter, in 1905. They named her Mary. In 1909, Ethel was born, a namesake of her famous actress aunt, Ethel Barrymore. Tragically, baby Ethel died in infancy in 1910. There was a third child born in 1916, also named Mary, but she too died in infancy in 1917.

What happened to the first Mary is not known, but it is said she was not mentioned by either Lionel or Doris after the age of eight years! Did she also die? In those days it was not uncommon to give a child the same name as a child who had predeceased it. If the first Mary was born in 1905 and then was not mentioned ever again after the age of eight, it would make her death date around 1913—*if* she did indeed die. The second Mary was born three years later, in 1916. Now, here's the question: Would a family name two of their children the same name if both children are still living? The answer: No!

Ethel Barrymore admitted in her autobiography to physically seeing baby Ethel in 1909, so it's certain that Ethel did exist. However, Lionel Barrymore refused to admit he ever had children and Doris Rankin refused to ever speak about her ex-husband or any children that she may have had with him. It was as though these children never existed, yet there is proof that they did. At least there is proof that Ethel existed because her aunt saw her with her own eyes.

Three daughters, two dying in infancy and one not talked about past the age of eight? It's a Hollywood mystery almost a century old. The truth about the fate of these three Hollywood children has been taken to the grave. No one will ever know. It's unfortunate that so many questions are often asked when it's too late to find out the answers

Preface

from the people who could tell it, thus solving the mystery once and for all.

Again, to all the people involved in this book: Thank you for answering the questions, telling the truth and for not leaving behind anything to wonder about once it's too late to ask.

Introduction

Many children of Hollywood stars followed in their famous parents' footsteps. Some succeeded and some outshone their parents, but most of them never lived up to the standard expected of them by their parents or the public. Comparisons are made, standards are expected and, more often than not, everyone is disappointed. Some children of Hollywood stars were so disappointed in their own lack of success that they saw no way out of their horrible feelings of failure and ended their own lives. There are others, of course, who succeeded both in the movie industry and in other varied careers.

This introduction reveals the memories and thoughts of several other children of Hollywood stars who don't have their own chapter in the coming pages of this book. Also included here are several excerpts and interesting stories told by the more successful second-generation actors of today. Still, even the successful few who maintain their famous family names have carried their fair share of burdens. These are their stories.

After choosing a number of horror roles that enabled her to make full use of her lungs, Jamie Lee Curtis was only twenty when she was labeled Hollywood's, "Scream Queen." Such movies as *The Fog, Prom Night, Terror Train*, and, of course, *Halloween* made her the number one victim of B horror films of the 1970s and 1980s. Of course, she has the acting gene, if there is such a thing, in her blood. With her father being none other than Tony Curtis and her mother being Janet Leigh, what other career could she choose? One might label Janet Leigh as the original "Queen of Scream." That title came to her after just one horror film, *Psycho*!

Playing the victim to Anthony Perkins' psychotic character Norman Bates in the now infamous shower scene in Alfred Hitchcock's

Introduction

George Burns, Gracie Allen and son, Ronnie Burns, are all smiles.

Psycho, Janet Leigh made her mark on the film industry forever. Hitchcock knew the impact the shower scene would have on audiences, and he wanted to get it right. There were no fewer than seventy camera setups over a seven day period. With so much footage shot, it's hard to believe the final edit came in at just under a minute of screen time.

The result? In one forty-five second scene, Janet Leigh became a cinema icon. Some forty-plus years after the making of *Psycho*, the scene still holds up and it's still shocking. Janet's eldest daughter, Kelly, has never seen the shower scene. She's watched *Psycho* many times but always leaves the room the moment she sees her mother's character step into the shower. As an adult, she certainly knows the difference between make believe and real life. It's just too shocking a scene for a daughter to watch and she can't bring herself to witness her mother being mutilated. For Kelly Curtis, it's a little too close to home, a little too realistic. It proves that Hitchcock did his job well.

Introduction

An interesting fact about *Psycho* is that Hitchcock, once again at his brilliant best, needed something to emulate blood in the shower scene. Because the movie was to be released in black and white, it didn't matter what he used; it could be any product and any color. As long as it resembled the consistency of blood, it would work. He searched for weeks to find something that looked to be the same consistency as blood and eventually he found it in his own refrigerator—chocolate syrup. That's right, chocolate syrup was used as Janet Leigh's spilled blood! Even after knowing that behind-the-scenes secret, that shower scene never gets any easier to watch.

It was only fitting for Jamie Lee Curtis to follow in her mother's footsteps. Being the progeny of not one but two star parents, it couldn't have been easy. In *Hollywood Dynasties* by Stephen Farber and Marc Green, she recalls some of her childhood moments. "No matter what we did," Jamie Lee says, "there would always be someone saying, 'Stop, Janet, let's take a picture of you and your two beautiful daughters.' Nothing was normal as we know it." Jamie explains further, "We did Disneyland with a VIP tour. When we went skiing, we always had a private instructor to get us to the front of the line so we wouldn't get mobbed. To this day I have a terrible fear of crowds. I can't go to a rock 'n roll concert because I just freak out."

Michael Douglas, actor son of Kirk Douglas, is now accustomed to the same treatment by adoring fans that his father used to receive when Michael was a child. Now he understands it. Back when he was a child, however, it wasn't so easy. In *Hollywood Dynasties* he explains why. "What is hard," he says, "is to try to understand the amount of public loving and praise that a personality gets and measure that against some of the deprivation that you feel."

It's interesting to note that most of the memories in this book come from big annual events such as Christmas and birthday parties. I'm not at all surprised about those memories being strong in the minds of these children of Hollywood stars. Each event was a spectacle; the massive grounds surrounding the Hollywood mansions were more often than not turned into a mini–Disneyland for these parties. The only problem was that the children were never dressed to enjoy it. The girls would have perfectly curled hair and wear the latest designer dress, starched to perfection. The boys would be dressed in sailor suits with slicked-down hair parted to one side, and all would be guided to each

Introduction

The Douglas Dynasty—Kirk Douglas poses with his equally famous son, Michael Douglas.

Introduction

activity and photographed for the latest fan magazine. If the star parents of other Hollywood children happened to stick around for the party, the photographers would have a field day. It was not your typical birthday party. For that reason and that reason alone, it is no wonder those memories are still with them, even after all these years.

In his book *I Couldn't Smoke the Grass on My Father's Lawn*, Michael Chaplin, one of the many children of Charlie Chaplin, remembers back to those lavish Beverly Hills birthday parties and gives a first-hand account of what they were *really* like. "Those typical Beverly Hills children's birthday parties with chauffeurs and nannies bringing a slew of rich young neighborhood kids carrying flashily wrapped presents for the lucky celebrant were commonplace. There'd be kids' games, and inevitably some brat would fall down and cut a knee or tear a dress and be carried of to its limousine bawling its lungs out."

Some movie star parents protected their children from the limelight while others used them as publicity props, constantly posing for publicity photos that projected an all–American wholesome image. In the case of Judy Garland and her daughter Liza

Judy Garland on the set with her very young, but still very recognizable daughter, Liza Minnelli.

Introduction

A happy family shot of Judy Garland with her children. From left, Joey, Lorna and Liza.

Minnelli, as Liza began to blossom into a performer in her own right, Judy no longer looked upon her as a proud mother should. Liza was now a rival, and in the same industry at that. Judy Garland would often bring Liza, along with her other children Lorna and Joey, onto the stage after one of her performances. They were all thrust into the spotlight at a very early age. Judy's own mother, Ethel Gumm, was the textbook "Hollywood mother" pushing her daughter to excel, to lose weight, to look pretty—all at a cost. Ethel put all three of her daughters on the vaudeville circuit and eventually it was Judy who made it big. Ethel had succeeded in making at least one of her daughters a star but eventually that mother-daughter relationship crumbled. A lot of

Introduction

resentment and bitterness on Judy's side saw Ethel die alone. She had not spoken to the daughter she made famous in years.

Strangely, Judy played out the same "Hollywood mother" scenario with Liza. The only problem was that Liza was soon overshadowing her mother, and envy and jealousy overtook the motherly pride that Judy should have naturally felt for Liza's success. She even went as far as dismissing Liza's talent to the media and would often express that her other daughter, Lorna, was a far more gifted performer.

Usually by age ten, and sometimes younger, the children would be shipped off to boarding school, only coming back to the family home on summer vacations. In his book *Don't Tell Dad: A Memoir,* Peter Fonda sarcastically commented about his time in boarding school, "What kind of parents would send a kid away at six to make his own bed?!" Peter Fonda is perhaps the most honest of the star children. Speaking candidly about the way a family like the Fondas, who by all accounts are often referred to as "Hollywood royalty," can be affected by media lies and innuendoes, his anger at the lack of control he has over what is written about his family is apparent.

As previously mentioned, Fonda's explosive book, *Don't Tell Dad: A Memoir,* included comments such as, "So many people have written about the Fondas. So many crass writers have made a lot of money 'detailing' the 'history' of my life and the lives of my sister [Jane], father [Henry], mother, and daughter [Bridget]. These plagiarists and poachers have been trivializing our lives, but the Supreme Court and I will in turn count on the First Amendment to give me full rights in exposing these minor assholes for the yellow journalists that they are. But their versions of our history remain out there in the public conscience as 'truth' and there is very little I can do to defend us."

It's a given that the general public are fascinated with movie stars, but Arthur Marx, son of Groucho Marx, was shocked when his friend Dean Jr., Dean Martin's son, asked him a question that he didn't expect to hear, at least not from him. In his book *Son of Groucho*, Arthur recalled the conversation.

"What's it like having Groucho for a father?" Dean Jr. asked.

"Don't you know?" Arthur replied. "Your father's a celebrity too."

"Yes, but your father's one of the Marx Brothers!" exclaimed young Dino.

With movie stars often divorcing and remarrying, the children of

Introduction

the stars were commonly introduced to new boyfriends and girlfriends which subsequently led to new stepfathers and stepmothers. Tarquin Olivier, son of Laurence Olivier and stepson of Vivien Leigh, remembers his first meeting with his new stepmother in August 1946. He was just ten years of age, and with both his father and stepmother leaving their respective spouses in order to be together, there were many fences to mend.

If Tarquin's memories are anything to go by, it seems Vivien Leigh had all the charm of Scarlett O'Hara in real life, too. Tarquin remembered their first meeting in his book, *My Father: Laurence Olivier*. "She [Vivien] was enchanting. She looked at me with love, called me 'Darling' and gave me a delicious kiss on each cheek. She asked me what things interested me. I told her music, playing the piano and shooting rabbits with my Uncle Jack. She made me feel they were precisely the things which interested her too. I felt discovered, understood, and cherished. She was a master of that art, but in all the years that have passed since that first conversation, I have never personally had any occasion to doubt her thoughtfulness. She, whose passion had deprived me of my father, did all she could to bring us together."

David Niven, Jr., eldest son of British actor David Niven, had a tragic childhood. His mother, Primula, died at twenty-five years of age, the result of an accident at the home of Tyrone Power. During an after dinner-party game, Primula Niven opened a door thinking it was a closet. It was dark and her one step forward caused her to fall down a flight of stairs into the cellar. She never regained consciousness and died a few days later in the hospital, leaving a grieving husband and two young sons behind. Despite the tragedy, David Jr. remembers his dad as a devoted father who, despite his own grief, raised his children with the perfect balance of love, respect and discipline. David gave a glowing tribute to his father in Thomas Hutchinson's *Niven's Hollywood*. "As a father he showed no favoritism and was always there whenever we needed him. He never insisted we be 'the best' only to do 'our best.' He instilled in us the value of family unity, the importance of loyalty, humility and honesty. He loved us very much and I only hope we gave him as much love and pleasure as he gave us. In spite of the fact that we won't see him again, he will always be in our hearts and we will miss him tremendously."

I have already mentioned the mysterious events surrounding

Introduction

Lionel Barrymore and his children, but the Barrymore dynasty continues down many different roads, all of them bumpy. Some call it the "Barrymore curse." After compiling the history of the Barrymore family, I agree that title is no exaggeration. John Barrymore's daughter Diana wrote one of the first Hollywood children books way back in 1957. It was entitled *Too Much, Too Soon*—the perfect title.

Diana's parents separated when she was very young. She was mostly raised by governesses and had no memory of her father before her ninth birthday. She rarely saw her mother due to her busy New York society schedule and therefore had no real connection with either of her parents. When her father did re-enter her life when she was thirteen, he had no perception of how to act like a father so he simply took her bar hopping with him. It was an activity that no doubt led to her battle with alcoholism.

Diana pursued her own acting career and she did show some promise at making it. She probably would have succeeded had it not been for the constant comparisons to her famous family. She recalled that while she made her first movie, *Eagle Squadron*, in 1942, "The makeup men groaned about my face.... Why, the Great Profile's daughter has no profile!"

Alcohol was, by far, a much stronger desire for her than the pursuit of acting and she was consistently arrested for drunken behavior. After squandering the family fortune, she was at such a low point in her life that she stole food whenever she could in order to survive. In 1960, at age thirty-eight, Diana was found dead in her apartment. Three empty liquor bottles lay next to her. The autopsy report showed she had died of a lethal cocktail of alcohol and sleeping pills.

Following the release of Diana Barrymore's book, Edward G. Robinson, Jr., released his story to the world, entitled *My Father: My Son*. A constant headline in the 1950s, Robinson Jr. was arrested for drunkenness, writing bad checks, robbery, assault and battery. His wild ways put a smear on the family name and his mother expressed her opinion of him clearly in her will. She stated that his "unforgivable" conduct toward her, Gladys Lloyd Robinson, had caused her to cut her son out of his entire $756,000 inheritance. She left him no cash, no property, nothing of value. He received a tea set, a baby chair and a painting of himself as an infant. He died in 1974, just one year after his father. An alcoholic since the age of eighteen, his death, reportedly

Introduction

of natural causes, was somewhat helped along by his addiction. He was only forty years old.

There are only a handful of Hollywood children who have made it in "the business," as it's so often called. Those strong personality types who can shine on their own and step away from the shadow of a star parent are the survivors. However, there are many who don't get that far. Charles Boyer, Jr., walked into his Los Angeles apartment one evening and shot himself through the head. A few hours earlier he had lost his job as production assistant on one of his father's television programs. He felt he had failed. Paul Newman's son Scott suffered drug and alcohol problems throughout his teenage years. In 1978 he, too, was discovered dead in his apartment. He had succumbed to an "accidental" overdose of drugs and alcohol.

Mercedes McCambridges' son John died in a tragic murder suicide in 1987. He shot his wife, his children, and then himself. The offspring of Louis Jourdan, Jennifer Jones and David Selznick, Gregory Peck, Ethel Merman and Dana Andrews all committed suicide and two of Bing Crosby's four sons from his first marriage to Dixie Lee committed suicide by gunshot.

Suicide has affected many and when we look statistically at a broad range of people there are certainly going to be tragedies within any family. However, the stars are stars because they wanted to be. The children of the stars are the innocents who have no choice in the matter. They are the children of a star parent and that makes them famous from the day they're born. The pressures of that life, those expectations, and the feeling of not being able to live up to the expectations of a parent who sets such high standards have to contribute to the wavering mental states of those who are not strong enough to step out from the shadows of a parent's prospering career.

According to Farber and Green's *Hollywood Dynasties*, when Jeff Bridges, son of Lloyd Bridges, decided he wanted to become an actor his father simply called up his own agent and demanded "You will represent my son." Not that Jeff Bridges isn't a talented actor; he is, in fact, and one of my all-time favorites. My point is that the path or the doors to potential stardom are opened with ease when you have an already famous name to carry you through. What you do from there is your own doing, but many second-generation actors got their start, probably over more talented or at least equally talented contenders,

Introduction

Jonathon, Gregory, Stephen and Greta Peck share a happy family moment. Tragedy would later strike the Peck family when their son Jonathon (seen here on Gregory's knee) would commit suicide by gunshot. He was just thirty-one years old.

simply because they were the son of or the daughter of you know who.

Many star children did branch out into other fields of the arts. Jack Haley, Jr., Alan Ladd, Jr., David Niven, Jr., John Wayne's son, Michael, and Paul Newman's daughter, Susan, have all dabbled in producing. Carrie Fisher, daughter of Debbie Reynolds and Eddie Fisher, did both. She excelled in both acting and producing. Groucho Marx's son Arthur became a writer, as did Burt Lancaster's son Bill and Keenan Wynn's son Tracy. John Huston directed his father in *The Treasure of the Sierra Madre*. They made history in making the film together and broke all records after they both took home Academy Awards for Best Direction and Best Actor. It was a family victory of the highest order.

Introduction

Of course, John's daughter Angelica Huston is a talented actor in her own right. It is a family legacy, three generations down the line. Robert Montgomery's daughter, Elizabeth Montgomery, followed in her father's acting footsteps and went on to become everyone's favorite witch, Samantha, in the long-running 1960s television series *Bewitched*. Jayne Mansfield's daughter, Mariska Hargitay, is a successful second-generation actor, currently starring in the smash hit weekly crime series, *Law and Order: SVU*. Angelina Jolie, the daughter of Jon Voight, is a movie star in her own right, surpassing her father's fame and popularity all before her thirtieth birthday.

In *Hollywood Dynasties*, Jamie Lee Curtis explains the perception of "normalcy" for a star child. "For me, if Sammy Davis or Kirk Douglas walked into the house, that was normal. So the outside world seemed exotic to me. And when I first moved out of our home in Benedict Canyon, I moved to a little house in the San Fernando Valley. That was my dream—a house in suburbia." When Jamie was making *Trading Places*, she was engaged to producer J. Michael Riva, who by the way just happens to be Marlene Dietrich's grandson. She stayed at Dietrich's apartment in New York for the duration of the film shoot and was literally starstruck over the things that her apartment contained. In the same interview she said, "Little things, like jewelry boxes with her initials. You don't see that kind of thing anymore. Now everybody uses Sportsac. Those little things are not essential. People will live without them. But they were nice, they were special."

It really doesn't seem that "Old Hollywood" was blinded by the strange, excessive, lavish lives of the children of the stars. The media saw the regimental routines and the lavish lifestyles that these children lived on a day-to-day basis. In fact, it was partly for the media's benefit that this whole lifestyle was created in the first place. All of it was for publicity. Still, even back then it was considered somewhat weird to see these children pulling off a perfect adult persona; after all, they were just kids. An article in *Esquire* magazine in 1957 touches on the topic. Aptly titled "Beautiful People," it went on to explain the exact role a child plays in that Hollywood environment.

> Children have become so fashionable in Hollywood that anybody who is anybody has at least three or four (if for one reason or another they have none of their own, they adopt them in clusters), and they all have impeccable manners. They shake hands with each

Introduction

A glamorous shot of Marlene Dietrich with her daughter Maria Riva, circa 1943.

guest, remembering the name—they pass the caviar without spilling a single egg, they answer politely when spoken to, and, eventually, duly admired and appreciated, they file gracefully out again. Conscious of the rowdy awkwardness of your own friends' kids, you have a wild, fleeting conviction that these poised and charming moppets must really be well-trained midgets in disguise, rented for the occasion. But no, they are bona fide children, and although many of them go to boarding school both winter and summer, from an early age, and at home are cared for by nurses and maids, nevertheless, they exist: living, visible, well-publicized proof that movie stars are, as they themselves so often tell you, just normal homebodies, leading quietly sumptuous lives surrounded with family devotion.

Even today, the Hollywood adoption trend is becoming more and more fashionable. That word "fashionable" seems an odd way of describing the addition of a child to any family, but in many instances it is simply a case of it being fashionable to be a mother but not so

Introduction

Robert Wagner, Natalie Wood and the adorable Natasha Gregson Wagner.

fashionable to lose the Hollywood figure by bearing a biological child. One would expect, or at least it would seem, that the abandonment of a child by its natural parents and the adoption of that same child by a parent with a multi-million dollar bank account would be a blessing. But is it really?

Introduction

It's party time! Lucille Ball and Desi Arnaz with their young children, Lucy and Desi Jr. The children are well behaved but the family dog just isn't cooperating for the photograph. What's that famous saying? Never work with children and animals....

Introduction

Little Al Jolson, Jr., finds his famous parents, Al Jolson and Ruby Keeler, extremely funny.

In her book *Detour: A Hollywood Tragedy*, Cheryl Crane, daughter of the original "sweater girl," Lana Turner, remembers a brief but telling conversation she had with her mother when she was a little girl. "I asked mother one day why she always went away. She told me it was because she worked, so I asked her why she worked." She said, 'Well,

20

Introduction

baby, just who do you think pays for all those dresses and toys and riding lessons you love so much?'" Cheryl remembers wanting to tell her mother that she'd give up all that stuff in a minute, if only she'd just stay at home, but she didn't.

Instead, Cheryl would find the comfort that she craved by sneaking into her mother's wardrobe just so she could smell her clothes. She continues, "I have seen all the posed press photos from that era. They show her [Lana Turner] gazing adoringly at the baby bundle in her arms or leading me somewhere by the mittens, but they inspire in me no sense of memory whatsoever, no recollection of the warmth of a cuddle or the softness of a kiss. Most of the time mother was off somewhere making movies or on a holiday. As for when she was at home, until my sixth year, I rarely saw her." It's ironic that the one thing Cheryl missed most cost nothing monetarily, yet her mother worked constantly in order to make enough money to give her daughter everything ... everything but her time.

Kate Burton, daughter of Richard Burton and actress Sybil Williams, was just three and a half years old when her father fell madly in love with Elizabeth Taylor. In a March 2003 interview with Sam Marlowe, Kate remembers back to her father and stepmother's time together. "Dad's relationship with Elizabeth was wonderful, but also tumultuous," she says. "And the media were on them morning, noon and night. It was awful." Despite those outside pressures, her father and Taylor did all that they could to give Kate a balanced life. She concluded, "Dad and Elizabeth lavished us with love. It was dreamy." Now in her mid-forties, Kate Burton is a prominent stage actress. She divides her time between the Broadway stage and London's West End. After leaving Brown University Kate spent a summer with a drama student friend. Ironically, it was that experience and not growing up with the likes of Taylor and Burton that gave her the acting bug. Also in the March 2003 interview with Sam Marlowe, Kate remembered back to the day that she told her famous father of her career choice. "Dad was horrified," she laughed, "but I said, look, let me give it a try. If it doesn't work out, I promise I'll do something else." She didn't need to; it worked out—it worked out just fine. According to Kate, her father was a very proud audience member at many of her performances.

In trying to decide if being the child of a movie star is an advantage or a disadvantage, I think Michael Chaplin summed it up best in

Introduction

Are all mothers supposed to look like this? Elizabeth Taylor with her sons Michael Wilding, Jr., and Christopher Wilding on her lap.

his own book, *I Couldn't Smoke the Grass on My Father's Lawn.* "To be the son of a great man can be a disadvantage. It is like living next to a huge monument; one spends one's life circling around it, either to remain in the shade, or to avoid its shadow. But then people brought up in an orphanage, when trying to find out where they stand in rela-

Introduction

tion to the world, often spend the rest of their lives searching for such a monument."

History has told us that the so-called "privileged life" can be a tough existence. One would hope that the errors of star parents of times past can be amended in this future generation of star babies. Don't get me wrong; there are many stories in this book that reflect true parent-child love, without a doubt. Not *all* of Hollywood's children are mere props or publicity ploys. Judge for yourself. Each story is different; each story is fascinating; each story takes you to a place you've never been before—straight into the lives of the children of Hollywood.

1

ARTHUR MARX

* Only Son of Groucho Marx * and Ruth Johnson

Outside of a dog, a book is a man's best friend. Inside of a dog, it's too dark to read.
—Groucho Marx

The name "Groucho" instantly conjures up thoughts of a stooped walk, fake moustache, black-rimmed glasses, and flickering eyebrows. In fact, that famous cheap plastic disguise of the black glasses and big nose was modeled after Groucho's character. Those all too familiar wisecracks were his trademark and let's not forget that famous cigar that in actual fact was more of a cleverly placed prop than a nasty habit.

Groucho Marx was a man of moderation. Yes, he smoked a cigar, but never to excess. He drank every once in a while, usually at a party thrown by himself. Even then, a party he threw would often see him leaving his guests by no later than ten o'clock to go to bed. He always encouraged them to stay on and drink and have a good time, which they often did—usually long enough to see Groucho re-emerge by morning. He once remarked, "I intend to one day throw a party where I never even come out of the bedroom to begin with. Everyone seems to have a much better time after I've gone to bed."

He refused to buy anything unless he could afford to pay for it in full. This included his first house. Unlike his brothers Harpo, Chico, Zeppo and Gummo, he was not one to go to the extreme in anything he did. There were only two exceptions—his work and his family. In February 1920, Julius H. Marx, aka Groucho, married Ruth Johnson, a dancer who had recently joined The Marx Brothers' vaudeville act.

Harpo, Groucho and Chico take a break in filming and manage to find the correct chairs to sit on, too!

A year and a half later, on July 21, 1921, Arthur Marx was born. In true Groucho style and seeing no humor in the gesture, Ruth's proud husband presented her with a box of cigars.

Being the only son of a world-famous comedian, an icon even, has to be looked upon as a tough job. Arthur Marx seemed to do his job well: a writer, a producer, a husband, a father, a son of one of the greatest comedians of our time. He did okay.

In a combination of memories taken from *Life with Groucho* and *Son of Groucho*, Arthur Marx tells of his relationship with a man whom he simply called Padre, a nickname Arthur and his sister Miriam had given him since learning Spanish in school. It's the story of a man caught up in a world before his time; it's the story of a son whose father was more often his best friend than his worst enemy. It's the story of many outside influences, mainly women, trying to break down the

1. Arthur Marx

family unit and family inheritance that stood to fall into the hands of Arthur, Miriam and Melinda (half-sister) upon Groucho's death. Lastly, it's the story of a man who, in his own stubborn way, loved his family, his work, his audience and his brothers till his dying day.

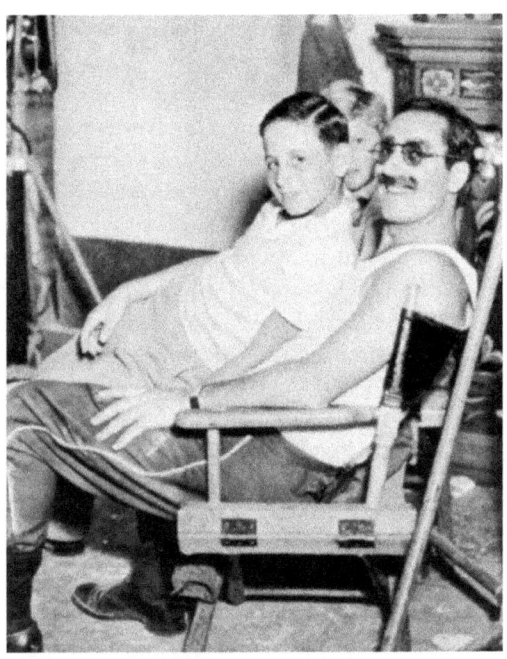

A young Arthur Marx on the set of *Duck Soup* in 1933 with his dad, Groucho Marx (courtesy Robert Bader).

"The years have blurred my earliest recollection of my father. I'm not exactly sure when or where it was that I remember seeing him for the first time. Although it's difficult for me to differentiate between what I actually remember about Groucho in those days and what I've been told, I seem to recall seeing a man of his description hanging around when I was still in a crib. He was about thirty at the time, gaunt, bushy-haired and bespeckled, and for some reason my mother always called him 'Groucho.' There was no such thing as a nurse or housekeeper to look after me. For a while there wasn't even a house or, for that matter, any kind of permanent place to stay—for what purpose I didn't know. Soon after we settled into a spacious but not very luxurious apartment on Riverside Drive. Following that our next extravagant family purchase was a seven-passenger Lincoln sedan for $6,000. The car seemed as tall as it was long, it had windows separating the driver's compartment from the back seat, and it was loaded down with all kinds of nickel-plated trimmings.

"The Lincoln was delivered at the stage door of the Casino Theatre one Wednesday afternoon during the matinee. Groucho was pretty excited about it. At one stage of his vaudeville career he and his brothers had all owned motorcycles and had traveled from town to town on them, sometimes transporting chorus girls on the handlebars. But this was his first full-sized motor vehicle.

"Chico was on the stage doing his piano solo when the Lincoln arrived, and the Napoleon sketch was to follow. But Groucho couldn't wait for the show to be over before trying out his new car. Figuring Chico would be on for another ten minutes, he hopped into the Lincoln and, dressed as Napoleon, went for a spin round the block. The Lincoln performed smoothly, but Groucho had not counted upon traffic being so heavy, nor had he taken the one-way streets into consideration. About the time the Napoleon sketch was to start, he was wedged in between two trucks three blocks from the theatre, and he was still trying to find a street where he could make a left. 'Chico had to play fourteen encores,' he later said. 'And this was pretty difficult, since he only knew ten numbers.'

"In his desperation to get back to the theatre he made an illegal left turn and, of course, a policeman stopped him. One look at Groucho dressed as Napoleon was enough to convince the gendarme that he was a refugee from Bellevue's psychiatric ward.

"'But I tell you I'm one of the Marx Brothers,' insisted Groucho, 'and I'm due on the stage right this minute.'

"'If you're one of the Marx Brothers,' said the skeptical cop, 'let's hear you say something funny.'

"'If you're a policeman, let's see you arrest somebody!' retorted Groucho.

"There was no reason why that line shouldn't have landed him in the nearest jail, but evidently the policeman felt that only a Marx Brother would have the nerve to say such a thing and not only let him go but escorted him back to the theatre. The following Sunday Groucho, sportingly dressed in a pair of long pants, said, 'Ruth, let's go for a spin in our new car.'

"It was a beautiful spring day, and my mother and I were looking forward to an outing in the country as we climbed in the front seat. But we got no further than Central Park. There, Groucho parked the Lincoln under a tree and alighted.

"'Why are we parking here?' asked my mother. 'I thought we were going for a ride.'

"'Riding on Sunday is for yokels,' he answered.

"He forthwhile produced a duster, a jar of car polish and some rags. 'I have to polish the car. You and Arthur can sit on the grass and play.'

"Stripping down to his undershirt, he labored for the next three hours and even polished the nickel plating. Passers-by must have thought we were the chauffeur and his family out for a jaunt while the master was away at Southhampton or Glen Cove for the weekend. After the car was as shiny as Groucho could make it, we piled in again and went back to the apartment. That is how we spent every Sunday for the first year we owned the car.

"Though you wouldn't suspect it from the way he spent his Sundays, Groucho was the toast of New York in those days. I just wasn't aware of it. All I knew was that the other children on the block had fathers who went to work every morning and came home at six o'clock. Mine hung around the apartment all day like a bum, read or played guitar, or took me for long walks in the park. Finally, I went to him and told him that my playmates wanted to know why he didn't go to work in the daytime like the rest of the fathers.

"'You go back and ask them what their fathers do at night while I'm in the theatre,' he advised me. 'On second thought, maybe you'd better not. It's an unfair question.' Actually, there were a great many advantages, I discovered, to having a father who was available during the day (except of course on Wednesdays and Saturdays, when he played matinees). And I think the other children in the neighborhood appreciated having him around too. Groucho loved children—and was never so busy that he couldn't take time out to entertain them. He'd sing and play guitar for us, he'd participate in our games, he'd treat the neighborhood to ice cream cones, and he loved to engage in long conversations with my friends. One of his favorite pastimes was story telling. If other children were around, they could get in on it, too. But always, before leaving for the theatre in the evenings, he made it a point to sit down in the massive chair in front of the fake fireplace, light up a cigar, and tell me a special bedtime story.

"Generally he'd stick to the tried and true classics, but they weren't very true when he got through with them. He'd keep the same story structure of the original, but it would be so full of jokes you'd hardly recognize it. It would be part Robert Benchley, part Ring Lardner, and part (big part) Groucho Marx. I was pretty young to appreciate the humor in his stories, but what difference did that make? He told them well, and he could always manage to stretch a ten-minute story into an hour. And when bedtime is fast approaching, that's more important than actual content.

"The other children who heard his stories were a little mystified by them, too, but they seemed to enjoy them just the same. They liked being with him. And it wasn't because he was a celebrity, because I don't believe many of the children (or even the grown-ups) in the neighborhood realized he was a star (I know I didn't).

"Riverside Drive and 161st Street wasn't a very theatre-conscious community, and besides, he wasn't easily recognizable in those days. He didn't wear a moustache in private life, and only his close friends and people in theatrical circles knew him as Groucho Marx. Outside the theatre he still clung to Julius H. Marx (he didn't change it officially to Groucho until years later), and from appearances he could have been an ordinary young businessman, except, as I say, that to most people he apparently had no business. His glasses and habitual intense expression gave him a studious look, he lived modestly, displayed no theatrical mannerisms, and he stayed in the background as much as possible."

Being the child of Groucho Marx is one thing but there are many extensions of that. The bonus was that Arthur was also the nephew of Harpo, Chico, Gummo and Zeppo. At age six, one of Arthur's favorite things to do was to meet his father after one of his matinees and have lunch. Not just any ol' lunch with Dad but lunch with his equally famous and equally amusing uncles.

"Almost always Harpo, Chico, Zeppo and their wives would be at the table with us, and I enjoyed that immensely because no child could have more doting uncles than they were. They'd shower me with expensive toys, slip $10 bills into my pockets when Groucho (who disapproved) wasn't looking and spoil me in every way possible. Apart from presents, the Marxs were a hilarious group when they were together. They were loud, raucous, and never took anything seriously. The jokes would fly back and forward so rapidly you couldn't keep up with them. And all the brothers but my father were accomplished at the art of doing table tricks. They'd be springboarding silverware into glasses of water, making rabbits out of napkins, pulling cards from their sleeves, and perhaps shooting dice with sugar cubes.

"Groucho was the champion of children's rights. He believed that children were not born to be left out of things. He felt just as strongly in favor of our going on all trips with him and my mother as he did about having us at the dinner table with them. Whether or not we should accompany them on trips was always a good starting place for an argument, for, devoted a parent as my mother was, she usually preferred to leave us at home. After all, since she was the mother, much of the responsibility of looking after us fell on her. With us along, she couldn't be as carefree or relaxed on a trip as she would have liked.

"Groucho's appeal to children was universal, obviously beyond language barriers (Groucho could speak German but not French) as proved to be the case in Paris when he took me to a Punch and Judy show in the park along the Champs Elysée. He left me in the audience while he went out and took a walk through the park. When the show was over and he hadn't returned, I went out to look for him. I found him on the boulevard rolling hoops with a group of French children and apparently having the best time he'd had since we'd arrived in Paris.

"On the career front, Irving Thalberg's death had put a large gaping hole into MGM. Groucho and the Marx Brothers' relationship with Thalberg was that of complete understanding and loyalty. His death was mourned by all of them, both personally and professionally. With Metro now being headed by Louis B. Mayer and Groucho not liking Mayer's attitude of churning out film after film, whether they be good or not, it made for a rocky road on the work side of life. His home life was yet another story. Groucho wasn't very happy with his last three pictures at MGM, and he announced that when his contract was up, he was going to quit. During the last year under contract to Metro, he went to the studio as little as he had to and spent most of his time around the house, supervising its management, writing an occasional magazine article, and entertaining Miriam and me.

"So, what was bad for his career was good for us, for no adolescents ever had a better friend than Groucho. There were some unhappy moments, too, for this was the period when the chasm between our parents was beginning to widen quite perceptibly. The divorce clouds were only forming over these years. They didn't actually divorce until I was twenty and living away from home. In the meantime, I enjoyed a pretty average American adolescence, complete with the regulation amount of parents, a tomboy sister, dogs, report cards, braces on the teeth and no swimming pool. Groucho refused to put in a swimming pool (despite having the money and ample room to accommodate it). His theory was 'a pool created too many *new* friends who otherwise wouldn't want to be in your company without it.' In short, and in Groucho's eyes, a pool was a social nightmare!

"Of course I couldn't have a completely average American upbringing with a world-famous comedian as the head of the house. And Groucho realized this, too. In fact, he had long been aware of the pitfalls likely to be encountered by the children of celebrities, and he did his best to see that we had no more advantages or privileges than any of the other children in the neighborhood. If anything, he leaned a little bit in the opposite direction.

"In some ways, Groucho was almost mid–Victorian in his thinking. He was always very strict about the time I went to bed. On school nights he'd hustle me off to my room sharply at nine, even when I was a senior in high school. On Friday and Saturday nights he'd be a little more lenient. He'd let me stay out until ten or ten-thirty. But if I came in past then, he'd give me a long lecture the next morning on how a growing boy needs at least eleven hours sleep and threaten to take my car away the next time it happened. If he caught me, that is. Many nights he was out late himself and wouldn't know whether or not I came in a few minutes past the curfew. But on the nights he was home it was very difficult to fool him, for his bedroom was right over the porch cochere, which you had to drive through in order to get to the garage, and Groucho was a very light sleeper. He never failed to hear my car roaring under his bedroom. Deciding that something had to be done about this, I tried an experiment one night. I turned my engine off at the corner of our block and coasted down the hill, into our driveway, through the porch cochere and into the garage. I was sure I had fooled him, but as I tiptoed towards the house he stuck his head out of the window, wiggled his eyebrows at me, and said, 'I still heard you.'

"In most respects he treated Miriam and me more like close friends than children. He confided in us about his business and matrimonial problems, we had private jokes that nobody else understood, and he liked to take us with him wherever he went, provided we wouldn't be too much out of our element. Being around Groucho made it pretty difficult for Miriam and me not to be bored with the company of children our own age.

"Mother and Groucho were rapidly approaching the parting of the ways by 1941, and everyone in our household was perfectly aware of what was happening and expecting the worst. Although we weren't looking forward to such an eventuality, Miriam and I were beginning to wish our parents would get divorced, if this was the best they could do.

"There is no doubt Groucho would have been a very difficult man for the average woman to cope with around the house. Being something of an eccentric, and a male chauvinist to boot, Groucho was never easy to live with. But he and Mother managed to iron out, with a minimum of

1. Arthur Marx

friction, most causes of their earlier disputes. I watched my parents drifting further and further apart until I entered the Coast Guard in 1942. I was away when they made the decision to divorce."

A few months later Arthur received the following letter from Groucho:

> Your mother moved out today, and the whole thing was kind of sad. I was sorry to see her go, for I am still fond of her, but obviously this uncomfortable set-up couldn't continue. I said good-bye to her before she drove off in her car. It was one of those awkward, half-serious moments, and I didn't quite know what to say. Finally, I put my hand out and said, "Well, it was nice knowing you, and if you're ever in the neighborhood again, drop in." Your mother seemed to think that was a funny line; so for once in my life I got a laugh when I wasn't trying for one. The house is pretty quiet now with just Miriam and me rattling around fourteen rooms. Well, it's better than fourteen people rattling around two rooms. I'll let things drift along, anyway, for the present.

After the divorce, the coming years saw Groucho marry twice more and subsequently divorce twice more. Another daughter, Melinda, was born and because she was near the same age she grew up alongside Arthur's son Steve. All through Groucho's two new marriages and divorces and even the birth of another daughter, Arthur and Groucho generally remained the best of friends—that was, until Erin Fleming appeared on the scene.

As Arthur explains:

> "No woman ever succeeded in endangering my relationship with Groucho until Erin Fleming came along. In fact, I'd always been his confidant where his love life was concerned. As a matter of fact I'd been his confidant on most subjects, ranging from career problems to the travail he was having with my sisters, from his insomnia to how much money he had in the bank and to whom he was going to leave it to when he died.
>
> "After his third divorce, Groucho called me into his study one day and gave me the key to his front door and the key to his desk, where he kept his will and a list of all his financial holdings, which amounted to approximately two million dollars, not counting his house. He said, 'I want you to know exactly where it's all going when I kick the bucket.'"

Children of Hollywood

Left: An elderly Groucho Marx with his son Arthur standing in front of a painting of The Marx Brothers, circa 1972. *Right:* Still telling jokes! Groucho performs for his son, Arthur, at home, circa 1972. (Both photographs courtesy the late Samuel Perkins and Arthur Marx.)

Erin Fleming came out of nowhere. She was eventually hired by Groucho himself to be his manager. Here was an aging comedian, in poor health, being directed and told what to do and where to go by a twenty-something woman with ulterior motives. It was safe to say that Groucho was mesmerized by her, almost under her spell.

The family could plainly see Erin Fleming driving new cars, wearing new clothes, even living in a separate house down the street from Groucho, all of which was funded by him. No amount of talking to him seemed to do any good, either. Arthur had tried on a number of occasions only to have Groucho side firmly with Erin against him to the point of them not speaking for lengths at a time. Always at some point, usually at Groucho's request by phone call or telegram, Groucho would contact Arthur and ask to see him again. Groucho always would greet Arthur with a huge hug and a kiss, as if nothing had ever happened.

1. Arthur Marx

Arthur would time his visits so that he would be less likely to bump into Erin. She controlled Groucho in many ways but not in the most important way. Groucho was never happy about not seeing his children and she knew it. His children also knew it and Groucho knew it and in that way—that "family way"—Erin Fleming lost the fight that she wanted so much to win.

The last two years of Groucho's life saw him mainly bedridden. He would get out of bed on occasion to eat, but that's all. Erin would be with him almost constantly, obsessively, and any family visits would be planned meticulously around her not being in the house. On August 19, 1977, Groucho Marx slowly and peacefully slipped away with his family by his bedside. Erin Fleming left the room as Groucho's family arrived. Arthur explains:

> "I kissed him goodbye on his forehead, which was still warm. The doctor closed his eyelids and then pulled the sheet over his face. And then we all had a good, long cry. I knew he didn't want a funeral; he considered them barbaric. He had told me that many times. He just wanted to be cremated and he didn't care what became of his ashes. A memorial service was held at my house on that coming Saturday afternoon."

Groucho's brother, Gummo, had passed away just four months earlier, but since Groucho's health was failing, his family didn't feel it neccesary to burden him with the sad news of the loss of another brother. Zeppo was the last of the Marx Brothers to say goodbye, passing away on November 30, 1979.

Because of Elvis Presley's sudden death just three days prior to Groucho, his passing went with little media coverage. *Elvis Presley—Dead* was splashed across the front pages of newspapers everywhere. Groucho was lucky to get a subheadline, if any headline at all. Given his understated wishes on how he preferred his final goodbyes to be, he wouldn't have been offended in the least.

Not one to let death interrupt a good joke, Arthur tells of a note his father wrote and he found after Groucho was cremated. "A few days after Groucho was cremated and his ashes interred in a vault in Malinov & Silverman's cemetery in the San Fernando Valley, a letter addressed to me was found among his effects. In it he had requested that he *not* be cremated. He preferred to be buried at the Westwood Cemetery alongside the body of Marilyn Monroe!"

Children of Hollywood

★★★★★

The same old Groucho. Always wanting the last word, the last joke, even from beyond the grave. Unfortunately, the last word on Groucho's estate was a long way off in coming. Court battles against Erin Fleming went on for more than a decade after Groucho's death. It was both an emotional and financial drain on the family members left behind to deal with it, and the end result was less than satisfying.

Justice was eventually done and Erin Fleming lost. Compensatory damages and punitive damages in the hundreds of thousands of dollar range were awarded to the Marx family, but it wasn't really a win. Most of the court costs and lawyers fees from eleven long years of battling ate up what was rightfully theirs. The remainder of Groucho's estate was finally distributed to his family in 1988—a mere fraction of what it started out to be at the time of his death eleven years before.

2

BILLY, ALEX, JIMMY AND MINNIE MARX

* Children of Harpo Marx * and Susan Fleming

I'd like so many children, that whenever we go out, there can be one in every window, waving to us.
—Harpo Marx

Harpo Marx was the lovable mute Marx Brother who didn't have to say a word to get a laugh. His trademark curly red wig, rumpled top hat and long trench coat, along with his amazing ability to play the harp—hence the name Harpo—made him famous. His only communication was usually the honk of his beloved horn. The decision for his character not to speak came from a critic who noted that Harpo was brilliant until he actually spoke. The Marx Brothers took note of this criticism and from that moment on, Harpo never spoke in character again.

Harpo chasing a pretty girl was another stock standard routine in most movies as was a solo scene of him playing the harp. He was a self-taught harpist, and a good one at that. Years later he discovered that he'd actually taught himself to the play the instrument the wrong way. However, when he became famous, musicians would often ask to learn it "his way," the Harpo way. His innocent mistake soon became another method of playing the hauntingly beautiful instrument, not only for Harpo but for many other budding musicians of his day.

As mentioned before, in all of The Marx Brothers' films, Harpo's character was a notorious skirt chaser. It was quite the opposite in real life. Harpo was a devoted husband and father. He was married to the

A classic shot of the lovable Harpo in character.

2. Billy, Alex, Jimmy and Minnie Marx

same woman, Susan Fleming, for exactly twenty-eight years. He passed away on September 28, 1964, their twenty-eighth wedding anniversary, after complications following open heart surgery.

Harpo and Susan adopted four children during their marriage: Billy, Alex, Jimmy and Minnie. I was so taken, so touched, with the loving story of their adoptions, I just had to include it in this book. So many parents are afraid to be truthful with their adopted children, but Harpo and Susan made a point of explaining to the children exactly how they were chosen to become a member of the family from a very early age. Right from the moment they could understand it, Harpo and Susan wove the tales of their adoptions into an adventurous bedtime story that was told to them for many, many years.

This is "The Story," as it came to be known, told by Harpo and Susan Marx and excerpted from the best selling *Harpo Speaks!* by Harpo Marx. I think after reading it you'll agree that it almost makes you feel like you've missed out, not being chosen by this family. Billy, Alex, Jimmy and Minnie were the lucky ones. This is their bedtime story, mostly true, a little spiced up for a child's enjoyment, and guaranteed to bring a smile to your face.

I'll let Harpo tell it from here:

> "Susan and I decided we would tell our children they were adopted as soon as they could understand any speech at all. It had to be the very first thing they learned about life. We'd seen some pretty sad cases, where parents were afraid of the children they had adopted—afraid, as they put it, that the kids 'might turn on them'—and kept putting off telling them the truth. When they were told too late, the kids really did turn, full of resentment and a feeling of being unwanted. The results were tragic—unhappy early marriages, delinquency, even alcoholism.
>
> "Billy was fourteen months old when he joined the family and he already knew by the time he learned to talk that he had come from someplace else. Before he was able to ask questions about that 'someplace else,' we told him all about it. He accepted it for what it was—a fact of life. It was like learning that the sun went down at night, night was the time for sleep, and that Mommy loved Daddy and they both loved Billy just as much—nothing more, nothing less.
>
> "Alex, Jimmy and Minnie each came home to us as babes in arms. We started telling them where they had come from when Alex was two, and Jimmy and Minnie were scarcely a year old. We told it in the form of a

true adventure bedtime story. By the time they were four and three, they couldn't go to bed without hearing 'The Story,' as we all came to call it. They used to sit around Susan and me on the bedroom floor, curled up in their bunny-type pajamas, while we told 'The Story.' We played it for suspense, like an old-fashioned cliff-hanger, and how they loved it!

"Alex's eyes would be glittering because he knew he came first. 'Poor, poor Billy,' Susan would begin, 'growing up sad and lonely, not having a little brother to play with. We had to find a little brother for Billy—not any little brother but the right one, whose name would be Alex and who would have yellow hair and pink cheeks. Well, we looked and we looked. We looked at this baby boy and that one, but no—not one of them was Alex. Then one day Dr. Hirshfeld called on the telephone and said, "I think I know where you can find him!" So Daddy and I packed our suitcase and got on a train and rode all day and all night, and then we got off the train and rushed to the place that Dr. Hirshfeld told us about. There they showed us a little boy. We looked at him .' " Susan would pause for effect. Alex would be hunched over and shivering from the terrible suspense.

"'...and what do you know! It was Alex! We bundled him up and took him on the train with us and all three of us traveled all night and all day and then we came home and Billy and his little brother weren't sad and lonely any more.' Alex would let out his breath and smile with relief. He'd been found! Now it was Jimmy's turn to squirm and hold his breath.

"But Billy was six years older than Baby Alex, and he would run out to play with the older boys, and now Alex was going to be sad and lonely if he didn't have a little brother to play with. So we began looking and looking for a little brother for Alex—not any little brother but the right one, whose name would be Jimmy and who would have bright, shiny brown eyes. Well, we hunted all over. People would show us babies, and they said, 'Is this the one you're looking for? Is this the one?'

"But none of them was the right one. We began to think we would never find Jimmy. Then one day Dr. Hirshfeld called on the telephone and said, 'I've heard about a baby boy, and I think he's what you're looking for.' So, Daddy and I got on the train, and this time we rode three days and three nights, and we said, 'Wouldn't it be awful if we got there and the baby they showed us wouldn't be Jimmy?' Well, we got off the train and rushed over and they showed us this baby, and oh, my goodness.

"Susan would shake her head. Jimmy would be biting his lip and clench-

2. Billy, Alex, Jimmy and Minnie Marx

ing and unclenching his hands. '...It wasn't our Jimmy. We started to leave, and then they said, "Maybe we showed you the wrong one. Maybe this is the one you're looking for?"'

"And what do you know—It was! It was Jimmy! Jimmy would smile and clap to hear he had been found at last, but Minnie would be beside herself waiting to hear the end of the story. The excitement would be so unbearable for her it was absolutely delicious.

"This is where I usually took over. 'Alex had his kid brother now and somebody to play with,' I would begin, 'but what Alex and Jimmy wanted now more than anything else in the world was...'

"'A baby sister!' Minnie would whisper breathlessly.

"'...a baby sister. Not just any old baby sister, but a little doll named Minnie who was happy and gay and who wanted three brothers, the same as they wanted her. Well, it's not easy, you know, to find a baby girl like that. We hunted and hunted, all over town, and looked at all the baby girls, but we couldn't find Minnie. Then one day Dr. Hirshfeld called on the telephone and said, "Hurry over fast! I think I've found the one you're hunting for!" So Mom and I hurried over fast, and Dr. Hirshfeld showed us this little girl. And what do you know! It wasn't Minnie at all.' Minnie would stuff her hand in her mouth so she wouldn't blurt out the ending and spoil the mystery.

"So we came home, feeling sad, and told Alex and Jimmy we hadn't found their sister, and maybe we never could. Dr. Hirshfeld called up again and again, but every time we went to look it was the wrong baby girl. Then one day, Aunt Gracie Burns called us up all the way from New York City, and she said, 'I think I've found the girl you're looking for!' and we said, 'What's she like?' and Aunt Gracie said, 'She's a little doll, happy and gay,' and we said, 'Yes! That sounds like our Minnie.'

"Well, we were in such a hurry to see her that we couldn't wait. So we didn't go to New York on the train. We told them to bring Minnie to us on an airplane. And the very next day a nurse got off the airplane and brought the little girl to us. But the minute we looked at her, she began to cry and yell, and her face got red and she wasn't happy or gay at all. 'You'll have to take her back on the airplane,' we said. 'This isn't Minnie. You brought us the wrong baby.' But then do you know what happened?'

"Minnie's eyes would be shut tight. She'd be nodding her head and wiggling all over the joint trying to contain herself. 'What happened was, the little girl fell fast asleep; she was so tired from the long airplane ride.

Children of Hollywood

And I looked at her, and in her sleep she was smiling a happy and gay smile, and she was the most beautiful little girl you ever saw. I yelled, 'Hey, Mom! Come here quick! It *is* her, after all! It's Minnie!'

"When we finally recognized her and decided to keep her, Minnie would be exhausted from the ordeal, exhausted but walking on air. Now all three of them had been found, they had something wonderful to take to

Top: A shot of Harpo Marx's young children. Left to right: Bill, Alexander, Jim and Minnie. *Above:* A recent shot of Harpo Marx's children. Left to right: Alexander, Minnie, Jim and Bill, all grown up. (Both photographs courtesy Bill Marx.)

2. Billy, Alex, Jimmy and Minnie Marx

bed with them and dream about, and there was seldom any squawk when the lights went out. Alex, Jimmy and Minnie never tired of hearing 'The Story.' Long after they outgrew bedtime stories they would ask us to tell the "The Story" at least once a week. When they reached their teens they still wanted to hear it a couple of times a year. By then, of course, Susan and I had worked it into quite a show. What with all the touches and gimmicks we'd added over the years, we could have followed Alfred Hitchcock and kept an audience holding onto their seats.

"I was the same kind of father as I was a harpist—I played by ear. But I've been lucky on both scores. The harp has given me a decent living and my children have given me more pleasure than I ever thought a man could possibly have. What rules we had as a family stemmed from the fact that all of us has been adopted by each other. We've always had equal amounts of gratitude and respect mixed in with our love for each other. Susan, an only child who never had any roots, and I, a lone wolf who got married twenty years too late, were adopted by the kids as much as they were by us.

"However, Alex was about twelve when one day he came to me while I was playing the harp. He looked troubled. I stopped playing and asked him what was eating him.

"'Oh nothing, Dad,' he said. He stared at the harp pedals like he'd never seen them before. He didn't know what to do with his hands. I reminded him of our rule. No holding back. If he had something to say, out with it.

"'Well, Dad,' he said. 'We've been talking about "The Story," Jimmy, Minnie and me. And, well, there's something that none of us ever said to you that we ought to have.

"My heart was in my throat. Maybe the truth was coming out, after all these years. Maybe we'd made a big mistake. Maybe we had told the kids, too much, too soon. I said, 'What is it you want to say, Alex?'

"He finally got up the courage to look straight at me. He took a deep breath and said, 'Thanks. Thanks for adopting us.' My heart went back where it belonged, and it's stayed there ever since."

3

Maxine Marx

* Daughter of Chico Marx and Betty Karp *

> *What's the shape of the world?*
> —A rhetorical question that Groucho
> and Chico would ask each other.

He was born on March 22, 1887, and was given the very official name of Leonard Marx. The first of the Marx Brothers had arrived, and the world would never be the same! He was known to the world as "Chico," a name given to him because of his love for the ladies. Women were commonly referred to as "chickens" in those days, so his name became a shortened version of that term. However, his name is commonly mispronounced as "Cheeko" because a typesetter once left the "k" out of "Chicko" in a news article. The brothers just decided to keep it that way, and he was known as "Chico" from then on.

He would play the Italian of the group, adopting his phony Italian accent as his character trait in honor of the many Italian immigrants who grew up in his neighborhood. Not content with being "just a Marx Brother," Chico discreetly took over the group's management, originally controlled by their mother Minnie. His charming ways secured the brothers their first international performance in London. He was instrumental in getting them all to make the move from vaudeville to Broadway with much success, and he negotiated their lucrative MGM movie contract with Irving Thalberg.

In a documentary entitled *The Unknown Marx Brothers,* Maxine remembered one of her father's tactics when it came down to making group business decisions. "The boys voted on all projects, everything. Daddy knew whoever spoke to Harpo last got his vote, so he made sure he waited until Groucho talked to him against the project and then Pop

3. Maxine Marx

Chico Marx and his daughter, Maxine, on a film set, circa 1938 (courtesy Maxine Marx).

talked to him and convinced him to vote with him. I always felt Groucho figured that out, but if the project flopped, he could say, 'Well, I was against it!'"

An accomplished pianist, Chico, like Harpo, had his own unique way of playing his chosen instrument. Mostly self-taught, Chico would rather gamble his piano lesson money than pay his music teacher. His daughter Maxine tells that story a little later. An avid gambler from the age of twelve, Chico gambled on anything and everything. His daughter Maxine once said she would be traveling in the car with him and they would be approaching a traffic light when he would say, "I'll bet you that traffic light will change by the time we get to it." For Chico, everything was a gamble; everything had its odds. If a bet could be placed then Chico would be the first in line to lay down his cash.

In the revealing documentary *The Unknown Marx Brothers*, Maxine Marx, his only child with first wife Betty Karp (they were married for more than twenty years), shared many Marx Brothers moments as well as some personal moments with her dad Chico and her equally famous, albeit wacky, uncles.

"Chico, my father, was born after the firstborn child died; his name was Manfred. Because Chico came after that, Minnie, my grandmother, was very attached; she adored him. Chico caused trouble from the time he was quite young. He got into gambling very early. He was a compulsive gambler by age twelve!

"My grandmother would give him fifty cents a week for piano lessons and maybe he got to the piano teacher once out of four times that he was supposed to be there. He'd gamble the fifty cents on the way to the teacher. However, Daddy was a great ragtime pianist and he had fun at the piano, but Harpo was a really great musician, an extraordinary harpist. Chico joined the act quite by accident. He was in the same town that his brothers were in and when he saw they were playing there he bribed the guy in the pit who played the piano to let him stand in for him. When his brothers saw him in the pit they started throwing things at him and he threw things back at them. The audience thought it was hilarious and he joined the act.

"My father was enormously optimistic about everything, that was the gambler in him. Groucho, on the other hand, was always very pessimistic so when Chico came up with the idea of doing a Broadway show, Groucho was terrified. He said, 'Why should anybody go see us on Broadway for $3.30 when for 55 cents they can see us in vaudeville?'

"Chico said, 'Because, Groucho, we're too good for vaudeville, we belong on Broadway.'

"There wasn't a day that went by that Daddy didn't call Groucho on the phone. They never said anything to each other. Daddy would say, 'Hi Grouch, what's new?' Groucho would obviously say, 'Nothing,' and Daddy would say, 'Fine, bye.' They did this every single day; they would always touch base."

The Marx Brothers were smart showman. They knew exactly how to test an audience reaction, even before shooting a scene. They would take the script for the proposed movie ahead of time. All of the gags would be set out for them, and before they made the film they would go on the road and act out the scenes on stage in front of a live audience. That way they could instantly see what worked and what didn't. If something didn't get a laugh it would either get tossed out altogether or be rewritten and retried on stage one more time. When they performed each scene they'd clock the laughter response time so that when they shot the film, they'd know how long to wait before saying the next line. That way the audience wasn't laughing over the next joke. It was a perfect rehearsal routine and it made for a string of hit movies.

Maxine was lucky enough to sit in on as many live shows as she could and she never tired of seeing the same routines over and over again. The same routine would often be a little bit different each and every time because they never ever stuck to a script. Timing was everything so if an ad lib could be squeezed in and that meant getting an extra laugh, then in it would go. Maxine remembers:

"As funny as they were on film, they were a hundred times—a thousand times—funnier on stage. And they were unpredictable; things would happen on stage that were so wonderful. On the second or third day of one of their performances, I thought to myself, 'Gee, the second show and there's nobody in the audience except a few drunks, guys in overcoats and a few ladies of the evening.' I thought, 'I'll go and get my hair done.'

"So I went out and I came back and went backstage and Daddy and Harpo were waiting for me and I said, 'Hi,' and they said, 'Well?' I said,

'Well?' and they said, 'WELL....?' I really didn't know what the hell they were talking about and I looked at Daddy and I looked at Harpo and Harpo said, 'I told you she wouldn't know!' and Chico said, 'I was sure you'd guess.' And I said, 'No, what? Guess what?'

"It turned out they had changed parts. Daddy played Harpo and Harpo played Daddy and they did it all for me and I wasn't there. That was one of the biggest disappointments I've ever had in show business. It was a heartbreaker because they would never do it again.

"A couple of years before my father died, I had just split from my husband and I was having a hard time financially. I was talking to Daddy about it and he said, 'Gee, I wish I were Groucho so I could help you.'

"I said, and I'm so very glad I said it, 'I wouldn't trade you in for any of my uncles. You're the best in the world.'

"I've always been so happy that I said that to him. Anyway, he was getting sicker and sicker and sicker and we all knew it was only a matter of time. He had a near brush and my mother had me fly out because we thought he was dying but he recovered from that attack. Everyone had lived through so many near deaths with Daddy that I think when he finally did die, they were just kind of relieved because he was very, very ill. When it finally does happen it's kind of a relief. At the funeral Jimmy Durante looked awful and I heard him say, 'Well, that's the end of it, there'll be no more Marx Brothers.'"

Chico Marx died on October 11, 1961. He was first into this world and first out of it. If you look at that fact logically, that's probably the way it goes and probably even the way it should be. However, no amount of justification really makes Chico's loss any easier because his death meant the end of many things, in more ways than one. As Jimmy Durante put it, it was the end of it. It was the end of a

A photograph of Maxine, circa 1995 (courtesy Robert Bader).

brotherly partnership that lasted many decades. It was the end of an era for Hollywood comedy—period.

The laughing was over and it was a time for tears. Chico was gone and so were "The Marx Brothers." There's no doubt the world is a better place because of their existence and, thankfully, the brilliance of digital technology and the preservation of priceless images enables a whole new generation to continue to enjoy the Brothers Marx over and over and over again.

4

JOAN BENNY

Daughter of Jack Benny
and Mary Livingstone

A scout troop consists of twelve little kids dressed like schmucks following a big schmuck dressed like a kid.
—Jack Benny

Jack Benny's story of how he and his wife Mary came to adopt their daughter Joan became a family favorite for years. It's only fitting that it be told here, in Jack's own words, just as if he were telling it today. Besides, it's the perfect introduction for his daughter Joan Benny, as she continues with her own story.

Her own memories of her childhood as the daughter of one of the most well-known faces and voices on American television and radio are all here. Joan found a complete 400-plus-page manuscript after her father's death. She knew he'd been writing here and there but she had no idea he'd completed an entire book's worth of memories. Those memories, along with some of her own, became the best selling book *Sunday Nights at Seven*. With Joan Benny's permission, some of her favorite memories are taken from that book and retold here.

From 1934 through 1965 and spanning radio all the way through to television, the American public tuned in for their weekly dose of laughter and mayhem on *The Jack Benny Show*. Here, in Joan Benny's own words, she fondly remembers her dad, Jack Benny. There is no doubt that she was and still is "Daddy's Little Girl." Now, let's start with Jack and that story.

"Mary and I decided to adopt a daughter in 1934. Joanie was about two weeks old the first time I saw her. She was long and skinny and wrinkled

4. Joan Benny

Daddy's little girl! A young Joan Benny practicing the piano with her dad, Jack Benny (courtesy Joan Benny).

all over her face and tiny arms. Her little legs looked crooked and were wrinkled all over, too. Her skin was puckered, there were big red blotches on her cheeks and her eyes were very blue. She was bawling so loud and she looked very mad. I couldn't believe my eyes. 'Is this the one you picked?' I asked Mary.

"Mary was smiling a secret smile, 'Yes', she said. 'Isn't she darling?'

"'How can you want to adopt a funny looking thing like that one?' I asked

"'I can't help it,' Mary said. 'I just love her!'

"She became very beautiful and I fell in love with my daughter before she was living with us even two days. She completed our lives. As she grew older she came to look like me and Mary. She had my blue eyes and my love for music and Mary's face and figure and manner of talking and smartness. Anybody would take her for our natural daughter. I feel as though she is ours and always has been ours. We told her she was adopted from the very beginning when she was too young to understand because we wanted her to get used to the idea of what it meant to be adopted. We did not rear Joanie in the permissive style that was fashionable then in Beverly Hills. Mary and I firmly believed that every child must be guided and disciplined and that the children of show business celebrities were more vulnerable to temptations than other children.

"Being the softie that I am, it fell upon poor Mary to do the dirty work of disciplining little Joanie. As a child, Joan was always coming to me and complaining about her mother making her do this or do that. Once, at age seven, she was seething with fury, 'I'm so mad at Mama,' she said, 'I'm just never going to talk to her again. I hate her, I hate her!'

"So, I put her on my lap and told her how when I first saw her I thought she was so ugly and how it was Mary who had wanted her so and how much Mary loved her and that these rules she hated were for her own good and necessary for her own happiness. Not long after I had this little heart to heart with Joanie, one morning she said suddenly out of a clear sky, 'Daddy, I love you very much.'

"I said, 'Joanie, you don't love me as much as I love you.' And then—mind you, she wasn't more than seven or eight—she remembered our little talk and answered with, 'Yes, I do. I love you more because I loved you all my life and you didn't love me until the second day.'

"That story of my arrival was a family favorite for years. Today I am often asked what it was like to be adopted. How would I know? I've never been anything else. A silly question and a glib reply. The truth: I consider

4. Joan Benny

myself one of the most fortunate people in the world. My adoption was hardly a secret. How could it have been when in 1934 my parents were well on their way to stardom? *The Jack Benny's Adopt Baby Girl!* That headline hit many fan magazines and newspapers of the time. No, I couldn't read then, but I knew even before I was able to understand that I had been adopted. I knew it just as I knew I had blue eyes and blonde hair. My parents handled it very matter of factly, never making it unusual or a mysterious occurrence, and since my best friend Sandy Burns as well as her little adopted brother Ronnie (George Burns and Gracie Allen's children) were also adopted, it must have been five or six years, or at least until I was questioned about it by outsiders, before I knew there was an alternate way to have babies. I thought if you wanted a baby you went to an orphanage and picked one out.

"In 1938 Beverly Hills was a rural community and what is now the commercial center or triangle that includes the famous Rodeo Drive was then a quaint village. Today there isn't ten feet of space in Beverly Hills that hasn't been built on, but then, although there were houses standing on either side of us, looking out from the front across the street, three large vacant lots ranged all the way to Sunset Boulevard.

"For a treat when I had been good, my nanny, Signe Bensen, known to all as 'Bens,' would take me for a walk across those lots up to Sunset to buy me an ice cream.

"Bens was tall and blonde and Scandinavian and she always wore a nurse's uniform. Of course it was Bens' job to eat with me when I was very little. And I didn't like to eat. I pushed the food around on my plate and occasionally took a small mouthful, which I chewed slowly. My parents were smart; they didn't eat with me then. When I ate dinner with Bens, Daddy would put on an impromptu show for me. From where I sat I could see straight through the dining room to the main hallway. Pretending he didn't know I was watching, he would slowly march back and forth across the space between the doors, as if he were crossing a little stage. He would glue pieces of paper to his eyelids with spit and make funny faces as he walked by in profile. Then he made believe that he was going down a flight of stairs by kneeling lower and lower and crouching down as he went across until he was out of sight. Then, seconds later he returned, starting in a crouched position and then getting taller and taller and taller as he went up the invisible stairs. It may have been ridiculous, but at age four or five, I thought it was hilarious!

"Christmas was the most exciting event of the year, not only because of all the presents but because it was the one occasion in which I was allowed to fully participate. About a week before my parents and I went to pick out a tree. It had to be nine or ten feet tall, silver tip, and it had to be green. Given those facts I could pick the one I liked best. It was delivered to our house and placed in the bay window in the library, looking out at the front lawn, and could clearly be seen from the street.

"When I was about five I made up my mind I wanted a red tree. Red was my favorite color. Daddy and Mother and I were at the Christmas tree lot looking at the green silver tips and I begged and begged, 'Couldn't we have the tree sprayed red?' Mother's answer was a definite no. Our tree had to be green. 'That's final!' she said.

"Then Daddy had an idea. (Yes, he spoiled me terribly.) 'Let's get Joanie a little red tree for her room.' And they did.

"Each year for the next few, until I outgrew my penchant for things red and switched to blue (no, I never got a blue tree), a two-foot red Christmas tree sat on a table in my bedroom. I was allowed to trim it with the leftover balls and tinsel from the big tree. The trimming of the big tree was a major production. The butler strung the lights, Bens stood on a ladder decorating what I couldn't reach, I did the bottom. The most beautiful of the ornaments was the top one—a large silver star with small flame-shaped light bulbs at the five tips. A light hidden inside the center shone through the cut out words: *Merry Christmas*.

"When the tree was decorated the gifts had already begun to arrive and were placed underneath. By the day before Christmas they fanned out to cover at least half the room—most of them for me. I think in those early days I must have received at least one hundred presents. It took more than an hour to unwrap them. Some were from friends and some were from parents, but many came from business associates to show how much they *loved* me. Of course I couldn't tell which was which but I didn't care. A present was a present. Some were lavish, some were trinkets, some came from people who didn't know what to buy for daddy—he had everything—so they bought a gift for me instead. At this point you may be wondering why the granddaughter of Meyer Kubelsky had a Christmas tree or, in my case, two!

"At that point in time and in Beverly Hills it wasn't very unusual. My memory may be faulty but I seem to remember most famous families, Jewish or not, had trees and celebrated Christmas then. It wasn't really a religious thing, more like just an excuse to celebrate and exchange gifts. My parents' real religion was show business.

4. Joan Benny

"With my four children I've always celebrated Christmas. too. And taught them carols and read the related stories in the New Testament. To me, it isn't important whether or not one believes in Christ as the savior—the Christians do, I as a Jew don't—but the story of his birth is lovely nonetheless, and for children, what with Santa Claus and the tree trimming and the festivity and the presents, it's the most exciting event of the year. Besides it's important to one's education to know about all the world religions and beliefs, not just your own.

"Another highlight of those early years was summertime. Everyone had a pool. Our pool measured 30 feet by 60 feet; the Burnses' was about the same; and some, like the one across the street and Jack Warner's, were Olympic size. Like most of the others, ours had tile sides, tile gutters and tile stripes running the length of the bottom. Some pools had mosaic designs such as fish or flowers scattered along the sides or bottom. Not ours—we had an octopus! Not just a cute little plaque. Nothing so trivial. Our octopus was fifteen feet in diameter. Set in a pastel blue tile octagon, "Ollie" had great tentacles with little brown suckers at their tips. The tentacles undulated and rippled with the movement of the water. As much as I loved to swim and as difficult as it was for my mother to get me out, that *thing* terrified me.

"Fortunately the pool was large enough for me to avoid Ollie by swimming close to the edges, looking straight down or straight ahead. Sometimes, when I was feeling brave, I managed to swim over him with my eyes closed. But he was always there. I complained a lot. Finally, in desperation, my parents decided to do something about it. They didn't want poor little Joanie to be frightened and so one winter (I must have been about seven), at great expense, the pool was drained and the black tiles in the eyes were replaced with pastel shades of green and tan. The pool was refilled and the problem solved.

"'There now, you won't be scared anymore, will you, sweetheart?' Daddy said.

"'No,' I replied. 'I guess not.' What Mom and Daddy didn't realize was that I never minded the black eyes, it was those ever-wavering, menacing tentacles that had me panic stricken. But what could I say after they had gone to so much trouble? They thought they had done the right thing, and now I simply had to learn to live with it. As I grew up I got used to it. In fact throwing and diving for coins on Ollie became a favorite sport. Today I think of our octopus with nostalgia.

"Unlike today, we were on easy terms with sightseers and fans clutching their maps of movie stars' houses and the tour buses cruising the street. Eddie Cantor, Jimmy Stewart, Hedy Lamarr, Jack Haley, Agnes Moorehead, Jose Ferrer and Rosemary Clooney, Polly Bergen, and Lucille Ball and Desi Arnaz all lived within two blocks of us. In those days movie stars were relaxed and friendly and so were the tourists. They frequently came to our front door, rang the bell and asked for an autographed photo. A stack of pictures was kept in a drawer in the foyer table. Sometimes I answered the door, had a short chat and handed out a photograph. It was also perfectly normal for Daddy to answer the door himself if he was nearby. He enjoyed—or rather he loved—meeting his fans.

"The house next door to ours belonged to a family named Burr. It was also a white Georgian two-story brick, so of course the two houses were frequently confused by fans.

During the first few years as our neighbors, the Burrs dealt with the constant picture taking, ringing doorbells and interruptions with some equanimity but eventually it got to them. One day a large sign appeared in their driveway:

JACK BENNY DOES NOT LIVE HERE. HE LIVES THERE.

"Under the 'there' a huge arrow pointed to our house. I don't know whether or not we were responsible for the Burrs finally moving, but move they did and the house was bought by Lucy and Desi who moved in with their two small children. Now the fans could choose either house and not make a mistake.

"When it came to entertaining, my parents were no slouches. Their parties were frequent and lavish. During the late 1930s and early 1940s— the years when my parents held their spectacular New Years Eve parties— I was sent off to spend the night at my grandparents. By the time I was eight, I was finally allowed to remain at home and even allowed to invite a friend over. I loved to watch the frantic preparations, the tent for dinner and dancing being erected over the patio, the caterer's truck arriving with giant boxes of ingredients for the extravagant meal, the rental company truck with the chairs and tables and table settings, the florist with the magnificent centerpieces for the tables and vines to decorate the pillars, the dance floor being nailed together, and on and on. The place was a madhouse. I tried to help and not be in everyone's way, but I probably didn't succeed.

"Those glittering parties—I remember how beautiful the women were in their evening gowns and jewels and how handsome the men were in

4. Joan Benny

their dinner jackets. After a full day of 'helping' the crew, I scurried off upstairs, not wanting to miss watching Mom get dressed. There was as much commotion in her dressing room as downstairs. I had to stay in a corner to be out of the way of her hairdresser, maid, dressmaker. Then into Daddy's room to help him choose his cufflinks and studs. What would they have done without me? Mother and Daddy went downstairs just in time for the door bell to ring.

"And there was Barbara Stanwyck, slim and elegant with her husband, Robert Taylor. Then Frank Sinatra with his wife, Nancy. Van and Evie Johnson, George and Gracie, Stewart Granger and his wife, Jean Simmons, George Montgomery and his wife, Dinah Shore, Tony Martin (later with Cyd Charisse), Jimmy and Gloria Stewart, Ray and Mal Milland, Gary and Rocky Cooper, the Edward G. Robinsons, the Robert Montgomerys, the Humphrey Bogarts, Keenan Wynn, Danny and Sylvia Kaye, the Henry Fondas, Ronnie and Benita Colman, Bob and Dolores Hope, Al Jolson, Ronald Reagan and Jane Wyman, Ann Sheridan, Betty Grable—and on and on.

"The casts changed as the years went by—different airings reflected the occasional divorce and remarriage and new faces appeared as they also did on Hollywood movie screens, but the format of the parties remained the same. It began with cocktails, followed by dinner and dancing under the tent, and always ended with the best part of all and what made a Hollywood party unique: impromptu entertainment in the living room. Entertainers love to entertain, particularly when they are with their friends and colleagues and feel they can let their hair down and be silly and risqué.

"It didn't seem at all extraordinary for Dinah to start things rolling with a Sammy Cahn song. Then George Burns would get up and tell stories that made Daddy literally fall down and pound the floor. Jane, Van, Tony or Betty might sing, Danny Kaye would do a double-talk routine accompanied by Sylvia. Frank would knock 'em dead with a ballad or two or three.

"Going to the studio with my parents to watch the show on Sundays was another special part of my life. It wasn't like going to see where Daddy works. I used to go to Daddy's office and it was just an office. The radio studio was glamorous. But even more glamorous were the motion picture studios, and during the years that Dad made pictures I was allowed to visit him on set. I remember particularly Paramount and Warner Brothers. I couldn't get enough of it. In one of his movies there was a chorus line of girls wearing gorgeous white tulle and silver-spangled costumes.

They had big puffy sleeves, sweetheart necklines, tight bodices, and ballet-length skirts with layers of petticoats and yards and yards of material.

"I wanted one so badly. I must have been about five years old and I had a little wind-up Victrola in my room and my favorite activity was playing music and dancing to it. To be able to dance in that costume was my idea of bliss. So, I asked Daddy; he asked Paramount and sure enough, they made the costume for me. I even went to the wardrobe department to have it fitted properly. I danced in it and wore it to breakfast, lunch and dinner. It was a struggle to get me out of it at bedtime. I may not have been much of an actress on the stage, but alone in my bedroom there has never been in the history of theater a more beautiful, more graceful, more regal fairy princess.

"Some years later Daddy was doing a film at 20th Century–Fox. Carmen Miranda was then one of their biggest stars. I had gone about as far as I could go as Odette/Odile and was entering my Latin/Xavier Cugat period. You guessed it! A Carmen Miranda costume, complete with platform shoes, ruffled orange satin skirt, bare midriff blouse with big ruffled sleeves and high orange satin hat, bananas and all.

"My life was special, too, because when we went out we were treated differently. Daddy was recognized, and I was fawned over. People were a little nicer to me because I was Jack Benny's daughter. We traveled more than the average family, mostly to New York. I remember being there when I was seven or eight. Danny Kaye, one of my parents' closest friends, had just opened in *Let's Face It!* and Mom took me to a matinee. It was my first Broadway musical and I was thoroughly enthralled. I was hanging on every dance step, every lyric. Included in the many songs was one of Danny's famous patter numbers. I think it must have been Cole Porter's *Let's Not Talk About Love* because it's all full of different names of then-famous people. Knowing we were in the audience, he changed one of the names as written and sang 'Joan Benny' instead. When I heard it I promptly jumped up in my seat, turned around from my third-row seat to face the audience and yelled excitedly, 'That's me, that's me!'

"When Daddy died I was thirty-nine years old. On television and in the newspaper obituaries, wherever I was mentioned as a 'survivor,' I was referred to as his 'adopted daughter,' Joan. I tried very hard not to let it bother me. The fact of my adoption certainly never had before; it was simply a fact. But after all these years of loving and caring, I read 'adopted daughter' as if I weren't really his child but rather some kid he felt sorry for and took in.

4. Joan Benny

"Yes, it bothered me—a lot!—and for the very first time in my life. Daddy was gone and the press made me feel as though I was an afterthought. Why couldn't they have said 'his daughter Joan?' I never wept for him. There was no reason to. I still see Daddy frequently on television and hear his voice on the radio or on one of my many tapes. I miss his footsteps, his cigar, our phone conversations, the trips, the drop-in visits, but those things aren't so important. What's important is that he's still very much alive for me. He's just out of town playing a long engagement.

"How could I be sad? I can only be happy for him. He lived eighty full, happy, successful years. He had a wife and a daughter who loved him. He had hundreds of loyal friends and thousands of adoring fans. He had recently finished a gig and was about to star in a film. He didn't get old and doddering, grow deaf or blind or lose his memory. Not him. He went out a star. No, he was not an intellectual giant. No, he was not without his flaws. No, he was not the funniest man in person. No, he had some anger. He had his faults, but none of them, I thought, serious faults, and all covered up by the fact that he was so dear to those he loved. My dad wasn't perfect ... but he was as close as anyone I'm ever going to meet or have met."

A recent shot of Joan Benny, all grown up (courtesy Joan Benny).

5

GARY LEWIS

Son of Jerry Lewis and Patti Palmer

I've had great success being a total idiot.
—Jerry Lewis

Jerry Lewis would have to be considered the most well-known modern-day clown ever to come out of Hollywood. His zany, childlike antics were his trademark, whether he was teamed with his straight-man partner Dean Martin or solo in his own films. More often than not those solo films were written and directed by the man himself.

Martin and Lewis were a popular pair in the 1950s and early 1960s. Whether with Dean Martin or without, Jerry Lewis was ranked one of the top ten box office stars during that time. Brought to Hollywood by Hal Wallis, Martin and Lewis were already a successful comedy team in nightclubs all across America. *My Friend Irma* was their first pairing in 1949 and the twosome became an immediate hit with the filmgoing public.

Many more Martin and Lewis films followed, always with the same plot recipe. Martin played the smooth-talking straight man, Lewis played the bumbling idiot who gets them both into trouble and both of them usually end up with the girl by the time the end credits roll. It was a simple story but it always worked. Their last film together was *Hollywood or Bust*, after which they went their own separate ways. Lewis continued in film with a successful solo career, with many memorable films such as the original *Nutty Professor*. He is without a doubt one of the great Hollywood clowns. His unique style is a lasting reminder of how such simplistic comedy can bring so much pleasure to generations of filmgoers, some fifty years later.

Born in 1946, Gary Lewis is one of five sons from Lewis's first

5. Gary Lewis

A young Gary Lewis sits on his father's shoulders at a train station. His father is none other than screwball comedian Jerry Lewis.

marriage to Patti Palmer. Patti thought that Cary Grant was a terrific actor and wanted to name her oldest son Cary. The hospital where Gary Lewis was born made a mistake when they recorded his name as "Gary" instead of "Cary." To this day his name has always been Gary Harold Lee Lewis. Gary's family members, however, still poke fun at what was supposed to be his original name. For his fourteenth birthday in the summer of 1960 Gary was given a set of drums. Four years later he formed a group in the Los Angeles area with guitarists David Walker and Al Ramsay, lead guitarist David Costell, keyboard player John West, and Gary himself on drums and vocals. They called themselves Gary Lewis and the Playboys and eventually began playing at Disneyland. West Coast record producer Snuff Garrett signed them to a contract with Liberty Records.

Children of Hollywood

Garrett suggested to Gary Lewis that he have his famous father, comedian Jerry Lewis, use his connections to get the group a guest appearance on *The Ed Sullivan Show*. The arrangements were made and after their performance on nationwide television in January, 1965, the group became literally an overnight sensation. Their song "This Diamond Ring" shot up to number one and the pressing plants ran twenty-four hours a day but could not keep up with the demand for the record. The arranger on most of their recordings was Leon Russell, who would sit on the beach in Venice with Gary Lewis writing rock-and-roll songs that the group turned into smashing successes. By the end of 1965 most of the original personnel had left the group and been replaced. Keyboard player John West remained, and he played along with Tom Tripplehorn, Carl Radle, and Jimmy Karstein. The latter three were all recruited by Leon Russell from his hometown of Tulsa, Oklahoma.

In 1965 and 1966, Gary Lewis and the Playboys released seven songs that made the top ten: "This Diamond Ring," "Count Me In," "Save Your Heart for Me," "She's Just My Style," "Everybody Loves a Clown," "Sure Gonna Miss Her" and "Green Grass." In late 1966, the Selective Service derailed the huge success of the group by sending Gary Lewis his draft notification. He was inducted into the Army on the first day of 1967. Jerry Lewis publicly expressed his anger at his son's return from Vietnam. Gary returned from the war addicted to drugs and it was Jerry who supported and paid for Gary's rehab. Jerry blamed the U.S military for allowing and even causing Gary's addiction. He even released a media statement saying, "The U.S Military Service will never get their hands on another one of my sons again!"

Gary resumed his career on his discharge in 1968. However, tastes in music had changed and the group never regained the success it had achieved in the mid–1960s, but it had placed a total of fifteen songs in the top one hundred by the end of the decade. Gary Lewis fared better than the offspring of other stars who had taken a run at rock-and-roll. He is a talented singer, songwriter and musician. His party songs sold well in the mid–1960s at the height of Beatlemania, but the psychedelic mood that prevailed in the following years made his style of music out of vogue. Tom Tripplehorn, who performed with the group during its most successful period, returned to Tulsa when Lewis was

5. Gary Lewis

drafted and still makes a living playing rock-and-roll and blues guitar there. He is the father of actress Jeanne Tripplehorn.

Gary Lewis now lives in New York and still tours with his group known as Gary Lewis and the Playboys. The present lineup of Gary Lewis and the Playboys includes Gary Lewis, Rich Spina, Paul Sidoti, Michal Hudak, Darren Frate and Billy Sullivan. Gary still plays the drums and sings and he gives a somewhat frenetic, inspired performance. He really enjoys his music.

A recent shot of the band Gary Lewis and the Playboys. Left to right: Darren Frate, Rich Spina, Gary Lewis, Michal Hudak and Billy Sullivan (courtesy Gary Lewis).

Gary Lewis is the perfect example of a son successfully living outside the shadow of his famous father. Being the child of such a huge star as Jerry Lewis can't be easy. It is often difficult for the children of Hollywood stars to achieve notoriety with their own names. More often than not life is peppered with comments like, "Oh, you're Jerry Lewis' son."

Despite his father being the one and only Jerry Lewis, Gary has proven himself to be a talent in his own right. He's used his own name and his own inner talent to become known as Gary Lewis, of Gary Lewis and the Playboys. His lengthy career isn't built on being the son of a comedy legend; such fame is short lived. Gary's career is built on the fact that he's able to stand on his own two feet, and for many children of Hollywood stars, that's the toughest job of all.

*****

The following is a list of the most successful songs by Gary Lewis and the Playboys in order of release, from earliest to latest, complete with their highest place on the Billboard charts. Just reading the titles

Children of Hollywood

will surely jog your memory and start you whistling one of their catchy tunes!

1. (Billboard Hit No. 1) "This Diamond Ring" 1/16/65
2. (Billboard Hit No. 2) "Count Me In" 4/3/65
3. (Billboard Hit No. 1) "Save Your Heart for Me" 7/3/65
4. (Billboard Hit No. 4) "Everybody Loves a Clown" 9/25/65
5. (Billboard Hit No. 3) "She's Just My Style" 12/11/65
6. (Billboard Hit No. 9) "Sure Gonna Miss Her" 3/5/66
7. (Billboard Hit No. 8) "Green Grass" 5/14/66
8. (Billboard Hit No. 13) "My Heart's a Symphony" 7/30/66
9. (Billboard Hit No. 15) "You Don't Have to Paint Me a Picture" 10/8/66
10. (Billboard Hit No. 21) "Where Will the Words Come From" 12/17/67
11. (Billboard Hit No. 39) "Girl's in Love" 3/11/67
12. (Billboard Hit No. 19) "Sealed with a Kiss" 6/22/68

6

DAMON LANZA

★ *Son of Mario Lanza and Betty Lyhan* ★

> *I sing from the heart... I sing the words of a song and really feel them, from the top of my head to the tip of my toes... I sing as though my life depends on it, and if I ever stop doing that then I'll stop living.*
> —Mario Lanza

Mario Lanza was Hollywood's modern-day answer to Nelson Eddy. The man with the golden voice made just eight films over a ten-year period and is most commonly known for his brilliant portrayal of opera great Enrico Caruso in the 1951 film *The Great Caruso*. It was the top-grossing film of that year.

Born in 1921, he was discovered by conductor Serge Koussevitzky. After he became a well-known recording star he was swiftly signed by MGM. He debuted in the 1949 film *That Midnight Kiss* and followed soon after in *The Toast of New Orleans*, the latter film featuring one of his most famous songs, "Be My Love." After several conflicts with MGM he made his last two films in Rome for Titanus, for distribution by MGM at a later date. Due to ongoing battles with his weight and other various health complications, Mario Lanza died of a heart attack in 1959. He was just thirty-eight years old.

Much has been speculated about his death over the years, including persistent rumors of Mafia involvement. Here, Damon Lanza, his only surviving son, tells a moving story and settles those rumors, once and for all.

"My name is Damon Lanza, son of Betty Lyhan and Mario Lanza. I was born in Hollywood, California, on December 12, 1952. My parents had four children, two of whom have since passed away. My oldest sister Colleen (now deceased) was born on December 9, 1948. She was struck by a car and killed in August of 1997. My second oldest sister was born on December 3, 1950, and my younger brother Marc (also deceased) was born May 19, 1954. Marc was born with a hole in his heart and in June of 1991, he also passed on. He was only thirty-seven years old. So now, I am the only surviving son to carry on the Lanza name and it makes me proud to do so.

"Every time I remember my early childhood, I can remember my father always singing around the house. He sang to my mother and to us children quite often. My memories actually started when we arrived in Italy in the year 1957. There were so many people coming and going in our home. When we arrived in Rome we moved into the Villa Badaglio at 56 Bruxelles, which was the home that Benito Mussolini built for his Marshall Badoglio in appreciation of his conquest of Abyssinia and which is now the Chinese Embassy. I began to 'sense' that my father was someone important because he sang, but I didn't yet realize how important or significant that really was until the following year or so. My father made his first European movie in Italy, which was named *The Seven Hills of Rome*. He would take us kids with him whenever possible because he loved to be with us.

"I remember one time my mother and father were talking about taking us to the set and my father said to my mother to make sure that we were kept quiet. In trying to help my father's wishes when they started shooting, I would lean over to my brother and sisters and remind them to be quiet. Of course the microphones picked this up and later we had to be moved back to a more 'secured' position. All through this movie, I remember the vast numbers of people who surrounded my father, asking him questions, smiling, and touching him and seeing him do a lot of writing. I later learned that he was signing autographs.

"Both my parents seemed very happy then and I can remember them always smiling and laughing. There were many parties and many people coming to our home. I can well remember how we kids would sneak out from our rooms and watch all the people having fun. Of course we always got caught and returned to our rooms, but it was fun. We had a governess and servants to look after our every need, which was really neat.

"All our birthdays were events, to be sure. I remember one birthday in particular when Colleen turned ten and my parents gave her a surprise party. They brought about five clowns, Shetland ponies, magicians and

6. Damon Lanza

about fifty-five friends from school and of course many of their parents. My mother cooked a lot of the food as well as having some of it delivered from the nearest restaurant. This was almost a common practice for any of our birthdays. I remember many of our friends always asking us at school, 'When is the next birthday party?' Guess we were well known for our birthday parties.

"Christmas was no exception. In fact, our Christmas time was legendary in our neighborhood and school. My mother would have a 25-plus-foot tree delivered to our home many weeks before Christmas. She wanted us kids to enjoy the spirit of Christmas for much

Baby Damon Lanza in the arms of his proud father Mario Lanza (courtesy Damon Lanza and Bob Dolfi).

longer than just weeks. As my father was still on location daily, we kids and my mother would decorate the tree. When my father would return home and look at the tree, he would exclaim that something was missing, only to pull out some salami and cheeses to hang on the tree. Of course these did not last very long because whenever we had company come over, my father would always pull some of these off and give them to the company as a goodwill gesture. And what he did not give away, he would cut up for us to nibble on. Of all my memories of Christmas, the one strong memory that always stands out is when my father dressed up as Santa Claus. Of course his voice was a giveaway to us kids but to the rest of our friends, that was really Santa.

"My mother and father had a gift for every kid who came to our home and many of their parents as well. By this time I began to realize that my father's voice was important. I sensed that many people wanted him to sing and would ask him to sing all the time. Sometimes he would and often times he would not. However, he sang each and every night to us kids as he tucked us into our beds. First he would tell us a bedtime story that he himself would make up, not a standard bedtime story from a book. As we started to drift off to sleep, he would quietly sing 'Guardian Angels,' the song that Harpo Marx wrote, to us. I guess this was the association that I figured out about his voice and why so many people were always around him.

"By this time my father was doing a lot of traveling all over Europe doing concerts. When he came back home he would seem very happy and always had a smile. Although much of this time period is somewhat fuzzy, I do remember some sporadic instances when he returned home and although he was very happy, he would complain to my mother how he did not feel well. I can remember at times my mother would ask us to 'Let your father rest, he is tired.' I suppose this was because we would always be so happy to see him after he was gone for a while that we sometimes went into his room and jumped on the bed and woke him.

"I remember hearing a few conversations that pertained to their Hawaiian trip with Tyrone Power and his wife Linda Christian in 1950. My mother would start laughing as she reminded my father of that trip where they all had dinners and drinks and went to all the local luaus on the island. Years later, I came across fifty-four Hawaiian pictures of my father, mother, Tyrone and his wife and I could see why she was laughing so much. They were really humorous pictures; they had straws coming from their noses, ears and mouth. This was indeed a happy period in their life, or so it seemed. The concerts continued and I remember things began to change a little. I suppose that as a child, you see things differently or maybe you see only 'some' of the whole picture, but things seemed to change.

"Then came my father's next and last movie, *For the First Time*, which was filmed on the Isle of Capri. Zsa Zsa Gabor was in that picture also. I remember that my father was not feeling that well in those days and for the first time that I can remember, he seemed irritable—just not his usual self. The movie ended almost on schedule but my father by this time was not feeling well at all. On October 7, 1959, my father had a heart attack, which ultimately killed him.

"After a brief funeral in Rome, we came back to America for a second funeral in his hometown of Philadelphia, Pennsylvania, followed by a third in Los Angeles, California, where he lies today at Holy Cross Cemetery in Culver City. When we returned to America, we stayed with Ms. Kathryn Grayson for about three months. This was my parents' best

6. Damon Lanza

friend, bar none. We then moved into our own home close to my grandparents' home in Pacific Palisades. This was the home that my father and mother bought for them. Sadly, three months later my mother passed away, barely six months after my father.

"The Los Angeles Superior Courts awarded us children to my grandparents, Maria and Tony Cocozza. We then moved into their home. My grandparents were loving and caring people who loved us very much. By this time, I was hearing several different stories about my father and how he had died. For the first time, I heard the word 'Mafia.' This came from someone who later wrote a book about my father. Of course this was unfounded and later proved to be false but nonetheless had done its damage.

"Rumors were now being circulated that my father died under mysterious circumstances and that the Mafia had killed him. Nurses from the hospital where my father died were supposedly disappearing and chauffeurs were claimed to be missing. Why these people started this rumor is beyond me, but I suppose it was to sell their books. Research needed to be done and done right away.

"I approached my best friend Bob Dolfi to help me with my research, as Bob is the indisputable archive writer on Mario Lanza. Bob has been my closest friend since 1963. So Bob and I decided to travel to Europe to try and get to the bottom of this story. We went to Italy, Germany and England to research the truth. It took us three trips to track down all our findings but here is what we found out. Immediately after the filming of *For the First Time* ended, my father had his first heart attack on April 17, 1959, followed by a second one on August 27, 1959. His blood pressure was measured at 290. We uncovered several German doctors' letters warning my father

A recent shot of Damon Lanza, all grown up (courtesy Damon Lanza and Bob Dolfi).

to slow down his lifestyle and rest. They also told him that he needed to rest for about one month without even so much as speaking. Medical records showed my father had a serious case of phlebitis and gout. Bob Dolfi then flew to Italy and picked up some medical records that he uncovered. These records proved without a doubt that my father was severely ill. No nurse disappeared and no chauffeur disappeared.

"After we printed all this information in the book that Bob and I wrote, *Be My Love: A Celebration of Mario Lanza*, we were contacted and interviewed on *Mysteries and Scandals* which went to one hundred twenty-five million homes. We had positive proof that my father died of a heart attack. There was no Mafia involvement whatsoever.

"Bob and I are working together with Mr. Robert Parkinson (of the *Circus of Stars* TV show) on a Broadway musical show about my parents. In addition to this, we will be opening a one-man two-act show based on my father's Coca-Cola days in song. Today I live in Los Angeles and buy and sell restaurants with my partner, Bob Dolfi. Every year we travel to parts of Europe to visit the Official Friends of Mario Lanza Fan club in England. There are many fan clubs but the Rugby Fan Club is the one Bob and I are associated with. Every year the Mario Lanza Institute in Philadelphia has an annual Mario Lanza ball and fans from all over the world attend.

"There is even a Mario Lanza museum where a fan can purchase anything and everything on my father. In addition to this I am also the editor of our quarterly newsletter, *The Lanza Legend*. Bob Dolfi is the archive writer and researcher, and together we produce this newsletter that goes to twenty countries. Based in San Pedro, California, our honorary president is Mr. Al Martino. We have just started the official Mario Lanza website at www.lanzalegend.com and thanks to the Internet we are hearing from fans all over the world.

"We visit Kathryn Grayson monthly and sit and watch the movies my father and she made together. It brings back many memories from when we lived with her for that short time. I am thankful that we were able to put some of these rumors to rest about the Mafia and so-called disappearances of nurses and chauffeurs. There was no mystery to how my parents died. The world may remember my father as the world's greatest voice, but I remember my father as the world's best father."

7

ROMINA POWER

* Daughter of Tyrone Power *
and Linda Christian

The secret of charm is bullshit.

—Tyrone Power

Tyrone Power was once described by Daryl Zanuck as "the truest, handsomest, best of the lot." He was 20th Century–Fox's leading box office star from 1938 to 1948 and was considered the typical "all–American" stereotype. After a varied career playing such diverse rolls as Jesse James and Zorro and even a clever murderer in his last film, the critically acclaimed *Witness for the Prosecution,* Tyrone Power died doing what he loved best—acting.

During a dueling scene with fellow actor George Sanders on the set of *Solomon and Sheba* in Madrid, Power retired to his dressing room after experiencing severe chest pains. He convinced everyone that he just needed to rest. He was found moments later collapsed on the floor of his dressing room, still in costume. It was a heart attack. Although he was rushed to the hospital, it was too late. One of the world's great actors had died, long before his time, at just forty-four. His tombstone bears the masks of comedy and tragedy along with the simple inscription:

Goodnight, Sweet Prince ...
May flights of angels send thee to thy rest.

He left behind two young daughters, Taryn Power and Romina Power, and with his son, Tyrone Power, Jr., still only months away from being born, which makes the timing of his death seem an even

Children of Hollywood

Proud parents Tyrone Power and Linda Christian holding baby Romina (courtesy Romina Power).

greater tragedy—dying before his son and namesake ever knew him. On January 22, 1959, just two months after his father's death, Tyrone Jr. was born with black hair and a dimple in his chin. Tyrone Power's third wife, Debbie Ann Minardos, released a statement to the press saying, "He's beautiful, he looks exactly like his father."

Unusually, Tyrone Jr. was not the only child of a Hollywood legend born shortly after his father's death. John Clark Gable was born shortly after the death of his father, Clark Gable, and subsequently spent his life never knowing the man the rest of the world called "The King of Hollywood." The following memories are told by Romina Power, Tyrone Power's eldest child from his second marriage to Linda Christian.

> "I was born Romina Francesca Power on October 2, 1951. I am the daughter, the firstborn child, of Linda Christian and Tyrone Power. Since my parents fell in love in Rome, Italy, and because they were married in the church of Santa Francesca Romana they decided to name me in honor of where they were wed. They preferred Romina to Romana (after the church) and they invented this new name. My name has now become a common name in Italy, after me, unfortunately.
>
> "I was just seven years old when my father died and at the time I was in a boarding school in Mexico—Marymount, a Catholic nun's school in

7. Romina Power

Cuernavaca. My father had said he'd prefer us to stay with our grandmother in Mexico and have a Catholic upbringing as opposed to traveling around the world with our mother. I was not aware of my father's death. What is more, I was not even aware that my parents had divorced two years previously. I don't remember much of anything from around the time of my father's death, parents' divorce, etc. Some people have told me that maybe I've removed it from my memory because I didn't know how to deal with it. Taryn, my sister, remembers more and yet she is younger.

"The only memories I have of him are in my dreams during the 1970s and 1980s when I was doing research on a book on him—memories that I'd created in my own mind from stories that were told to me by other people who were there and remembered. My father was the type of person who would have played games with us and told us stories and made us laugh if he had the chance. I know he would have loved to sail with us. I do remember him taking us on his airplane. I visited him on several of his film sets in New York for *The Eddie Duchin Story* with Kim Novak and in California on *Abandon Ship*. The only way I know this is because I have photos of us together on location. I remember none of it.

"He had a few close, true friends: Cesar Romero, Orson Welles, Charles Laughton, Lawrence Olivier and Vivien Leigh, Claire Trevor and Gene Tierney. He starred alongside Gene Tierney in several films; they were great friends. I've heard from several mutual friends that they lived on the same street, Salt Air, for several years and took turns hosting parties at each other's houses. Several of his friends have told me that my father had a great sense of humor and even called them from overseas just to tell them a new joke that he'd heard.

"Many famous people would visit my father's home. I have several party photos with children of celebrities, clowns in the garden, the works. All things that any child would most likely remember because these were not ordinary children's parties, they were huge! Again, I remember nothing."

Romina has lived in Italy since she was nine years old, "too long" according to her, but she has had a long career as a professional singer there and is a celebrity in her own right. Now separated from her singer husband, Al Bano, theirs was a relationship that was frowned upon by Romina's mother. At just sixteen, Romina met Al in a cinema studio in Rome, Italy. Al was eight years her senior and an already established Italian pop singer himself. They soon fell in love and they were married, still against the wishes of her mother, in 1969. They soon began

Children of Hollywood

A young Romina on the film set with her handsome father, Tyrone Power (courtesy Romina Power).

singing together and released their first duet in 1970—"Storia Di Due Innamorati (Story of Two Lovers)"—onto the Italian market. Their diverse ability to record their albums in Italian, Spanish and English has seen them appear at many international song festivals around the world. They've released several albums together and solo and they're both well-known entertainers all over Europe. Romina explains further:

> "I liked singing when I was in boarding school in England when I was eleven. I wrote my first songs with Sarah, my best friend in school. I recorded my first single in Italy when I was just fifteen. I actually started acting professionally before singing; I made my first movie in Italy when I was thirteen. It was called *Menage All Italiana*. I absolutely love acting!"

7. Romina Power

Left: A proud Tyrone Power with his two daughters, a young Romina and baby Taryn. *Right:* Tyrone Power enjoying some pool time with his daughter Romina. (Both photographs courtesy Romina Power.)

Romina has four children. Ylenia was born in Rome in 1970; Yari, a son, was born in Rome in 1973; Cristel was born in Romina and Al's home in Puglia in the South of Italy in 1985; and Romina was also born at home in 1987. "My two oldest children have watched many of my father's films, they like to see their grandfather up there on the screen. My youngest know a little less. But I do constantly try my best to keep his memory alive with them.

Sadly, Romina's oldest daughter Ylenia disappeared in 1994 and has not yet been found. An attractive young woman with blonde hair and green eyes, she was the successful host of an Italian talk show. She traveled to New Orleans to do research on a book she intended to write. She never returned. Every year hundreds of young women disappear in the city of New Orleans.

"It's a mystery what happened to Ylenia," Romina says. "New Orleans is a dangerous city. I cannot believe that crimes like this happen on a regular basis in a country like the United States, yet nothing is seriously done about it. She disappeared in 1994. Since then we've had no news of her. I still have faith and hope that she'll return someday. One piece of advice I would give to young people who decide to travel the world: never travel alone, no matter how courageous you feel, never travel alone, *never!*

"As to my sister and brother, my relationship with them is great. Even though we have an ocean between us, there is an inner connection with the three of us. I like to say our hearts are in the same time zone. My sister Taryn lives on a farm in Wisconsin. We spent a month together last summer, and we phone each other often. My brother lives in L.A., and we also connect as often as we can. We met as adults because our mothers weren't on good terms. Our first meeting was when I was thirty-seven and he was thirty."

Romina Power, all grown up (courtesy Romina Power).

In conclusion, Romina tells of a favorite childhood story that makes her laugh, something she was told by a family friend from when she was a little girl.

"I've been told that when I was six years old, in London, my dad was acting in a stage play, and since I was considered very mature and well behaved for my age, I was allowed to go and watch him one night. Normally I was a very quiet child. In fact, that evening I was silent until he appeared on stage. At that very moment I stood up and screamed at the top of my lungs, as loud as I could, 'That's my daddy, that's my daddy!' I was in one of the balconies, and the play was a serious drama, so you can imagine the reaction of the public. My poor father, what must he have thought. I'm sure he was just as amused as everyone else."

It is somewhat tragic, as stated before, that Tyrone Power, Jr., wasn't born in time to meet his famous father. Yet, in some strange way, Romina was lucky enough to have had seven years with him but her memories are few. All that she knows of him is what she's been

7. Romina Power

told second hand. She knows only of certain things they did together by the collection of photos that she has in her family album. Like an amnesia patient, she is fed a past that she lived but fails to remember in her own head. She's entirely aware that she may have erased these memories from her head herself as a self-protection against any hurt she faced in losing her father at such a young age. Whatever the reason, she will always be Tyrone Power's daughter and he will always be Romina Power's father. Nothing else really matters.

8

JANET CANTOR GARI

★ *Youngest Daughter of Eddie Cantor* ★
and Ida Tobias

BRIAN GARI

★ *Son of Janet Cantor Gari and* ★
Grandson of Eddie Cantor
and Ida Tobias

A wedding is a funeral where you smell your own flowers.
—Eddie Cantor (*Kid Millions*, 1934)

Eddie Cantor did it all and he succeeded at it all, too—vaudeville, stage, radio, film and television. You name it, he did it. Nicknamed "Banjo Eyes" because of his big round eye-popping stare and standing at only 5 feet 8 inches in height, he may have been small in stature but his presence was almighty. His film career began with the silents, when he starred alongside the "It Girl," Clara Bow, in *Kid Boots*, a film version adapted from his success in the Ziegfeld stage production. His songs and jokes were just as well known. "If You Knew Susie" and "Ida, Sweet as Apple Cider," written for his wife Ida Tobias, were two of his better known songs. Of course, most of his fast, wisecracking jokes were directed at his wife and five daughters.

Unlike a lot of other stars, he made a successful transition to sound pictures, and most of his work was done under the watchful eye of Samuel Goldwyn. In fact, for a time Samuel Goldwyn owned the rights to *The Wizard of Oz*, and Eddie Cantor was seriously considered for

8. *Janet Cantor Gari* and *Brian Gari*

the role of the scarecrow. Of course, MGM eventually ended up with the final rights to the film and Ray Bolger was cast as the scarecrow. It's usually difficult to think of another actor playing a role that has been made so famous by someone else, but the idea of casting Eddie Cantor as the scarecrow was perfect. Had it gone ahead, he would have been just as good as Ray Bolger if not better. Cantor went on to star in many of Busby Berkeley's lavish productions. He's often seen surrounded by a group of beautiful dancing girls. He continued in film as late as 1948 and he was honored with a special Academy Award for his distinguished services to film comedy in 1956.

A pensive portrait pose of Eddie Cantor.

Here his youngest daughter, Janet Cantor Gari, tells her touching story of a man simply known to her as Dad. Over several days of constant communication, Janet happily provided me with a private peek into her childhood. She speaks truthfully and lovingly and, of course, there's a touch of that Cantor family humor thrown in every once in a while! In an interesting twist, her son Brian Gari also tells his story. I was lucky enough to have two generations both talking about one man: Eddie Cantor—father, grandfather and nonstop entertainer.

> "As a child I had the best of all possible worlds. I was both an only child and a member of a large family. Since the sister nearest to me in age is six years my senior, I was most definitely the 'baby.' My oldest sister was twelve years older and to me, therefore, an 'adult.' One of my other sisters once told me that she was sure our parents had created me to present the rest of them with a live doll with which to play, and play they did. I suppose I should have been terribly spoiled, but I responded to all

that love and attention by reciprocating with love and loyalty myself. It was also fascinating to me to be able to look into the future biologically and anticipate each change in my own body.

"My parents were both born on the Lower East Side of New York in 1892. My father, orphaned by the age of two, was raised by his grandmother, who left her own thriving little business in Russia and came to take care of her ailing daughter. Although she worked very hard at back-breaking jobs, she and her little grandson were often at the starvation point. My mother's father, a tailor by trade, saw to it that his six daughters and one son always had enough to eat, but no one even knew the meaning of the word 'luxury.'

"My father, frequently playing hooky from school, would watch my athletic mother doing high jumps in the playground, impressed by her agility and taken by her long, thick blue-black hair and bright blue eyes. By the time they were in their early teens, he was courting her by making her laugh, but her father didn't want his daughter to hang around with a 'bum like that.' He tried very hard to hold down a nine-to-five job but was always getting thrown out for making fun of the boss or showing up late or, if he had the chance to go to a vaudeville theatre, not showing up at all. Finally, when he got a steady job as a singing waiter in Coney Island, my grandfather relented and allowed them to 'go steady.'

"They were married in 1914 and went to London on their honeymoon, not because they could afford it but because my father was working with a partner and they had gotten booked into an English vaudeville house. When they returned to America, my mother discovered she was pregnant with Margie, my oldest sister. Margie spoke beautifully (she actually did everything beautifully) and Mother, who made up her own rules and came to her own conclusions about everything, always said Margie had the best diction in the family because she was conceived in England! Only two months after Margie was born, Mother found herself expecting again, but my father, steadily rising in his career, was on the road when Natalie was born. By the time Edna came along, however, he was appearing in *The Ziegfeld Follies* and was able to spend more time with the family he was building to take the place of the one he never had. Mother, having grown up surrounded by girls, accepted all her daughters as 'home.'

"After Marilyn's birth, I have a feeling she decided enough was enough, but six years later both my parents longed for a little baby around the house, so I made my entrance. My father was starring in the show *Whoopee* at the time, and my birth announcement read 'Mother doing well at the

8. *Janet Cantor Gari* and *Brian Gari*

Brooklyn Jewish Hospital; Father doing well at the New Amsterdam Theatre.'

"All my sisters had been born at home, but I was premature and it was a very difficult birth. When Mother came home from the hospital, she felt too weak to take on another child and she called an agency for a nursemaid to take over when the hospital nurse had completed her shift. Winnie entered my life when I was six months old and stayed until she got married on my eleventh birthday, after which I saw her at least once a week. Boy, did I give Winnie a few scary moments. I was a climber—trees, ladders, small mountains, etc.

"We lived on the top floors of the San Remo. I was never allowed on the roof area by myself, but one day, by golly, I managed to slip out of the office door alone. There was a decorative tower with a light in it about another story higher, and what should I find but rungs on the side of the building. Up I went, about seven years old and with the confidence and lack of fear that only a young child possesses. There just happened to be an electrician working on the light in the tower, and he called downstairs to say that someone's little girl was hanging off the building, twenty-eight stories above the street!

"Winnie, my nanny, came rushing out and coaxed me down as calmly as she could. She suggested that I not wave to her but keep both hands on the rung above and when I finally reached the bottom and jumped down beside her, she burst into tears and almost hugged the life out of

A two-year-old Janet posing the exact same way as her famous father, comedian Eddie Cantor (courtesy Janet Cantor Gari).

me. I thought she was nuts because I had just seen her about fifteen minutes before and there didn't seem to be any reason for the ecstatic greeting. She very wisely didn't scare me with any warnings but simply said that the management of the building had told them it was against the law for anyone but the electrician to climb up the ladder. 'Oh,' I said solemnly. 'I wouldn't want to break the law.'

"Poor Winnie! For the rest of her life she had nightmares about it, eventually substituting her own children teetering on the top of a mountain. We were so close and I loved her so much that when she died at eighty-eight, her two sons insisted that I sit between them at her funeral because I had really been 'her first child.'

"I don't remember the first two years of my life. I know that my father had made a million dollars in the stock market and that we lived in a huge estate in Great Neck, Long Island, but when the market crashed in 1929, he lost everything and owed about $250,000. He wrote two tiny little books, *Caught Short* and *Yoo Hoo, Prosperity*, which sold so many millions of copies that it paid off his debt and put him back on his feet. By that time the movies beckoned, and he made two silent movies before making the screen version of *Whoopee*.

"We had, of course, moved to Beverly Hills, California, but we came back to New York when he went on the radio (going to California only in the summer for him to make a film but back to New York for the school year). Those were the happiest years of my life. We lived in a duplex apartment in the San Remo on Central Park West, and my father had his office on the floor above, the top floor of the building. My folks had many wonderful parties, and although he would joke and sing with his fellow performers, it was my mother who was the life of the party.

"Far from being the shy person she was in public, she was witty and full of fun and they were a very popular couple. Because my father was so warm and affectionate at home, I don't think any of us realized how harmful it was being 'props' in his act. He was always making jokes on radio about marrying off his five daughters and attributing wise cracks to his 'baby daughter Janet.'

"Just recently a friend mentioned to me how cute she thought it was, and she was surprised that I had found it humiliating. All of us hated being lumped into what sounded to us like a bunch of unattractive burdens around his neck, but it never occurred to us to tell him so because he was completely different as a father. There was a hard and fast rule that everyone was to be at the dinner table at 6:30 every night. No one was allowed to go out (even on a date for the older ones) because he knew that it was the most likely time that we would all be together.

"Not only did we play word games and geography games and make up songs together but it was a time when my father could instill in us all the principles he held dear—that we are indeed our brother's keeper, that if we are taking up space here on earth, the rent we pay is responsibility toward others. We had been blissfully unaware of prejudice because in show business the only person who is considered inferior is the one without talent! He was way ahead of his time in speaking out against racial and religious hatred, and we have all been fighters our entire lives. When I was nine, my folks decided it was time to stop living in rented houses every time we went to California. They bought a house big enough for us all and moved us out there permanently. I was heartbroken. I hated leaving my friends and my school and vowed to come back when I was old enough.

"I had been writing music since I was six, and by the time I graduated high school, I was planning on a career in classical music. However, deep inside I felt that what I needed most was an identity of my own, and I switched from a college preparatory course to a course in office procedure. I learned typing and shorthand and even got school credit for a job in an office that I took after school each day. I earned $10 a week and therefore refused to take an allowance any longer. Because of midyear graduations, which I don't think they have anymore, I graduated at seventeen, and when a friend of mine left to go to an Eastern college, I left a polite note for my folks telling them that it was nothing personal but that I wanted to go home. I had saved $300 and saved even more by sharing a train berth with my friend, who was going to a college in Connecticut but who had to change trains in New York. When I called my folks, they were very calm, but they told me I would have to come home until I was eighteen, at which time they would buy me a ticket to make up for the one I had just used. When I arrived home in the evening, everyone was just sitting down to dinner. I put down my suitcase and tentatively peeked into the dining room. 'Sit down,' my father said with a wink. 'You're late.'

"I took another office job until I was eighteen, and then my folks and I ran away together! My father was about to do the Colgate show on television, and it was shot live in New York. This time I had a roommate—someone I knew well from school. We all got into a cab from the station, and my folks went to the Waldorf Astoria Hotel while my roommate Sunny and I went to a tiny little hotel right across the street. She and I both went job hunting the next day, first trying the same employment agency. We said we were qualified secretaries and that we'd like to work in an office connected with show business (her father was a writer/director). They immediately sent us to Universal Pictures, where they happened to have two openings. We could hardly believe our luck. What they didn't tell us was that the openings were in the legal department, about which we knew nothing whatsoever. For two years we took dictation and typed up contracts and reports without understanding a word. Fortunately, short hand is taken phonetically, so we just wrote down what we heard.

"Then Sunny got homesick and went back to California. I went with her, since it was my first vacation, and while I was out there, a friend called from New York to say that she and a partner were starting a stock company and that they would like me to play the lead in one of their first productions. I was thrilled and learned the entire script on the plane on the way home. It was a wonderful comedy part, and I got raves—even one from one of the most important Boston critics of that time—but when I got back to the city and began to make rounds, I looked only for more outlandish comedy parts and never considered auditioning for the ingénue. Those old jokes about 'marrying off the daughters' were nagging at my subconscious, and I didn't see how I could be pretty enough to play an ingénue.

"Instead, I got married, had my first song published and went on studying music and working as a secretary until I could no longer fit behind my typewriter with Brian about to be born. Brian and I were just reminiscing recently about going to see Judy Garland at the Palace when I was seven months pregnant. I was so small that I didn't really show, and we got all dressed up for that spectacular occasion. I told Brian I thought he became a songwriter that night because he was bouncing around in my belly and not missing a beat!

"My daughter Amanda moved to California about seven years ago. We don't get to see each other much, but she's singing her head off out there at one club or another, and she sends me videos of her shows along with hilarious e-mails. She is one funny person!

"Of course, Allison, her daughter, is the apple of my eye. I was the only sitter she ever had, and I baby sat very, very often. She's beautiful and smart and interested in philosophy and medicine, but she's not the least bit musical. In fact, she loves every single thing I write, even when I myself don't think much of it!

8. *Janet Cantor Gari* and *Brian Gari*

"My folks' friends were mostly the old New York crowd who had also moved to California—Burns and Allen, Jack Benny, etc. I had my first crush on Danny Kaye, and when I was sixteen and got my first driver's license, I would follow him all over Hollywood or park longingly outside of his house. My father said I would end up being arrested as a Peeping Tom, but I got friendly with the neighborhood cop, who knew my license plate by that time and would wave hello to me. I was too young to go to any of the lavish openings of any of my father's movies, but when he came back to the stage in *Banjo Eyes* after a twelve-year absence, I saw first hand what had made him a star.

"It was a musical based on *Three Men on a Horse*, and he made his entrance from inside a rolltop desk. He was given literally a five-minute standing ovation before he had even said a word, and the waves of love between him and the audience were palpable. He had always said there was no such thing as a bad audience; it just meant that you hadn't hit on the right thing yet. I think people loved him because he loved them. He truly appreciated the people who actually paid to see him and never got over it, in fact.

"No matter how important an award he was to receive for his charitable work or whatever, when he and my mother, all dressed up in evening clothes, would come in to say good night to us, he'd poke her in the ribs and say, 'Not bad for a little couple from Henry Street, eh?'

"Not bad at all, Dad, and I'm glad that little couple turned out to be my parents."

Janet's son, Brian Gari, a musician, has his own memories of Eddie Cantor, his grandfather. His is a different perspective, through the eyes of a grandson. His memories shed a whole new light on Eddie Cantor the man, the father, the grandfather, the entertainer. Although he was just twelve years old when his grandfather died, Brian has many memories of a guy who was just a bundle of fun to be around, his grandfather. He just happened to be Eddie Cantor.

"I started making trips with my family to the West Coast at a very early age. When I started school, we would end up spending every summer out there. It was a ball! I really didn't know I had a famous grandfather. I just knew he was a lot of fun. He tried out his old vaudeville magic tricks on me like making a banana go from ear to ear or turn into a quarter. He had a captive audience in me and a good laugher as well! His big trade-

Children of Hollywood

mark eyes were full of joy and his hair was as black as shoe polish (which he was probably using on it at the time).

"We had great times together. I used to love to watch cartoons at his house because NBC had given him one of the first color TVs. What an event that was for me to see my animated friends in living color—a far cry from my tiny black and white in New York. I'll never forget a particular lunch and movie with him. He asked what film I would like to see and I mentioned the Three Stooges' new one called *Have Rocket Will Travel*. Well, I couldn't have found a more perfect movie for grandpa and grandson—they were old friends of his! We went into Beverly Hills to have lunch (which was a cheeseburger and a milk shake) and then to Hollywood for the movie. I was only seven years old.

"My grandfather didn't have a swimming pool at his last home, but he didn't want his grandkids to miss out on one of the summer joys of a California trip. He instead called his friends Groucho Marx or Dinah Shore and sent my mother and her kids off to their houses for a day of swimming. This was such a different lifestyle compared to my city escapades.

A recent shot of Janet Cantor Gari and Brian Gari (courtesy Janet Cantor Gari).

8. Janet Cantor Gari and Brian Gari

In fact, it was similar in a way to my grandfather's experience as a kid. He only knew the streets of New York so he was given a chance to see the countryside when he was sent by the Educational Alliance of New York City to Surprise Lake Camp for two weeks. He said he had never seen that much green except on a pool table and supported the Camp for the rest of his life.

"Although there were sweet memories of my grandfather (and grandmother Ida), there were also sad memories. He had to have an oxygen unit in his bedroom to help him through his later years. His first daughter, Margie, passed away from cancer at the age of forty-four in 1959. Ida died in 1962. These deaths really took their toll on my grandfather. He finally passed away in 1964. His final letter that came to me in June of that year was ironic. He said he felt I would be the one to carry on the show business tradition in the family.

"Well, not only did I write all the songs for a musical that ended up on Broadway, but it was I who produced all the CDs and tapes that are currently available on the market featuring Eddie Cantor! I am so proud of preserving his work. Not only that, but a letter came from a fan asking if she could start a fan club in memory of my grandfather. It couldn't have been more perfect timing. The fan club was established in 1993 and has been growing steadily ever since."

Our memory of Eddie Cantor is in no danger of fading. Almost one hundred and ten years after his birth, his family lovingly helps to keep him alive for a whole new generation of fans. He's still alive in so many different ways, it's almost like he never left.

9

PETER FORD

* *Son of Glenn Ford and Eleanor Powell* *

If they tried to rush me, I'd always say I've only got one other speed, and it's slower.

—Glenn Ford

Being the child of one movie star parent is one thing, but being the only child of two star parents is a whole other story. Such is the story of Peter Ford, son of one of MGM's greatest musical stars, Eleanor Powell, and Hollywood's number one box office star of 1958, Glenn Ford.

At the age of thirty-three, Eleanor Powell gave up her career as a Hollywood dancer and actress to take on the new and, according to her, more important role of wife and mother. At the time of her early retirement, Eleanor was already a well-known, well-loved performer. Giving up her career for a life of domestic bliss to be married to a little-known actor by the name of Glenn Ford had studio moguls and fans in an uproar.

It wasn't until three years after their marriage, in 1946, that the public and studio heads knew who Glenn Ford really was. That was the year that *Gilda*, which starred Glenn and Rita Hayworth, was released. They would electrify the screen in what was to become a "classic." Glenn Ford had become a major star, overnight.

★★★★★

Born in Los Angeles, California, on February 5, 1945, Peter Ford was the product of a marriage made in Hollywood. It was a childhood of many privileges and opportunities that most children would never

9. Peter Ford

A young Peter Ford poses on the lawn with his equally famous parents Glenn Ford and Eleanor Powell (courtesy Peter Ford).

experience. One story Peter recalls is learning to swim. "When I was three my parents wanted me to learn to swim. A normal activity for most young children but my parents went about it a little differently. Instead of enrolling me in swimming class, they built an Olympic-sized swimming pool in our back yard. Not only did they hire a private swimming tutor to teach me, but one of my 'instructors' turned out to be an old friend of Mother's from her early days in show business, Johnny Weissmuller."

It was the same ol' story with tennis. For tennis lessons he was packed off to the Beverly Hills Hotel to play with Pancho Segura; for golf, Peter practiced in the back yard with the great Ben Hogan. It was certainly not the "average life," but Glenn Ford made a point to ensure his son Peter would not be overindulged to the point of being a spoiled brat, a common term that labeled many of Hollywood's children.

Children of Hollywood

The offspring of parents with standard everyday jobs would grow up with similar people coming to visit the family home. This was the same with Peter; however, his "family friends" who'd visit frequently were quite different. "Because of my mother's earlier Broadway background, I met many luminaries of the stage and screen at a very young age. Eddie Cantor and Sophie Tucker were regular visitors, as was Al Jolson, who my mother once briefly dated. One clear memory is of going to Pickfair, the social 'place to be' in those days. I remember sitting on Mary Pickford's knee as she told me stories. We were only a few houses away from Pickfair so it wasn't far from home."

Fred Astaire lived up the street and Charlie Chaplin was his next door neighbor. Peter recalls, "I will never forget the night that Charlie Chaplin, rushing down the street in his car, hit my beloved German shepherd, Bill. I suffered a lot of trauma over my dog's death. Any child would." The fact is, as a child, Peter didn't know these people were famous. It was really no different for him to have Clark Gable, Bette Davis or Barbara Stanwyck sitting at his dinner table. James Mason, another neighbor, was his regular baby-sitter when his parents were out for the evening. "My parents were entertainers and their friends were entertainers. It is amusing to think back on, now that I realize how significant these people were. I remember that nearly every weekend Mom, Dad and I would be posing for pictures that would accompany movie magazine stories that were being written at the time. As the only child of these two famous parents, I was often needed for publicity sessions. Today, my children get a kick of seeing their dad as a child in all these early publications."

Peter's parents were married in October of 1943. After the marriage Eleanor gave up her career to be a housewife and mother. She never really returned to films; the family was more important to her than her career. "After *Gilda* was released and my father was now considered 'a star,' my parents wanted to buy their own home. My father was under contract to Harry Cohn at Columbia Studios. Mr. Cohn was not known for his generosity, so Dad, working under his old weekly contract, couldn't afford it. Mom stepped in and went to London and appeared at the Palladium where she earned enough money for the down payment on the house. They purchased a huge twenty-two-room home on Cove Way in Beverly Hills." The previous owner had been

9. Peter Ford

Max Steiner, who composed and conducted the music for countless films, *Gone with the Wind*, *The Treasure of Sierra Madre*, and *Casablanca* to name just a few.

★★★★★

In 1952 Eleanor created and hosted a religious television show called *Faith of Our Children*. It was the first weekly religious show west of the Rockies. Peter appeared as a regular member of the Sunday school class for the four years the show aired. *Faith of our Children* won five local Emmys. Some of Hollywood's biggest stars at the time were guests on the program.

In a Hollywood sense, sixteen years of marriage is a long-term commitment. That was the length of time it took before divorce was mentioned in the Ford household and in 1959, at the age of fourteen, Peter's secure world crumbled around him. He recalls those times clearly. His father didn't want his son to become another Hollywood brat, and because of that fact he often went beyond what was necessary to instill a sense of discipline and responsibility.

> "There were many times when my friends wanted to play and Dad would insist I spend the weekend chopping wood and doing other chores. I was only excused if I was before the camera doing publicity. Conversely, my mother would indulge me by buying me ice cream and milkshakes to compensate for Dad's strictness. It was a battle between the two of them and I was the chess piece stuck in the middle. It became more strategic as the divorce grew closer. I'll tell you this, divorce can be very hard on children, and it was on me.
>
> "I was not handed a new car or a wad of money for the asking. I probably felt sorry for myself at the time, but now I appreciate that it's made me a better person for not getting the 'easy ride.' Sadly, many of my 'show biz' peers today are bitter, lonely or dead for lack of good parenting."

Some of his fondest memories are of him and his father building projects together.

> "We had a workshop with tools that he taught me to use. Among other things, we created a wonderful fort, with two bunk beds and even a World War II antiaircraft gun and turret on the roof, accessed by a secret trap door. It was the hit of the neighborhood."

Children of Hollywood

This pursuit of woodworking was a passion that most certainly spilled over into adult life and led Peter to create his own construction company.

"Dad might have been strict, but I owe him a great deal for some of the talents and qualities that I have to this day."

There were certain formalities in the Ford household. Peter remembers,

"As a child I would always have to dress in a shirt and slacks for dinner. Dad would, without fail, check my hands and fingernails at dinner to make sure they were clean. They had better be clean or dinner would wait until they were. Not only did I make my bed every day, but the quarter that my father inevitably dropped upon it needed to bounce the required two inches or I had to remake it. Needless to say, doing my chores and helping around the house was expected, and rightly so.

"I loved both my parents but at the time of the divorce, I had to choose where I would be living. I decided to live with my mother because she needed me, but that choice cost me the opportunity to be with my father for a very long time. Until the time of the divorce, my parents maintained separate living areas in the same house. My bedroom was right in the middle. I remember the lawyers coming and going and whispering about what would happen to 'the child,' but nothing was ever spoken about it to me out loud. It was a very stressful time. As much as my parents' parting hurt me, I was glad when the separation was finalized.

"Within days, my mother and I were left alone in a huge old mansion on a couple of acres of land. It was eerie; my dad was gone and with him the social life we once knew. Frank, the gardener, was the only other adult I saw for awhile at the house. We couldn't afford to pay anyone else to help maintain the household. After a few months, as a matter of survival, mom decided that she would need to go back to work, but this was not the story that was given to the press. She took out a large loan against the house to finance the return of dancing star Eleanor Powell. She said she was doing it because of a challenge from her son. In reality, she was doing it because we were broke!

"Over time, she developed an act and took it on the road. She was a success. At one time she was earning more than twenty-five thousand dollars a week. Not a bad paycheck, and in the early 1960s it was big money. However, there was a problem. All the money she made had to be plowed

9. Peter Ford

back to maintain the act. By the time the dancers were paid, the costumes were cleaned and the traveling costs were calculated, not to mention that everyone insisting on flying first class, there was a cash flow all right, but it was all going out. No profit!"

During those years when his mother was on the road, Peter lived by himself in the big house while he was going to college.

"Dad and I started seeing each other again; in fact I moved in with him for awhile. We did do some films together. In the mid–1960s Mom retired again, and I moved back home to help her maintain the old house. Sadly, although we struggled to keep it, the house had to be sold. We just couldn't afford its upkeep. Many nights we would sit down to a meal of Hamburger Helper and beans; we honestly couldn't afford anything else. The vegetables we grew in the yard that everyone thought were for show were not; we ate them.

"I really think mother did her best acting when it was time to sell the house. She was well prepared, and thinking back now, it is amusing. Because we couldn't afford anyone to help us, on the day of a showing mother and I would spend all day cleaning. She would purposely make the real estate broker's appointments toward the end of the day in order to give us enough time to make the place look immaculate. When they eventually showed up with their clients, hopefully potential buyers, mother would always make sure she was outside lounging in the sun by the pool. She played the part of the retired movie star perfectly. She was entirely believable reading a glamour magazine wearing her dark glasses, and doing her best Joan Crawford. Who would have believed that just minutes before she had been furiously cleaning the toilets, with me following behind with the vacuum and dust cloth."

It is a given that the only child of two people in "the business" would try his hand at the same profession. Peter did just that. Peter has worked in nearly two dozen film projects, both as an actor and a dialogue director. The first film on which father and son both worked together was called *The Americano* and was shot in Brazil in 1954. Peter's first speaking role was in *The Gazebo* in 1959, one of Glenn's favorite comedies co-starring Debbie Reynolds. In 1946, Director Charles Vidor used a photo of Peter who was "doubling" for his father Glenn in a photo on his office wall in the film noir classic *Gilda*.

Peter graduated from Chadwick High School in Palos Verdes, California, in 1962. He received an Associates of Arts degree from Santa Monica College in 1966 while pursuing a career as an actor and singer. Under contract to Capitol Records, Peter was mentored by the legendary Nat King Cole. Later, he recorded for Phillips Records, and the release of his single, "Blue Ribbons," resulted in appearances on many teen music television shows including, *American Bandstand*, *Hullabaloo* and *Ninth Street West*. He eventually formed his own group, The Creations, and they appeared in various local clubs as well as the Whiskey A Go Go in San Francisco and the El Cortez Club in Las Vegas.

In the summer of 1966, Peter and his group were scheduled to appear in San Diego on the bill with pop music stars Peter and Gordon. It was a major break but the unimaginable happened. Peter was struck with crippling arthritis. Within weeks he was totally bedridden. He was forced to give up everything he had worked so hard to gain. Just when it was within reach, it was taken away. Peter remembers back to those days.

> "I was told I'd most likely be in a wheelchair for the rest of my life. I remember being in excruciating pain. Some mornings I would have to crawl from room to room just to get around. Most doctors told me it was a hopeless case, I would be crippled from this disease, and I would never walk again. I refused to believe it and went about my own health regime to mend my broken body. I gave up all red meat, liquor and most other things considered 'bad for you' and eventually I was able to stand, then walk with a cane. It was agonizing to make such an effort but I had to. I refused to give up; there was too much at stake."

Peter went back to college. His singing career virtually ended before it had really begun, and there was no other choice but to go back to school. He was accepted at the University of Southern California (USC). Throughout those two years at USC Peter had to walk with a cane and crutches. It was at USC that he met his future wife, Lynda Gundersen. Both were English majors. In 1968, Peter graduated, cum laude, with a B.A. He was accepted to law school at USC, and Lynda went on to receive a masters in education and became a public elementary school teacher.

For Peter, law school was put on hold when in the summer of 1968 he was offered a job too good to refuse. He was asked by actor/producer George Montgomery to co-star with Chuck Connors and Cesar Romero in a western, *The Proud and the Damned*. It was filmed in

9. Peter Ford

A recent shot of Peter Ford and his wife, Lynda (courtesy Peter Ford).

Colombia, South America. Peter was suffering from arthritis, but he took the part. He was only able to complete the film with massive doses of medication. By necessity, Peter felt he had to try and make a living by a skill he knew well, carpentry. To try and work full time in the movie business was too physically demanding. He started doing small jobs for family and friends. It would soon be the start of a successful building company.

Peter and Lynda were married in his father's home in December 1970. Rita Hayworth, then Glenn's next door neighbor, was the guest of honor. Peter and Lynda's first home was a small rented apartment in West Hollywood. It was during this time that Peter, between building commissions, began working at 20th Century–Fox as a dialogue director. His first project was *The Mephisto Waltz*, starring Alan Alda and Jacqueline Bisset. Peter's association with Fox afforded him other acting opportunities, including a recurring role on *The New Perry Mason* television show.

While at Fox in 1972, he was invited to play a supporting role in his father's new TV series, *Cade's County*. The series ran for one year on CBS. Peter appeared as the forensic deputy, Peter Odom, in nearly every one of the twenty-six episodes. All through the filming, Peter was still suffering terribly from crippling arthritis. He continued his strict diet, medication and intense physical therapy and his condition became bearable. One night, after yet another heavy dose of steroids, he asked his mother to help him to pray for the release from the grip of pain in which he had been living. She did just that, and the next day he was, for the first time in years, without any pain. His doctor was amazed; Peter was amazed. All hope had been given up that he'd ever be completely cured and suddenly a miracle occurred. Soon Peter stopped all medication. More than three decades later, Peter remains completely free of the once crippling illness.

After *Cade's County* had ended, Peter was asked to join the Los Angeles County Sheriff's Department as a reserve deputy. He had played a sheriff in the forensic lab in the TV series and had been trained for his role by a technical advisor from the Sheriff's Department. Peter, who only months before was nearly disabled, was able to join the force in 1973. He eventually reached the rank of lieutenant and retired in 1996 after twenty-two years of public service.

During the mid–1970s, Peter continued to work in the film industry. It was in a nearly fatal airplane accident (in a scene with actor James Wood) while filming an episode of a television series at the time, *Barnaby Jones*, that led him away from acting and back to his love, building and working with his hands. Before he stopped acting, Peter appeared in eight films with his father. He starred as Wilber in a low budget film, *Wilber and the Baby Factory*; he had several roles in various television shows; had a singing career, and had even appeared in a play, *Member of the Wedding*, with Ethel Waters. Peter not only had the opportunity of working at every major motion picture studio but also had a speaking role in Frank Capra's last film, *Pocketful of Miracles*.

With Lynda teaching school and now also working in films, they both remodeled their first home. Funds were scarce, so they did all the work themselves. Peter did the building; Lynda sewed the drapes and painted the rooms. Their first child, Aubrey Newton Ford, joined the family in 1977. They sold their home and made enough profit to purchase another and remodel that. Eventually it became a pattern. Peter and Lynda decided to put all their energies into buying, remodeling and selling homes for a living. Before they stopped and moved in to care for Peter's father, they had renovated and sold seven homes.

9. Peter Ford

Peter's first major home building commission was for Walter and Rita Coblenz, producer of *All the President's Men* and *The Onion Field*. He took a partner into his company in 1979 and the Blackoak Development Company was born. Peter went on to build and remodel homes for many well-known clients: producer Steve Tisch; actress Mary Kay Place; producer Jerry Belson; super agent Jeff Berg; Don Simpson, producer of *Top Gun* and *Beverly Hills Cop*; Chuck Shyer and Nancy Meyers who wrote *Private Benjamin*; actress Jo Beth Williams; health guru Richard Simmons; actress Sally Kellerman; and Blake Edwards and Julie Andrews. The list is endless.

In 1984, Ryan Welsie Ford was born and their daughter Eleanor Powell Ford joined the family in 1988. In 1989 Peter took over the company and operated it as a sole proprietorship until his retirement from building in 1996. Peter's own company, Blackoak/Ford, was a respected custom residential construction firm working in Los Angeles. His work has been published in the most prestigious architectural magazines throughout the world. The Schnabel House, designed by noted architect Frank Gehry, was voted by the *New York Times* as one of the Ten Contemporary American Homes that matter most to Architects.

Today, Peter and Lynda support many charitable causes. Peter also serves as a member on the board of trustees of the Southwest Museum in Los Angeles and the Americanism League. He's a student and collector of Native American material culture and an avid reader, collects movie memorabilia from Hollywood's Golden Age, and maintains The Glenn Ford and Eleanor Powell Library and Archives. As a writer, he also has published numerous articles. His collection of photos personally inscribed to him, which he started as a child, is extensive. One expert who has seen his autographed photos said it was one of the most comprehensive collections he had ever seen. Peter had the rare opportunity of personally knowing most of the greatest figures of stage and screen from Hollywood's Golden Age. In addition, he is a public speaker dealing with issues of Americanism and patriotism as well as recalling his adventures as a participant in that starry cosmos known as Hollywood.

Peter's various interests led him to KIEV 870 AM radio, where for nearly three years he hosted a popular weekly nighttime political talk show. The station was sold in 1998, and he left the air. Peter has run twice for nonpartisan elected office. He received ten thousand votes in his first attempt and two years later, he received thirty thousand in a college board race, but in both elections he fell short of being elected. The outcome of these two efforts sparked considerable interest by many people who have encouraged Peter to seek partisan office in the future.

Peter is now retired but remains active in many endeavors: sitting on boards of directors, helping local charities and pursuing his hobbies. Peter's mother, Eleanor Powell, died in 1982. Today Peter, his wife Lynda, and their two youngest children reside with Peter's father in Beverly Hills, California. At the present time Peter is co-writing a biography of his father with Christopher Nickens entitled *Glenn Ford: A Life in Film*.

It does certainly seem Peter Ford not only survived being one of Hollywood's children but made his own way in the world, built a business, had a family and lived through the normal ups and downs that all of us endure from time to time. Through it all, his success was not because he was the son of two movie star parents; it was simply because he was Peter Ford.

10

SIR DOUGLAS FAIRBANKS, JR.

* *Son of Douglas Fairbanks, Sr.,* *
and Anna Beth Sully;
Stepson of Mary Pickford

> *I never tried to emulate my father. Anyone trying to do that would be a second-rate carbon copy.*
> —Douglas Fairbanks Jr.

Known as the "King of Swashbucklers" long before Errol Flynn, Douglas Fairbanks, Sr., was a silent cinema action hero loved all over the world. Mary Pickford was known as the "girl with the golden curls" or "America's Sweetheart," but together they were known as the King and Queen of Hollywood. Both divorced their respective spouses (in a somewhat nervous fashion) in order to marry each other, but they need not have worried because their public image remained as glowing as ever and they were commonly referred to as "Hollywood Royalty."

There was no other couple more powerful than Fairbanks and Pickford. Together they lived in their luxurious mansion Pickfair (named after both of them), and within one of the most lavish palaces in all of Hollywood, they entertained Hollywood's elite couples in grand ceremonies. It was the *in* place to be.

Both were shrewd business people (especially Pickford), and they soon realized it was in their best interests to set up a company, a movie studio that would give them full control of the distribution and release of their own pictures. So, along with D. W. Griffith and Charles Chaplin, Pickford and Fairbanks created United Artists.

Children of Hollywood

Considering the power the major studios of the time had over their stars, it was a bold and somewhat brave move to branch out in an independent direction. However, these four film pioneers made a business decision well ahead of their time, and it worked. Many actors of today create their own production companies in order to do the same thing, to maintain control over the release of their art form. Acting is now a business and the actors are now making it *their* business to make sure it's handled the way they want it to be.

In 1919, United Artists was formed by actors for actors, but considering that one of the major partners was a woman, Mary Pickford made it quite clear to all that she was a force to be reckoned with. One of the thirty-six founding members of the Academy of Motion Picture Arts and Sciences, Mary Pickford is also responsible for the annual award ceremony that honors talent and achievement in the film industry—the Academy Awards.

At the same time, Fairbanks Sr. was still displaying his swashbuckling abilities in films such as *The Three Musketeers, Thief of Bagdad, Robin Hood,* and *The Mark of Zorro*. His amazing athleticism and skillful sword fighting scenes were all carried out with expert arrogance and a victorious smile at all times. Mary Pickford was the shining light of cinema herself, earning some $10,000 a week by 1916 and more than holding her own alongside her talented husband.

However, as popular and successful as both were and as completely compatible as they seemed to be, after fifteen years of marriage, divorce reared its ugly head. The King and Queen of Hollywood were dethroned, but it was Mary who remained in her beloved castle, Pickfair.

Fairbanks Sr. eventually married Sylvia, Lady Ashley, and they remained together until his death in 1939. Pickford eventually found love again with Charles "Buddy" Rogers. She remained devoted to Pickfair for the rest of her life. Little Mary, as she was affectionately called, passed away at age 87 on May 28, 1979, some four decades after the death of her king and true love, Douglas Fairbanks, Sr.

Here, Sir Douglas Fairbanks, Jr., speaks about living up to his namesake and father, Douglas Fairbanks, Sr. He also speaks about his stepmother, Mary Pickford, and those golden days of Hollywood that are so often longed for in our modernized world. This is his story, his life as he knew it as the son and stepson of the King and Queen of Hollywood.

10. Sir Douglas Fairbanks, Jr.

Father and son golfing partners—the original swashbuckler, Douglas Fairbanks, and his son, Douglas Fairbanks, Jr.

Children of Hollywood

Unfortunately, he's no longer with us. Sir Douglas Fairbanks, Jr., passed away on May 7, 2000. He was a true old-fashioned gentleman who will be greatly missed. In *You Must Remember This* by Walter Wagner, Doug Jr. said,

> "I have no idea when I first became aware that my father was a motion picture star. I do recall that in 1915, when I was six years old, I visited him on the set and he had me photographed with a group of actors dressed as cowboys and Indians. I vaguely remember big sets behind me as I left the studio. Of course, I didn't realize the full significance of my father's position at that age. I was much more interested in the cowboys and Indians."

In a 1996 interview with Dan Lybarger, he said,

> "I do remember visiting the sets of *Robin Hood* and *The Thief of Baghdad*. The sets were pretty impressive in life just as they were on the screen. On weekends when nobody was in the studio, some of my schoolmates and I would go clamoring around the set, and we would play games and nobody would catch us."

Doug Jr.'s mother was Anna Beth Sully. She divorced Doug Sr. in 1918 and shortly thereafter he married Mary Pickford. The Sully family were a wealthy bunch, but they had fallen upon hard times and lost most of their fortune rather quickly. The ailing stock market and several bad business investments brought them close to ruin. The healthy divorce settlement from the broken Fairbanks marriage did nothing to pull them out of their financial woes and it was up to Doug Jr. to follow in his father's footsteps by playing the nepotism card in order to support them. Barely into his teens, Doug Jr. was given the overwhelming task of supporting his mother, grandparents, aunts, uncles, and just about everyone on his mother's side who had once lived off generations of inherited money. Now they had to work for a living, or at least Doug Jr. did!

After a humble apprenticeship as a prop hand and an extra, he landed his first role in the silent version of *Stella Dallas* when he was only sixteen years old. His role of a young juvenile received good reviews and the movie was a success, but the fame was fleeting. In *You Must Remember This*, Doug Jr. admitted how tough it was for him in those early days. "Early in the game I realized that I wasn't about to match my father's enormous success, a success he richly deserved."

10. Sir Douglas Fairbanks, Jr.

He may not have matched his father's fame but he gave him a run for his money. By the end of his career, Douglas Fairbanks, Jr., had made more than eighty films of his own. Despite his eventual success and despite his father's impressive record in the acting profession, Doug Jr. remembers his father being less than enthusiastic about his son following in his footsteps. In *You Must Remember This*, Doug Jr. said, "He wanted me to continue with school and lead a normal life."

The real reason behind his son's sudden interest in acting wasn't told to Doug Sr. for years. Doug Junior's career hadn't started out of an inner desire to act; it was just a necessary step in order to pay the family bills. Once he'd accepted the fact that his son was firmly involved in the acting profession, Doug Sr. would brag to his friends (and anyone who would listen) that his son had made it on his own, *without* his help. Yes, he had the Fairbanks name, and that may well have opened a few doors for him, but once those doors were opened it was his raw talent that got him to the next level. If the talent wasn't there those doors would have been slammed in his face, firmly and forever. Of course, having a famous name and a father with such success in the same business can also be a curse.

Not content with being "just an actor" it was Douglas Fairbanks, Sr., and his equally famous wife, Mary Pickford, along with fellow actor Charles Chaplin and pioneering director D. W. Griffith who helped form the film company United Artists. Ahead of their time, they realized if they could make their own films there was certainly no reason why they couldn't distribute them, too. By cutting out the middle man they increased not only their paychecks but also their overall influence in Hollywood. Suddenly they were in the film making business and all four were a force to be reckoned with.

The onset of sound made Doug Sr. reluctant to continue in the business he loved so much. He was part of the old school and that meant acting was a form of expression, in body and emotion, without the need for sound. Like many of his peers, he knuckled under the pressure of the advancing medium. He made a few sound pictures, but these pictures just didn't have that same Fairbanks spunk that shone through in his silents. The new phase of the industry just wasn't for him. In Wagner's book, Doug Jr. said, "Since silents were going out, my father preferred to go out with them."

Children of Hollywood

Douglas Fairbanks, Sr., was a bundle of energy. He exuded a child-like mischief that was merely trapped in a man's body. He was full of life and always on the move, just like his dynamic characters on film. Because of that boundless energy, it was somewhat of a surprise that he succumbed to a heart attack at the early age of fifty-six. Doug Jr. was at his father's bedside just a few hours before he died. His reported last words were, "I never felt better in my life."

Looking back, Doug Jr.'s career achieved modest success, but in comparison to his father, he had more downs than ups. It was the Howard Hawks–directed *The Dawn Patrol* (1930) that really made the studios (and the audiences) sit up and take notice. As a result of that film, Doug Jr. was given a new contract with film approvals that most actors only dreamed of getting. His contract stated that he would now receive his name above the title of the film, and he had the power to approve the story, cast and director of each production. He went on to form his own production company and like his father, he wasn't "just an actor." He was also a businessman.

As if that wasn't enough, he was a captain in the Navy during World War II, and after being knighted by King George the Sixth in 1949 for his support of Anglo-American relations, he was given the official moniker of Sir Douglas Fairbanks, Jr. He dabbled in everything and did everything well. He was not just a movie star; he was a producer, a screenwriter, even an author. His autobiography, *Salad Days*, was published in 1988 followed by the equally entertaining sequel, *A Hell of a War*, in 1993.

Despite his impressive resume, Doug Jr. was almost always compared to his father. If it wasn't for his easygoing nature, that comparison, that burden would have surely destroyed him. Instead, he spoke of his father with pride; there wasn't a hint of bitterness between father and son. In most of his interviews, he continued to praise his father's place in Hollywood. More importantly, he understood why questions like, "What was it like having Douglas Fairbanks, Sr., as a father?" were still being asked of him. He answered those questions year after year and with enough enthusiasm to make the interviewer think he was being asked that question for the very first time.

Doug Jr.'s most notable marriage was to the Queen of MGM, Joan Crawford. However, the demands of movie making and their blossoming careers took a toll on their relationship, and it ended after four

10. Sir Douglas Fairbanks, Jr.

years. Despite their divorce, they remained friends and frequently corresponded via letters and phone calls right up until Joan's death in 1977. Their relationship was easy and without strain; in fact she continued to call him "Dodo" (her pet name for him) long after their separation. Two subsequent marriages to "non-actresses" followed, but during his bouts with bachelorhood he was romantically linked to some of the most glamorous and influential women in Hollywood, including Marlene Dietrich and Tallulah Bankhead.

Even after his father's divorce from Mary Pickford, Doug Jr. would still stop in at Pickfair and visit with his ex-stepmother. He adored her and for that reason alone he saw no reason why his father's divorce from her meant that he should sever ties with Mary, too. In fact, their relationship continued right up until her death. In a *Classic Images* Online interview with Geraldine Hawkins shortly before his death, Doug Jr. remembered a particularly funny story from one of his many visits to Pickfair. As Mary got older, she would spend most of her time in her bedroom reading, writing letters and watching television. In between these activities, she would happily receive her visitors and happily reminisce about the "good ol' days."

Doug explains further, "As Mary got older she took to her bed and stayed there. Mentally she was fine; she was still humorous, very humorous, but she was weak and ill. I used to call on her and hold her hand in the bed and talk with her. She asked one time if I had seen Charlie Chaplin. Did I ever see Charlie anymore? And so I made up a story and said, 'Oh, yes, dear, I see him a great deal and he's always asking for you. He's so sweet about you...' It was not true at all, but I just thought it would cheer her up. I did see him, but we didn't talk much about Mary at all, but I told her that he inquired about her and was so sweet, and I made up a big story about him. She listened to me intently, then very weakly said, 'I still say he's a son of a bitch!'"

Even with his eventual success, Doug Jr. maintained that it wasn't his career that had given him his wonderful memories, it was the people that he had met along the way. In *You Must Remember This*, he concluded, "I would rather have been something else than a film star. I'm quite lazy by nature. I would have been the damnedest beach bum you ever knew!"

*****

Children of Hollywood

A debonair portrait of the now-deceased Douglas Fairbanks, Jr.

In 1939, six years after his divorce from Joan Crawford, Douglas Fairbanks, Jr., made another attempt at marriage and this time it was successful. On April 22, 1939, Doug Sr. was best man and witness at his son's marriage to Mary Lee Epling Hartford. She was his loving wife for 49 years and together they had three daughters, Daphne, Victoria and Melissa.

After Mary's death from cancer in 1988, Doug Jr. would wait three years before marrying for a third and final time. On May 30, 1991, Vera Shelton, a merchandiser, became the third Mrs. Fairbanks. They happily divided their time between New York and London for almost a decade. On May 7, 2000, just three weeks shy of their ninth wedding anniversary, Douglas Fairbanks, Jr., passed away. He was ninety years old. He is interred at Hollywood Forever Cemetery in the same crypt as his father, Douglas Fairbanks, Sr. Two charming swashbucklers together for all eternity.

*****

Some of Douglas Fairbanks, Jr.'s, most successful films and television appearances are as follows:

The Air Mail (1925) Sandy
Wild Horse Mesa (1925) Chess Weymer
Stella Dallas (1925) Richard Grosvenor
Padlocked (1926) Sonny Galloway
Broken Hearts of Hollywood (1926) Hal Terwilliger
Man Bait (1927) Jeff Sanford
Women Love Diamonds (1927) Jerry Croker-Kelley

10. Sir Douglas Fairbanks, Jr.

Is Zat So? (1927) G. Clifton Blackburn
A Texas Steer (1927) Farleigh Bright
Dead Man's Curve (1928) Vernon Keith
Modern Mothers (1928) David Starke
The Toilers (1928) Steve
Our Modern Maidens (1929) Gil Jordan
The Dawn Patrol (1930) Douglas Scott
Little Caesar (1931) Joe Massara
The Prisoner of Zenda (1937) Rupert of Hentzau
Gunga Din (1939) Sgt. Thomas "Tommy" Ballantine
Safari (1940) Jim Logan
Angels Over Broadway (1940) Bill O'Brien
The Corsican Brothers (1941) Lucien Franchi/Mario Franchi
Sinbad the Sailor (1947) Sinbad
Douglas Fairbanks, Jr., Presents (1953) TV Series Host (1953–57)
Circus of the Stars #4 (1979) (TV) Ringmaster
Ghost Story (1981) Edward Charles Wanderley

11

HARRY LANGDON, JR.

* *Son of Harry Langdon* *
and Mabel Watts

> *The oddest thing about this whole funny business is that the public really wants to laugh, but it's the hardest thing in the world to make them do it.*
> —Harry Langdon

Harry Langdon is most often described as one of "The Big Four," an exclusive club of comedy genius consisting of Charlie Chaplin, Buster Keaton and Harold Lloyd. He is usually billed fourth on that list of comedy genius simply because the other three were long established before him. With a unique character persona of a baby-faced, childlike character trapped in a man's body, Harry Langdon was a late bloomer in film. He was almost forty years old by the time he became a star.

Born in 1884, he was a known vaudevillian for twenty years before Mack Sennett discovered him and signed him up to do an amazing thirty comedies in just two years. It is said that legendary writer/director Frank Capra created the baby-faced character that made Langdon such a unique-looking performer. Chaplin was "The Tramp," Keaton was "The Stone Face," and Lloyd was known as "The College Kid." If Langdon was to make it he needed a getup and the boy/man character was it.

His popularity was at its peak and Warner Bros. set out to lure him across with a too-good-to-refuse offer of $6,000 a week. Not only did Langdon jump ship but he also took Capra and his director, Harry Edwards, along with him. He knew he wasn't a one-man show and it was a smart move. The Capra/Edwards/Langdon threesome created

11. Harry Langdon, Jr.

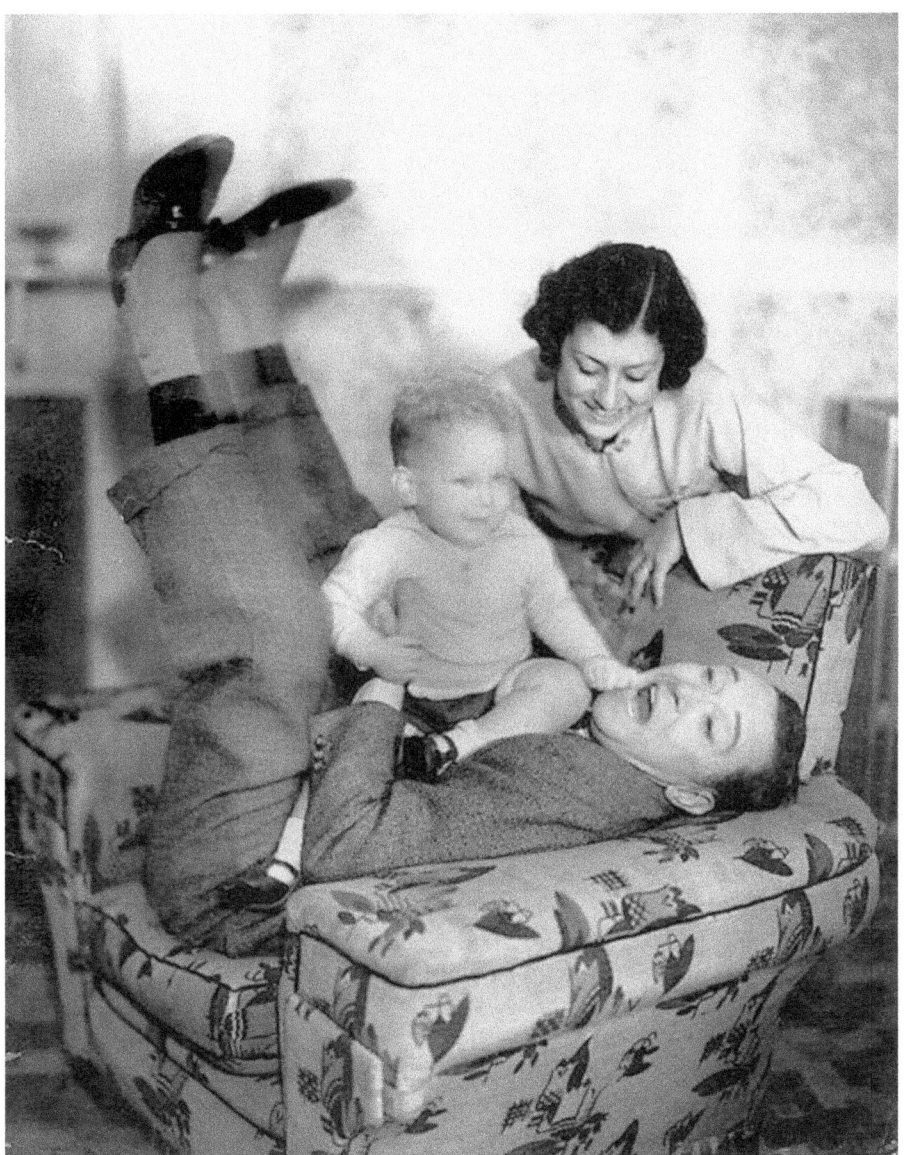

Baby Harry Langdon, Jr., spends some quality time with his father, Harry Langdon, while his mother, Mabel Watts, looks on with pride, circa 1936 (courtesy Harry Langdon, Jr.)

some of Langdon's greatest work at Warner Bros. *Tramp, Tramp, Tramp* and *The Strong Man* were both churned out in 1926 with *Long Pants* following soon after in 1927. To this day all three are considered to be gems. Langdon, however, soon forgot why he brought Capra with him to Warner Bros., and after the success of all three films he sacked Capra.

His following three "self-directed" films post Capra were all utter disasters. Letting Capra go was career suicide and it didn't take him long to realize it. His career soon floundered and sadly Harry Langdon is now too often referred to as "the forgotten clown." Some eighteen years after his last successful film, Langdon was still working and still trying to make a comeback. Unfortunately, he never made it. He died in 1944.

Harry Langdon's only son, Harry Langdon, Jr., was only ten years old when his father died. Here he remembers him to be full of fun, both on and off the screen. Harry Langdon, Jr., is himself an internationally renowned professional in his field. A portrait photographer with his own prestigious studio in Beverly Hills, he is the choice photographer for many A-list Hollywood stars.

With a Hollywood celebrity list too long to mention, Harry Jr. has created his own successful business, estimating to have photographed at least 10,000 people during his thirty-year career. Having photographed the likes of Cher, Henry Fonda, Katherine Hepburn, Robin Williams, Kirk Douglas and many more, Harry Langdon, Jr., is capturing his own slice of Hollywood on film. Faithfully following in his father's footsteps, he's just using a different kind of camera, that's all. In an interview that originally appeared in issue number thirty-five of *Cult Movies Magazine*, Harry Langdon, Jr., recalls what it was like to have "the fourth genius" as his father.

> "I'd have to say that my childhood was a pretty euphoric one. It seemed like we had fun almost constantly. A lot of other comedians came over to the house. Red Skelton was one of my dad's friends and he was there a lot. Vernon Dent was there often, and so was a British comedian my dad worked with named Charlie Rogers.
>
> "When we had our Canoga Park house it seemed like every weekend was open house, and of course Stan Laurel and Oliver Hardy were there many times. And other kids would come over and play with the grown-

11. Harry Langdon, Jr.

up kids, this house, full of comedians. Everyone was partial to musical instruments such as the banjo and accordion, and I can remember one time my dad and some of the others improvising some comic things with different instruments including a kazoo.

"My dad died by the time I was ten years old, so I was pretty young and impressionable during get togethers. I just somehow had the impression that all kids had fun like that and these get togethers with fun grown-ups was what life was like. That impression would get strengthened by trips to the outside world. My dad took me to Columbia studios and we saw Buster Keaton shooting a short comedy on the lot. My dad was working for Columbia also at that time. And I recall going to Hal Roach Studios and seeing that big lake right in the middle of the lot, plus a huge sky hung behind it. A lot of miniature work was done in that lake.

"Harry (my father) appeared with Edith Fellows in a stage show called *Out of the Frying Pan*, which was very successful in 1943. He took me backstage during that show, which was pretty impressive. But there again, it just led me to feel that all of life was a free and easy show business kind of life and that people had fun all the time. My dad used to like to take me to a theater on Hollywood Boulevard called The Hitching Post since it showed all Western films. I liked Roy Rogers and Hopalong Cassidy when I was a kid, and I think my dad liked them also since it gave him the chance to get away from film comedy. The Westerns also may have given him some ideas for comedies he was doing. I'd be dressed up sort of like a cowboy in my leather holster with a completely working toy pistol—something that is probably illegal or unwise in this day and age. The kids would give their guns and holsters to the cashier and they would hang all the guns up on the wall. We would get very engrossed in the films.

"We also went up to the rodeo in Newhall. My dad was friends with a woman named Patty Patton who raised thoroughbred horses. Again, this is an indication that he liked show people but also liked things beyond creating comedy.

"He had lots of other interests in the arts, such as painting and sculpting. My dad loved radio. He liked to listen to it, perform on it and go to live performances of it. Our family was in New York frequently, and we'd go to live broadcasts of the Fred Allen and Jack Benny shows. I recall sitting in the audience of broadcasts of *Texaco Star Theater* looking at the giant red curtain with the sponsor's insignia on it. Other comedians would come out before the actual show and warm up the audience, which usually numbered about five hundred people. There weren't too many

Children of Hollywood

Harry Langdon, Jr., waits his turn as his famous father, comedian Harry Langdon, swings away (courtesy Harry Langdon, Jr.).

shows using canned laughter in those days! And then the curtain would go up on Fred Allen and the audience would go wild. We also saw Olsen and Johnson live on radio.

"My dad was on Jack Benny's show. After we'd see a show or participate in one in New York, we'd all go to Sardi's Delicatessen. My dad loved that place. And again, he'd get the star treatment from the manager of the restaurant, which only served to reinforce that everyone was famous and people get treated like stars all the time. It was a magical time for me. I think he would have eventually gone into television the way Buster Keaton did, had he lived long enough. But when Harry died at the end of 1944, television was truly in its infancy, still in the experimental stages.

"My interest in drawing and carpentry came from the example my dad set. My interest in photography comes from my mother. When I was a kid in school, I was in the Cub Scouts and my dad would get involved with us doing plays for the school. He'd build sets, demonstrating and

11. Harry Langdon, Jr.

teaching us how to do the same thing. He'd get involved with rehearsing and directing the kids and help put on shows.

"I'd also watch him paint and draw. I was amazed at the speed at which he could do caricatures of people. He'd honed it down to a science during his days in vaudeville and was touring the country. He'd appear on stage, and then after the show he'd hurry out to the lobby and do cartoons for the patrons for a little extra money. People would line up, and naturally, the faster he could crank out the sketches the more money he would make. He used that experience to help entertain the soldiers in World War II. At the Stage Door Canteen where soldiers went for relaxation, many actors would come and sing and perform for the guys. My

A recent shot of famed Hollywood photographer Harry Langdon, Jr. (courtesy Harry Langdon, Jr.).

dad would do that and also do caricatures for the guys. I'd see twenty or thirty soldiers at a time lined up to get their picture drawn by my dad. I can do paintings and sketches, although probably not as quickly as my dad could.

"I had various hobbies while growing up. After my dad died, my mom got me interested in model balsa wood airplanes, and for a while that was my big thing. Then she got me a chemistry set that was made for kids, and I think she felt that getting me a darkroom kit was a natural extension of chemistry. So for a while I had a darkroom in our garage.

"At age fourteen I got a Model A car for $100 and started tinkering with that, but the hobbies became something of a problem. By the time I was seventeen or so, I think my mom felt I was socially challenged. I could do lots of things but wasn't very good at communicating with people. At age fifteen I became an apprentice carpenter and eventually joined the union as a journeyman carpenter. But my mom was worried about my social skills and at sixteen or so I was sent to Arthur Murray Dance Studios to meet girls. One thing led to another. I began to photograph some of my dancing partners.

"By age twenty I became an apprentice at a portrait studio in Santa Monica and learned the business and art in every detail. I'd worked at several studios and by the age of twenty-nine I went into business for myself in my own studio. I eventually worked myself up to having a respectable reputation and top-of-the-line client list. I think I'm a nonconformist with my approach to photography in the same way my dad was a nonconformist in his approach to film comedy.

"I think we all inherit a dominant gene or creative spark from our parents. In my case it was the theatrical and sense of adventure that came from my dad. In commercial photography they don't care who your father was; it's the kind of work you create that's important. I feel I've made my own place in this world. However, I feel that studying my father's work has helped me in my field, in creating images of the people who come to me to be photographed for movies or television.

"I can see how parents want their kids to succeed and reach public acclaim, and perhaps reach the parent's level of worthiness. That's a super feat when your parents are famous or unique. That's been my situation and mission. I think I've realized that worthiness, but it's taken a lifetime to do it."

12

LEATRICE GILBERT FOUNTAIN

★ *Daughter of John Gilbert* ★
and Leatrice Joy

Solitude is sweet; but how much sweeter to have someone to whom you may say: solitude is sweet.
—John Gilbert

Silents Majority correspondent Sheryl Stinchcum introduces us to the daughter of two silent stars. If the name Leatrice Gilbert Fountain doesn't ring a bell, her maiden name should. She was born "a Gilbert" (Leatrice Joy Gilbert), the daughter of matinee idols John Gilbert and Leatrice Joy, but her fame doesn't begin and end with her parents. Leatrice Fountain is a star in her own right. Throughout her life she has played many diverse roles: wife, MGM starlet, the mother of five, novelist, grandmother, and opera star, but she is best known as her father's biographer. Her book *Dark Star: The Untold Story of the Meteoric Rise and Fall of the Legendary John Gilbert* is the most detailed, colorful, and dependable source of biographical data available on the brilliant actor aka "The Great Lover of the Silver Screen."

It seems paradoxical that Leatrice "Junior," who resembles her father in so many ways, should be named after her mother. Like her father, she has large cinnamon-brown eyes, a winning smile, and more than her share of magnetism. To put it simply, she radiates what a discerning talent scout would call "star quality."

Had she chosen to follow in her parents' footsteps, Leatrice Fountain no doubt could have become a great film star. In fact, she did have a brush with stardom. She was too old to play the lead in *National Vel-*

vet (by the time MGM got around to making it) and too young to play Scarlet O'Hara's sister in *Gone with the Wind*, but she was the right age to play Jimmy Stewart's pubescent sweetheart in *Of Human Hearts* (MGM, 1938). The film is shown frequently on Turner Classic Movies.

Born in 1924, she is moderately tall and slim with a girlish, gravity-defying figure that women half her age would envy, but her most distinguishing characteristic is her rich and arresting voice. It is difficult to talk about Leatrice without repeatedly referring to her father, whose vivid, indelible image remains enthroned in her heart. Not only has she immortalized him in *Dark Star* but she currently introduces his films, which are increasingly shown on the big screen with a full orchestra in the United States and Europe. Thanks to his daughter's untiring efforts, John Gilbert will always be remembered as one of the most talented film stars of the twentieth century.

With thick black hair spilling over his large shadowy eyes, the brilliant, versatile, and dangerously handsome actor seemed destined to wear the crown of success among Hollywood's elite, but in actuality he began life as an abused, unwanted child. Making his own way into the world as an adolescent with virtually no one to guide him, he showed up at the Ince-Triangle studio in Santa Monica in 1915 with dreams of becoming an actor. He was tall, lean, and terribly hungry but never lost sight of his starry destiny. Years later he would recall: "My expression was to be a complete projection of my inner self on an entirely mental plane, with nothing visible but a shadow of me thrown on a screen." In 1915 he played an extra in his first film, *Matrimony*. The following year, stealing scenes right and left, he graduated to a bit part in *Hell's Hinges*, starring William S. Hart.

In 1917 he landed his first leading role in *Princess of the Dark*, and by 1921 he was not only starring in screenplays but writing and directing them. Still, he was not exactly a household name—that is, not yet. Leatrice Joy was the bigger star when Gilbert married her in the early 1920s. As DeMille's favorite leading lady (his replacement for Gloria Swanson), she received rave reviews for her starring role in *Manslaughter* (Paramount, 1922) with Thomas Meighan, but her film career had really begun in 1915. She made six films for the NOLA Film Company in New Orleans, her home town, before heading northeast in 1917. She worked with Roscoe "Fatty" Arbuckle and doubled as Mary Pickford's stand-in before moving to the West Coast.

12. Leatrice Gilbert Fountain

In California she was cast in comedies with Billy West (a Charlie Chaplin imitator) and made a handful of films—*One Dollar Bid* (Paralta, 1918), *Three X Gordon* (Paralta-Hodkinson, 1918), and *Ladies Must Live* (Mayflower Photoplay Corporation, 1921)—with husband-to-be, Jack Gilbert. She landed her first major role in *Bunty Pulls the Strings* (Goldwyn, 1921).

As her popularity soared, she became a trendsetter, showcasing ultra-feminine Adrian gowns on one hand and sporting mannish clothes on the other. Her bobbed hair started a fad among a generation of flappers. Over the course of her career, Leatrice Joy starred in dramas, melodramas, and comedies. She played a spoiled society girl in DeMille's *Vanity* (1927), an ultra-efficient business woman in *For Alimony Only*, and the proverbial tomboy in *Eve's Leaves* (MGM, 1926).

Also featured among her best-known films are *The Ten Commandments* (Famous Players–Lasky, 1923), *A Tale of Two Worlds* (Goldwyn, 1921), *Java Head* (Famous Players–Lasky, 1923), *Made for Love* (DeMille, 1926), *Triumph* (Paramount, 1924), and *The Clinging Vine* (DeMille, 1926). It was this film that inspired Katherine Hepburn to become an actress. She wanted to be like Leatrice Joy.

John Gilbert finally began to surpass his wife in the arena of fame after he left Fox (where he had starred in *Monte Cristo* (1922), *St. Elmo* (1923) and *Cameo Kirby* (1923) and signed a contract with MGM in 1924. Stardom followed his role in *The Merry Widow* in 1925, but the best was yet to come. That same year he played an American doughboy in the World War I classic *The Big Parade*, the most successful film of the silent era and, in fact, the most successful film until *Gone with the Wind*.

During his years at MGM, he starred with (and sometimes courted) Hollywood's most beautiful leading ladies including Lillian Gish; Norma Shearer; Renee Adoree, who played opposite him in more films than any other actress; Joan Crawford; Eleanor Boardman; and, of course, Greta Garbo, his legendary live-in lover. Gilbert and Garbo co-starred in four sensual films, beginning with *Flesh and the Devil*, which featured one of the first horizontal love scenes in the annals of film. By 1928 John Gilbert was the highest paid actor in Hollywood.

A few years later, his career took a mysterious, downhill turn with the shadow of MGM's Louis B. Mayer dogging him all the way. The explosive, well-documented fight that created a wall of hostility between

Gilbert and Mayer took place September 8, 1926. The whole thing started when Garbo, who preferred "living in sin" to marriage, stood Gilbert up at the altar. Gilbert was understandably despondent and vulnerable when Mayer confronted him in the restroom.

"What's the matter with you, Gilbert? What do you have to marry her for?" he insensitively remarked. "Why don't you just sleep with her and forget about it?"

Gilbert spontaneously lunged at him, grabbed him by the neck, and banged his head on the wall. Someone pulled them apart, and Mayer shouted, "You're finished Gilbert! I'll destroy you if it costs me a million dollars!"

From then on, Gilbert was often denied the roles he really wanted to play. After making the transition from silent films to talkies, he began receiving inexplicably bad reviews. A rumor began to circulate in print that his voice was more or less effeminate—unfit for talkies. Nothing could have been further from the truth. Gilbert had a splendid baritone voice. He made eleven talkies between 1929 and 1934 and would have made more, but his health deteriorated after he made his last film, *The Captain Hates the Sea* (Columbia). Had he lived, he might have portrayed Rhett Butler with David Selznick's blessing.

It is perhaps catastrophic that John Gilbert and Leatrice Joy divorced in 1924. Although they were opposites and their marital problems were critical, they never stopped loving each other. Gilbert thought that Leatrice was the loveliest woman he had ever seen, and she, in turn, found him "breathtaking." Even so, misunderstandings caused a breakdown in their relationship, prompting "the wronged wife" to file for divorce. However, before it was finalized, Gilbert become a father, fulfilling one of his dreams.

In contrast to the sociopathic rogues he played in *The Show* (MGM, 1927) and the talkie *Downstairs* (MGM, 1932), Gilbert was a kind, sensitive, generous human being. Having always wanted a family, he had persuaded his wife to become pregnant, and the result was Leatrice "Junior." He called her "Tinker Bell," and to prove that he thought of her as a princess, he gave her a crown with seed pearls and rhinestones. He also gave her a dog and a pet lamb, but he wasn't around as much as she would have liked. Leatrice spent her childhood living with her mother, who eventually remarried. Nevertheless, her dashing father captured her imagination. His Spanish hacienda was sit-

12. Leatrice Gilbert Fountain

uated high on top of a hill, and during her formative years she envisioned him as the "Prince in the Tower."

The title fit. Gilbert had played Prince Danilo in *The Merry Widow* (MGM, 1925) and Prince Gritzko in *His Hour* (MGM, 1924), but his princely aura was not limited to the screen. Leatrice learned at an early age that in spite of his failed marriages (four of them) and human frailties, there was something regal about her father off screen as well. It is not much of an exaggeration to say that Jack Gilbert was magic. Once when Leatrice found herself in a life-threatening situation off the coast of Malibu, her elusive "prince" seemed to materialize from nowhere, just in time to save her.

Years passed during which Leatrice rarely saw her father, who was depressed and aloof because his career had stalled. Impulsively she wrote him a letter, addressed to MGM, requesting an autographed picture. He responded with a personal note and a spray of flowers and offered to send a limousine to bring her to his hacienda. Beginning with that magical day when she visited him in his hilltop "castle," Leatrice came to know and understand the Prince in the Tower, perhaps better than anyone who knew him. Her firsthand observation revealed a congenial, upbeat father who differed dramatically from reports that he was a recluse as well as an unredeemable drunkard.

In his poetic, spell-binding four-part autobiography ("Gilbert Writes His Own Story," *Photoplay Magazine*, June–September, 1928). Gilbert wrote, "Solitude is sweet; but how much sweeter to have someone to whom you may say: Solitude is sweet." Throughout 1935 young Leatrice filled a void in his life and he in hers. Discovering the many things they had in common, father and daughter developed a close relationship—but it was not to last. Eleven-year-old Leatrice was devastated when on January 9, 1936, her Prince in the Tower died of heart failure. In her own words, "[It seemed] like the end of the world."

Gary Cooper, John Barrymore, Sam Goldwyn, Myrna Loy, Marlene Dietrich (Gilbert's last girlfriend), and other celebrities attended the funeral. Afterwards, Dietrich took Leatrice under her wing for several years and treated her like a princess. "I adored your father. Let me adore you," she told her.

In *Dark Star*, Leatrice chronicles her father's tragically short life (in which he packed in ninety-seven films) and her parent's ill-fated marriage and highlights her own stirring relationship with "a slightly tarnished movie star," a phrase Gilbert used to refer to himself. But her book is not the end of the story. Here, in two separate interviews with Sheryl Stinchcum (The John Gilbert Appreciation Society) and Jimmy Bangley (*Classic Images*), Leatrice gives new insight into her own life as the only child of not one but two Hollywood parents. Affectionately referring to her father as "Jack," she tells the inside story of life as yet another Hollywood child.

> "My father had a kind of intensity that burned like fire (or acid, depending on his mood). He was unpredictable, volatile. Rowland V. Lee, the director and Jack's early friend and roommate, once said of him, 'It was like living with an elemental. You never knew what mood you'd find him in or where it would take him.' He had a temper, usually under control, but it could explode, not in physical violence (except for Louis B. Mayer) but in verbal fireworks. Stomping out of the house and, of course, drinking accompanied his mood swings. I suspect he was manic-depressive and would have been helped by the medications they prescribe these days. He suffered through an agonizing childhood that must have affected him later in life, but he may have had a chemical imbalance also. If so, that would have contributed to his alcoholism as well. We have a greater understanding of mental illness now than we did in the 1920s. A lot of other gifted people might have been saved.
>
> "My parents were both very young when they decided to marry, in their early twenties. She was four years older than he (or six, depending on what year he was really born; it's still uncertain), and they were both extremely ambitious. Jack suffered a cruel childhood of neglect and poverty and was left on his own much of his early life. He had very little formal education and spent the rest of his life becoming educated. He went to work in the movies when he was fifteen years old.
>
> "My mother came from a sheltered background. Although the Civil War had ruined the family financially, they managed to survive. She grew up in a comfortable house on Esplanade Manor in New Orleans. Her father was a dentist, and she attended the Scared Heart Academy there. After graduation she became starstruck and went into the movies when a small company came to New Orleans in 1917. All Leatrice wanted in life was to be a star. Acting came second. Stardom was all.
>
> "Leatrice was radiantly beautiful; she was described as a glass of fine champagne and a perfect flower. She was southern, gracious, soft spoken and, at the same time, showed a devilish side that was irresistible. She

12. Leatrice Gilbert Fountain

A young Leatrice with her actress mother, Leatrice Joy (courtesy Leatrice Gilbert Fountain).

fell madly in love with Jack and he with her, but they were doomed from the start. He was badly damaged from his early life, insecure, and a little crazy, but he was a serious actor devoted to his craft, highly self-critical, irreligious, and determined to be an intellectual and he sought out people who knew more than he did and tried to learn from them. Mother was deliciously frivolous and a devout Christian Scientist. She disapproved of drinking and smoking, loved pretty clothes, trusted anyone who offered advice except her husband, and every time she began a new picture she left him and returned home to her mother. His bookish friends and drinking companions bewildered her. She did not understand what they were talking about, thought they were boring, and called them 'stuffed shirts.' Many of them were English and she didn't like that either. They were 'stuck up' and spoke with affected accents.

"Every time she left him, Jack went out with other women and she dated other men like Tom Mix; Tommy Meighan; and the great Irish tenor, John McCormack. There were tearful reconciliations, many good intentions for the future, and more fighting and misunderstanding. Jack wanted a child. She didn't. She was intent on her acting career and could not afford the risk. In those days the image of a married star was unacceptable to most audiences and to all studio heads. Being a mother was unheard of. Still, she did produce me. Jack was unfaithful, or she thought he was, and she filed for divorce several months before I was born. It was the end of their stormy marriage. Although they talked about going back together several times, it never happened. Then he met Garbo!

"My parents had very little in common besides their youth, their love of the movies, and a powerful physical attraction. Garbo was so elusive, she was harder to pin down than he was. She would slip away to walk alone on the beach or drive for hours across the desert or into the mountains. Or she would withdraw into herself, and although she was with him physically, she would be light years away in time and space. He tried to include her in his intellectual interests, ordering books, reading out loud together, going to art exhibits, encouraging her to talk with his circle of friends (who were mostly writers), but she could only go along so far and then she quietly disengaged. I don't believe Garbo was in the least scholarly, but with him she tried. What Jack was looking for, or what he needed most, was a wise, nurturing, maternal, loving woman. He never found one.

"My father's affair with Garbo was doomed from the start because Jack demanded total commitment, which Garbo could never give to any man or woman. He was so insecure himself that he required an ironclad relationship to give him the confidence he needed. I think Virginia Bruce tried to give him that, but by then he was out of control, drinking and fatally depressed, his career destroyed. She didn't have a chance.

12. Leatrice Gilbert Fountain

"Marlene Dietrich was just incredible to my mother and me. She was so kind, considerate, and sweet to me. She loved my father truly and was his last girlfriend. In fact, she was with him when he died. A lot has been written about this supposed meeting with John Gilbert and Garbo with Dietrich the day when he died, and it's all lies. Supposedly Dietrich was jealous and Gilbert and Dietrich had a row. One book even quoted me as the source of this outrageous lie. It angers me, all these fictions about my father. Anyway, back to Marlene. She was wonderful and very stylish and beautiful. She was so sweet to Mother and me when Father passed on. She also knew of a will that my father made (she saw it with her own eyes!) leaving everything to me. His last wife, Virginia Bruce, hired his last crooked attorney, and the two of them destroyed or repressed it or whatever. Anyway, Marlene kept up the good fight and encouraged my mother to fight Miss Bruce and the crooked attorneys. Mother dropped it, and Marlene was furious. She was looking out for me and my dear departed father's last wishes. I'm sure Marlene's daughter, Maria Dietrich Riva, has some legitimate gripes about her world-famous mother, but she was always fantastic to me, my mother, and, of course, John Gilbert.

"My father's outside interests away from film were varied. He was interested in American history, especially the westward movement and the Indians, but was not particularly curious about Europe or Asia. He read everything written by Ernest Thompson Seton and was an early animal rights activist. I don't know about his taste in art. He had a lot of paintings around, and I seem to remember they were rather dark and Spanish looking. And he had a stunning bronze statue of a nude woman (Dolores Del Rio) sitting on his coffee table. He was interested in fabrics and dyes, in magic tricks, and chemistry. He was a better-than-average chess player. He studied the stars and liked to pick out the constellations and planets. He was curious about evolution and plant propagation. He designed an extensive cactus garden with many rare varieties, worked in it himself, and grew all kinds of trees up and down his mountainside.

"We had a lot in common, including a similar sense of humor. We laughed together at offbeat things. He didn't do well with authority and I don't either. He never pretended to be anything he wasn't, and I hope I'm that kind of person. I shared his deep sympathy for animals. He always had them around—dogs, cats, even a tiny monkey he rescued while on a trip through the Panama Canal. I think I inherited my abiding sense of curiosity from him. I'm still learning anything that comes my way, from cereal boxes to the Internet!

A young Maria Riva (left) with her childhood friend and John Gilbert's daughter, Leatrice Gilbert (right), enjoying a shopping trip with Maria's mother, Marlene Dietrich (courtesy Leatrice Gilbert Fountain).

12. Leatrice Gilbert Fountain

"I'm not very much like my mother. She was not my role model. Leatrice was constantly 'on stage' and we were her audience. I felt I could never really get to know her and never knew what she was thinking or feeling. It was all a performance. This was devastating for a child who needed some kind of reality to grow on, to learn, and to try to understand how to get through the world. It's hard to describe, but I'm still not sure what my childhood was all about, except that I was awfully glad when it was over. Actresses, as a rule, do not make particularly good mothers. Yes, many of them try. She certainly did, but the powerful drive, the ambition and talent that make them successful actresses rule out the very different requirements of being a mother. I think there are only a few exceptions to this.

"Children have nothing to compare their present experiences with. I didn't know what a 'normal' childhood was like. I only knew mine, and it came in two distinct chapters. During my earliest years, I lived in Beverly Hills with my mother. We had a constantly changing cast of servants and nurses for me. I would no sooner get used to one—be it 'Fraulein,' or 'Miss Vanneman,' or 'Hilda,' or 'Nursie' (an amiable young Swedish woman)—than she would vanish and another starched white uniform would appear to wake me in the morning and bring breakfast up to the nursery. I remember the feeling of loss and confusion and feeling bereft as each newly loved acquaintance would disappear without explanation and the anxiety I had of getting to know the next one, hoping always that I would make a good impression. I don't ever remember wondering if I would like her. That did not seem to be the point. My mother would appear from time to time, always beautiful and affectionate, like a visiting princess or a young queen. I would watch from the open door of my room as she descended the stairs, dressed in a lovely beaded gown, wearing her diamonds and sleek bobbed hair, and greet whomever she was going out with that evening. She was very elegant and merry, full of fun—above all, beautiful.

"My father was an absent legend. I was told he lived 'in a tower on the hill above our house.' There was indeed a tall water tower up there, and for years I believed that was his castle and that one day he would come down from his tower and find me. Later I discovered that he lived on an ordinary street in a house up behind the Beverly Hills Hotel. It was a Spanish house perched on a mountain top with great views of Los Angeles and far out to the Pacific Ocean in the west. He appeared occasionally for my birthday, always a time of huge excitement.

"Mother gave me enormous birthday parties, inviting all her actor friends' children. Once we had a magician who arrived with a helper, 'Bozo the Clown,' who gave us presents and then made them all disappear. There was a woman ventriloquist with a talking doll dressed to look like Charles Lindbergh. Another time we had child tap dancers who were called Meglin Kiddies and appeared in the movies. In particular I remember Josephine, a tiny monkey who came to all my birthday parties with her keeper, Tony, who played a street organ. He was Italian and spoke very little English. He let Josephine sit on my shoulder, and she hugged my neck and squeaked in my ear. We gave her dimes and she'd pop them into the pocket of her red velvet jacket. It was reported in *Photoplay* that Our Gang Comedy entertained at my fourth birthday party. Unfortunately my memory of their coming is dim. I was more impressed with the monkey.

"When I was seven, my mother retired from the movies and married a Los Angeles businessman. We moved away from Beverly Hills to what was then called the Wilshire district, and I went to Third Street Grammar School. It was quite a change. No more news photographers! No more fancy parties and fewer celebrities coming and going. It was 1931 and the Depression was creeping in. Instead of rotating nurses, Mother hired a governess to look after me. I guess by sheer blind luck she got an Englishwoman, Miss Gladys Hunter, who stayed for the next five years of my life. That was the greatest consistency I had ever known.

"She was a real daughter of the British Empire. She hung pictures of the little princesses, Elizabeth and Margaret Rose, on my bedroom walls, and if I misbehaved she would ask in a sorrowful voice, 'Leatrice, what would the dear Queen say if she could see you now?' Since in those days that was the formidable Queen Mary, it usually brought me swiftly into line. She was kind and firm and she always made sense. She taught me how to eat fruit with a knife and fork, how to deal with doilies and finger bowls, and all kinds of formal table manners. She made everything a game and I enjoyed it. We were good friends. After Miss Hunter left, I went as a boarding student to Westlake School for Girls and made friends, some of whom I have to this day. So, it was an odd childhood, hardly tragic, but different from most.

"I remember Jean Harlow very well. She was a Christian Scientist and my grandmother was her 'practitioner,' or healer-advisor, and my uncle was her agent. I knew Charles Laughton and his wife, Elsa Manchester; early stars like Conrad Nagel; the producer Sidney Franklin; Greer Garson; and Spencer Tracy. I had a huge crush on him, and at age thirteen hoped he would wait for me. Joan Fontaine asked me for tea a few times. She was patient with a shy and starstruck teenager. I met Clark Gable and admired Mickey Rooney (didn't know him well but he was always kind) and Judy Garland.

"I was particularly fond of Ava Gardner. We were both in our teens, and although she was the most beautiful woman at MGM or anywhere, she never made you feel that she was conscious of it or gave a damn what she looked like. She was natural, charming, and warmhearted. Once we went out together for publicity pictures. They took us to a deserted beach to photograph us playing in the surf with a big red beach ball. There was Ava in a glittering white latex suit, looking like a goddess with long wavy hair and a voluptuous body; and there I was, straight up and down like a boy, with short-chopped black hair and a two-piece leopard print bathing suit (I had nothing worth mentioning on top!). It was the most humiliating day of my life. Fifty years later a fan approached me in London at the Dominion Theatre with one of those pictures. I nearly hit him!

"My father's career seemed to end shortly after the 'talkies' came in and this created the rumor that my father's voice was so highly pitched that sound film completely destroyed him. Some people suspected my father's decline was, at least in part, a case of studio politics and closely connected to an attempted merger at the time between William Fox and Loews, which indeed, it turned out to be. The reason the myth of 'the canary voice' continues is that it is almost impossible to destroy it. People like to believe in myths and archetypes. It satisfies a need. It's a fable: John Gilbert, the Great Lover, was destroyed by his squeaky voice. It's a better story than the truth.

"Jack adored the movies. There was no part of their production that didn't interest him or that he couldn't do. He was happy just to walk around the lot and watch what was going on. The technology fascinated him, and he had opinions (not always welcome by his associates) on any topic concerning the business. He was the original 'movie person.' Leatrice lived in a fantasy of stardom, of recognition, of luxury, and of importance that became an obsession as she grew older, long after her career had dwindled away. Her need for that kind of stimulation and excitement never faded and kept her going, making tours, lecturing on early Hollywood, doing readings, and showing her films. It gave her an activity she enjoyed up to the time of her death. Two months before she died, she stood in her beaded gown and glittering three-inch heels on the stage of

Radio City Music Hall blowing kisses to a worldwide audience on *The Night of a Hundred Stars*. It was a proper ending for a star.

"As for the haircut, it happened by accident. She and Father were separated, she was making a picture, and (as usual) had gone home to live with her mother. One day she spied him driving down Hollywood Boulevard and followed his car. He stopped and went into a barber shop for a haircut. She followed him, climbed up into the next chair, and said she wanted a haircut too. (There were no unisex barbers in those days!) Well, the barber cut off her waist-long black curly hair into a normal man's haircut (in mid-picture!), and she and Jack got back together again for another go in their tumultuous marriage. DeMille nearly fired her!

"My mother adored DeMille as a director, and she played a beautiful waif in his epic biblical telling of *The Ten Commandments*. I remember her telling the story about *The Ten Commandments* and how DeMille managed to divide the Red Sea for the Israelites to pass through. It was always kept the darkest secret, but mother told me that it was done in miniature, using gelatin.

"By 1931, she accepted a marriage proposal from a Los Angeles businessman, William Spencer Hook, whom she married. She then retired gracefully, but reluctantly, from the business she loved. I don't believe she was ever completely happy again. Stardom was her life's goal, and her brief moment in the spotlight was the culmination of all she desired. Considering that she lived for another fifty-five years, it borders on tragedy and a waste of a gifted and beautiful woman.

"My own movie career is brief and not memorable. I made one picture when I was twelve, *Of Human Hearts*, with Jimmy Stewart, Walter Houston, and Ann Rutherford. It was a Civil War story with John Carradine playing Lincoln. It shows up on TV from time to time. For six months when I was seventeen, I was under contract to MGM and appeared in tiny parts in a number of films: *Kismet, Hitler's Hangman, Thirty Seconds over Tokyo, We Were Dancing, Random Harvest, Reunion in France,* and *Calling Dr. Gillespie*. I don't remember them all. My fellow starlets were Donna Reed, Ava Gardner, and Janis Paige. I later fled MGM. The place and the life terrified me and I've never regretted it. About that time my best friend, a young man called Skipper Daly, was shot down over the Pollezzi Oil Fields in Rumania and, in an emotional reaction and still in shock, I joined the army (the Women's Army Corps) and served at Fort Des Moines until the war was over. Then I went to New York and never lived in California again.

12. Leatrice Gilbert Fountain

"When I was fifteen, I studied voice in Los Angeles with Marshall Rusk, a coach from New York, and later in New York with Walter Cataldi-Tassoni. We sang operas all over New York, in workshop productions mostly, plus some more elaborate stagings. I appeared with Patricia Brooks and Andre Dobrianski in *Rigoletto* singing Madalene. Patricia later sang at the New York City Opera. She was a tiny, blond coloratura with a sparkling voice, and Andre sang with the Metropolitan Opera for many years. By that time I had produced five children and realized that as much as I loved to sing, it was too late. I had other responsibilities. I still go to the opera every chance I get. I sang Musetta in *La Boheme*, Santuzza in *Cavalaria Rusticana*, Suzuki in *Madame Butterfly*, and Azucena in *Trovatore*."

Stinchcum concludes, we have not heard the last from the progeny of John Gilbert and Leatrice Joy. The Gilbert family tree is blooming in all directions and thriving. Leatrice Gilbert Fountain has many talented offspring gifted in art, music, writing, acting, and other skills. Her daughter Lorin Hart, who looks like Leatrice Joy, is a folk/blues/country/pop singer and songwriter. Lorin has been on the Los Angeles club scene and coffeehouse circuit for about ten years. Leatrice has four good-looking sons. The oldest, John Gilbert Fountain, lives in Ireland where he studies art. Anthony, a musicologist, is an archivist at Sony Music Entertainment. His purview is Masterworks, the classical line of Columbia Records purchased by Sony Music years ago. Christopher is a lawyer with a flair for writing fiction (the next John Grisham perhaps?). He's written several unpublished novels. The youngest son, Gideon, is a successful realtor in Greenwich, Connecticut. Witty and charming, he has also had film work in the past.

A recent shot of Leatrice Gilbert Fountain (courtesy Leatrice Gilbert Fountain).

Children of Hollywood

The starry genes don't end with the third generation but extend into the fourth. David Britten Prior, the great-grandson of John Gilbert and Leatrice Joy, is a rising star in the film industry. He played an alien in *Alien Resurrection* and recently wrote and plans to direct a crime thriller called *Cain Rose Up*. He did the rewrite of *Immortal Kiss* (a vampire screenplay) and wrote, produced, and directed a short called *Forever After*.

Finally, Leatrice sums up her fleeting relationship with her father. Although their time together was brief, it is apparent that he left a lasting and loving impression on Leatrice long after his untimely death. An array of John Gilbert photos are displayed throughout her Connecticut home, and she still talks about him with love and pride.

> "My father wrote to me once and said, 'You fill a great void in my life.' I didn't know him at all before, so it was entirely new and a pleasure that still moves me to tears. He was so stiff and unaccustomed to children when I began going to visit him, and gradually ... very slowly ... he got used to having me around, found out that I was a real person and not unlike him. Then we began laughing together and enjoying each other's company. We were just getting to that stage when he died. It was a shock. I had not been told he was ill. He always looked well when I was with him, and it simply never occurred to me that anything could happen. I never got over it. I never will."

13

CHRIS COSTELLO

* *Daughter of Lou Costello* *
and Anne Battlers

VICKIE ABBOTT WHEELER

* *Daughter of Bud Abbott* *
and Betty Smith

> "Now, on the St. Louis team we have Who's on first, What's on second, I Don't Know is on third."
> —Abbott

> "That's what I want to find out"
> —Costello

Abbott and Costello. Anyone who mentions that twosome, even today, is bound to get an instant smile and a favorite childhood memory of watching their comic genius on screen. They proved that "opposites do attract." Two buddies happened to get themselves, and each other, into more trouble than enough, yet enough trouble to make it funny.

Bud Abbott was the tall, thin, wisecracking straight man. His pal, Lou Costello, was the exact opposite. Lou was the short, fat, innocent whipping boy for Abbott. His trademark cry of "Abbbbbottttttttttt!" was heard in every film. He was always looking to Abbott to smoothtalk him out of one predicament after another. It was that simple comedy that made them who they were; they made America laugh in a time of war. In fact, that popularity carried them through the post war and many, many years beyond.

Children of Hollywood

Their teaming was quite by accident. In 1936, Lou Costello was performing in a burlesque house when his straight man fell ill. Bud Abbott just happened to be at the club, working as a coat clerk. He agreed to stand in as Lou's straight man for the night but from that night on they were a team. They clicked.

They were, and still are, one of the greatest comedy teams ever to come out of Hollywood. Together they were the number one box office attraction in 1942 and they stayed in the top ten for another eight years after that. Their fast-talking, completely confusing, trademark "Who's on first?" routine is considered a classic American skit and is dedicated to America's favorite sport, baseball.

One of their finest and most successful films actually teamed together two very different genres, comedy and horror. *Abbott and Costello Meet Frankenstein* featured Glenn Strange as Frankenstein, Bela Lugosi as Dracula and Lon Chaney, Jr., as the Wolfman. Teaming the most successful comedy team of the moment with three of Hollywood's most notorious monsters proved to be the perfect recipe. The movie was a smash hit.

Lou Costello made a point of mentioning his home town of Paterson, New Jersey, in almost every television show and most of his movies. Alfred Hitchcock usually had a walk-on role in most of his movies, too. It was a personal touch, their trademark, and it was fun for the audience to sit and wait for the moment to come.

Bud Abbott and Lou Costello had a partnership spanning twenty-one years. They made thirty-seven films together and performed on almost every other medium in the business—radio, vaudeville, burlesque, movie houses and, eventually, television. Their last film together, *Dance with Me Henry*, was made in 1956. In 1957, the movie-going audience changed their tastes in film and Abbott and Costello went their separate ways. Lou Costello died just three years later, in 1959. Bud Abbott followed in 1974.

Here, Lou and Anne Costello's youngest child, their daughter Chris, tells of her life as a "Hollywood Child." Sometimes sad, sometimes happy, her story once again proves the theory that seems to be so commonplace among the lives of the people whose job it is to make us laugh. Comedy is often tragic and it is too often the comedians and, in some cases their children, who bear the brunt of such tragedies. In Raymond Strait's *Star Babies*, Chris Costello explained what it was like

13. Chris Costello and Vickie Abbott Wheeler

growing up in Bud and Lou's world. So, when I approached her about this similar project, I was thrilled when she kindly offered to retell her story for *Children of Hollywood*.

"My mother and father both died during my year of going from elementary to junior high school, but I remember them both very well, especially my father with whom I was very close. People think because I was only eleven when he died that I really don't have a lot of memories, but it was a very close relationship—very close.

"Before I was born my father and mother had two other daughters and a son. Their son, Lou Costello, Jr., was the last child before me. He drowned in the family swimming pool and because of that, when I came along four years later, I was born into almost protective custody. That attitude on the part of my father was very beneficial to me after he was gone. When he died I felt he had given me enough love and memories to last a lifetime. He was a beautiful father. Many people I know can't say that about their parents.

"When I think of my childhood I think of my father and that always concludes with memories of Christmas. That's the hardest time for me, Christmastime. My father loved Christmas. He was like a child who truly believed in Santa Claus. At one of our San Fernando Valley homes Christmas became an event. My father had the place lit up like a sound stage with moving reindeer on the roof. There were bubbles floating up from the chimney and a huge movie screen up on top of the house where he would be showing film clips. Traffic was always jammed up for blocks with people trying to see our home. I remember George Gobel, who lived across the street from us, always opened up his television show with, 'Here I am and this is the show.' Every year during the Christmas season he used to put up a sign out on his front lawn over which he hung a single light bulb. The sign read: Well, here I am—and there's the show. An arrow pointed across the street to our house.

"Dad also loved trains. Our entire backyard was outfitted with train tracks and an actual train that seated maybe five or six people. He drove it around the property—he and David Rose, the composer, who lived down the street. They loved to get out there and fiddle around with that train; both were train nuts. One Christmas he bought me a train set that was laid out across the pool table. It was my train but I couldn't play with it. He had to play with it. That was his baby—Daddy's toy.

"It was easy to be his daughter because he loved children more than

Children of Hollywood

Chris Costello gets a ride on the back of her famous father Lou Costello, as his long time comedy partner Bud Abbott cheers them on (courtesy Chris Costello).

anything in the world. For example, one night he was out Christmas shopping with my mother, and a little girl in the toy department was crying for a doll. Dad overheard her father explaining that they could not afford that doll. Dad went to the woman behind the counter and slipped her the money for the doll. He said, 'Wrap it up and tell her it's from Santa Claus.'

"Other times when he would pick me up at school, I'd be tired by three o'clock and want to go home. When I came out to the car it was mobbed with kids from the school—all talking to my father and having a great time. That always meant I was late getting home and it left me less time for playing before bedtime, but he just couldn't run away from a fan or say, 'I'm too busy.' He used to tell my older sister Carol, who went through the same thing, 'Those people are the people who put me where I am.' He loved his fans."

In a *Classic Images Online* article by Jenn Dlugos, Chris remembered back to being on the set of *Abbott and Costello Meet the Mummy*.

"It was a very colorful set on a sound stage and I was sitting on the sound stage with my two cousins, Tony and Joe. The actors were breaking for lunch and all of a sudden 'The Mummy' started walking toward us. We all let out screams. I'm twelve years younger than my sister so she remembers a lot more than I do about being on the film sets. The Abbott and Costello meet the Universal Monster films were always very colorful sets, which is something you don't end up seeing in a black and white movie. What really got her was seeing all these monsters sitting in directors chairs smoking cigars, chewing gum and reading the newspaper. That was absolutely amazing to her.

"The biggest business mistake that my dad and Bud ever made was not taking the opportunity to buy Universal Studios. Back when the studio was really fighting to keep its doors open, they were offered the chance to purchase it, but they turned it down. After we heard that story, we just kind of banged our heads against the desk and said, 'OH MY GOD!'"

"At home, my dad was a very quiet family man. He had that unbelievable way of turning on a switch to bring on the comedy. If he threatened to spank me when I was bad and if I cried, he would automatically start being funny—walking into the wall, tripping over his feet, anything to get me to stop crying. His over protectiveness didn't help my early career ambitions much. As a kid I always was very starstruck for the movie industry. I wanted to be in pictures. My biggest disappointment with my father

Happily posing for the camera, a young Chris Costello is pictured with her parents, Lou and Anne Costello (courtesy Chris Costello).

13. Chris Costello and Vickie Abbott Wheeler

came when he was filming his last picture with Bud Abbott, *Dance with Me Henry*.

"They were shooting on location in Calabassas and he had me and a bunch of kids out one day. I desperately wanted to be in that movie to a point of making sure I got in view of that camera lens. He promised me I could ride on the carousel and be an extra. When he finally did put me up on the pony I realized they had wrapped for lunch and there were no cameras on me. That was very disappointing.

"Another time I was thwarted by my own inhibitions. I was about six when I had the chance to play Baby Snooks. About six months earlier I'd had my tonsils out and it was a horrendous experience for me. When I found out there was a scene in which Baby Snooks had her tonsils removed I came totally unglued and locked myself in the bathroom on the day we were supposed to go into the studio to tape it. My father was very angry, and it was one of those times when I became 'your mother's daughter.'

"My older sisters, Carol and Paddy, tell me he was very strict in some ways. They went through some scenes I missed because he was gone by the time I reached that age, but he was a very Italian father in every sense. Don't wear lipstick until you're sixteen. If you were out with a boy and parked outside before going in (more than five minutes) he'd be out on the porch flipping the light switch on and off. One time he even came out to the car when a boy brought Carol home and rapped on the window. He said, 'Don't you think it's about time you came in now?' She was so embarrassed. There he was in his plaid bathrobe and house slippers with a big cigar.

"He always had the cigar. Often it was not even lit. That intimidated some of my friends, but never me. I always respected my father but I never feared him. School friends were a little frightened the first time they met him because he was not an outgoing-type conversationalist. People expected him to be the man on the screen and he wasn't that at all away from making movies and doing radio and television shows. I remember my mother telling me that one of the reasons why he never really disciplined us per se—like physically spanking—was because he was afraid of his own strength. I don't think he had it in him to be able to do that.

"My mother? Very strict. She came from a conservative Scottish background. The most important things in her life were her family and her marriage. I don't think she would have cared if she lived in a twenty-two-room mansion or a one-bedroom flat—just as long as she had her family.

She was a woman who had servants, yet at seven or eight in the evening you might find her scrubbing a floor because of some imaginary splash of water. She was also an excellent cook and my father always said that one of his greatest pleasures in life was being able to sit down to one of her fabulous Italian meals—just the family. And she dearly loved doing that for him on the cook's night off. She learned from his father, who was a great Italian cook.

"On the home front I was a triple A. Academically I was a big flop. Growing up I was a mischief-maker of the first order. Never to the point of being harmful to anyone else, but I was one of those children who had a tendency to get a little wild. I can remember throwing one of the nun's bells over the hedge into a reservoir at Our Lady of the Valley School, ditching classes and hiding in the chapel, and once setting off the fire alarm in school. Not until I got into high school and found my way into music did I take any of it seriously. That's all I wanted then—music. I didn't want to go to college because I wanted to be out there singing. I've never missed it.

"My father was very realistic about education. I think he provided the best that he could for his children—if they wanted it—because he didn't come from the wealthiest of parents and he valued education. His father made a living but was never wealthy. His advice was that even if we wanted to get into the entertainment business, we should get an education in case things didn't pan out. Then we'd have something to fall back on. That's one bit of his advice that I didn't take.

"As realistic as he was about practical matters, he was totally unrealistic when it came to giving. He was generous to a fault. They used to have a saying about him at the studios: that he had long arms and short pockets. If somebody needed a loan for a sick wife or kids he'd ask, 'How much?' Nobody knows how many operations he paid for—for people he didn't even know. I don't think anybody really knows about the private life and family of a comedian. There's no glamour, so the feature writers pass them by favoring cleavage and handsome faces.

"When my father died we had already sold our ranch in Canoga Park and were temporarily living in an apartment in Sherman Oaks until our new home on top of Longridge Terrace was completed. I was going to school at St. Jane Frances. I can vividly recall one night when my father and I went up to Longridge Terrace to look at the progress of the new house. It was an evening I'll never forget. We drove up the hill and only the framework was up. It overlooked the entire San Fernando Valley. It

13. *Chris Costello* and *Vickie Abbott Wheeler*

was a clear beautiful night. God, it was gorgeous! My dad stood within the framework where the sliding glass doors were to be. He always had a tendency of rocking back and forth on his heels (a habit I have since acquired). He stood there with his hands in his pockets, rocking back and forth, and looked out over the valley. After a short silence he turned to me where I was standing beside him and very softly said, 'You know, someday, Chrissy, I'm going to be up here among the stars.' It was the last time he ever saw the place and is a moment stamped indelibly in my memory.

"The home was finished after Dad died in March of 1959, and my mother and I moved in, but it was never the same without him. After he died she just gave up the will to live. Theirs was a beautiful love story. I remember Mom taking our pictures of him and surrounding herself with them and with the memories of their life together.

"My mother had a drinking problem, just as my father had been a somewhat compulsive gambler. Human frailties. I never knew a lot about my father's gambling, but I was painfully aware of my mom's drinking, although I couldn't understand why. She seemed to have everything, just as I did. It is tough being married to a celebrity and I think Lou Jr.'s death had a lot to do with her drinking. People made her feel guilty about it. Some people made her feel like she had committed a crime against my father because she hadn't saved the baby's life—my God, she was the child's mother. It was her loss, too. My mother just wasn't strong enough to handle all of that without help, and her help came from drinking.

"They never had a moment's peace—my mom and dad—until they were alone in bed. Our home was always filled with people. People I'd never seen before crowded around the bar and the pool. Sometimes Mom would ask, 'Do you know that person out by the pool?' Our place was overrun with the leeches and the hangers-on. Her home was like a transient zoo. I now understand what she went through.

"All of that added to my confusion in growing up. I wanted to have a mother like other kids' mothers. When I'd leave for school she'd be fine, but when she picked me up she might be drunk. Just before she died she went out and did the type of Christmas shopping that might be reminiscent of the 'old days' in our home when the entire theater would be packed to the ceiling with gifts. She was trying to make everybody happy that Christmas. Paddy had three kids and was going through a divorce and Mom wanted to make it look like everything was normal, for a while anyway.

"She was out three nights straight, just buying and buying and buying. She died the days the lights were being strung up outside the house. I was twelve years old and it was hard to put those gifts under the tree—hard. Mom was killed by a combination of a heart attack, alcohol, and just losing the will to live. There are so many beautiful things to remember about my mother. I have to pinpoint things because I was so much closer to my father and only during the period between their deaths did I get in any way nearly as close to her. I was like Daddy's little girl, yet I can remember her sticking up for me in every instance. She was always in my corner.

"I recall one time in Catholic school a nun was giving me a very hard time and Mom went to the school and met the sister head on. Using an old expression, she'd picked up from her own mother, she told the nun, 'If you don't treat my daughter right, I'm going to pull your black mutch right off your head!' Mutch is an old Scottish term for a veil.

"Like my father, my mother was a very tender, giving person. I had a kitten once and some kids across the street were target shooting with a BB gun and they hit my kitten. My mother ran outside in nothing but a bathing suit, scooped up the kitten, got in the car, and drove to the vet. She stayed with it—it died, but she stayed there until it was all over. My mother loved to touch, to hug. My father was not that way. He was not a touching person, but my mother was warm and loving in that sense.

"Once I wanted to go to church on my own, so I took my bike and rode all the way down the hill to St. Jane Frances Church, which was fine. Riding back was something else. I got home and was just dripping wet and my face was red. I was totally exhausted and she took me into her arms and really cared for me. That's something I'll always cherish about my childhood, too.

"When Mom was not drinking she was a fun person. After my dad died I used to sleep in her bed and we would watch TV together and have baked bean sandwiches, which she loved. We were like two schoolgirls. She often told people, 'Someday when Chrissy grows up I think we're going to be fabulous friends.' I think we would have been. It's amazing to me when I hear people talking down about their parents. I want to scream out to them 'Be thankful to God you've got your parents!'

"Even the things you didn't like about your parents seem like nothing after they're gone. Paddy told me about a time she approached Mom in the kitchen and told her, 'Mom, you've been drinking too much again. I think it's about time that you told me what's wrong.' Mom stood in the

13. *Chris Costello* and *Vickie Abbott Wheeler*

middle of the kitchen and raised her hands up before her face. She started to sob uncontrollably and left the room. She tried but couldn't get it out. She just trembled and sobbed and the words wouldn't come.

"I recall once hurting my mother and not even knowing it at the time. I came home from seeing *Some Like It Hot* and told Mom that I wanted Marilyn Monroe as my mother. It just sliced right through her and I'm sure she went straight to the bottle. Other times it might be something more humorous. It was gossiped about our family that Betty Hutton was once very much in love with my dad before he had married my mother. Whenever I would complain about something unnecessarily, one of my mother's favorite squelchers was, 'Well, you could have had Betty Hutton for your mother.'

"One Halloween my father dressed me up like him. We got a little argument going because I didn't want a cigar. He put the derby on my head and shoved the cigar into my mouth; I pulled it away and took a stand. 'I'm not going to put that cigar in my mouth because it will burn my tongue.' So he took the cigar, but every time we'd stop at a house when we went trick-or-treating he would shove that damaged cigar back in my mouth just before someone opened the door.

"The things that are difficult about being Lou Costello's daughter are not things that were his fault. I loved my father and had great respect for him, but being his daughter looking for work I began to feel I'd never get my own identity. He once told me when I asked about someday getting into movies, 'It's interesting sweetheart. I can help open the door, but once you walk through it's got to be your talent that sustains it.'

"The death of my parents, my mother especially, put a great burden on the three of us girls, each in a different way. Paddy and Carol were already out on their own, but something had to be done to accommodate me. I was too young to do a solo number. With Paddy coming off a divorce I just naturally fell into her care. That didn't really work, either. Paddy was still very young, in her early twenties. Having a twelve year old on her hands was not exactly the best medicine for her own problems. So after a while with Paddy, I lived with Carol and then went on to boarding school because they thought it would be good for me. The discipline and supervision were something they decided I needed but they could not give me at that point.

"It came at a time when I was ready to break loose. I was a brat. Oh boy, was I a brat. I loved my sisters, but I was just at that age—just a rebel. For a while I hated God for taking my parents. I even stopped going to church. Since then I have left the Catholic faith and am now a Methodist.

"After my parents' deaths there was all the business of settling their estates. There were insurance and trust funds and all that sort of thing. A lot of people said my father was not a businessman, and in many senses, he was not. He got in with the wrong people, but he started a corporation called Television Corporation of America, which still handles all the distribution of the fifty-two film shorts he left. So there certainly was some business sense in that man. My sisters and I still have an interest in that.

"In the beginning, to prevent a second tragedy, my parents wanted me to learn to swim early. I was quite small when my dad took me to Eunice Knight Saunders Swimming School where I learned to be a fish. It used to scare the hell out of me because I always would get water up my nose. I would get in the pool and say to my dad, 'Dad, I can't swim. I'm going to drown. I'm going to drown.' Of course, I was just kidding around, but I failed to understand why he never laughed at that. You didn't joke about drowning in our house. When I was small, I remember there were times when they would lock the door to my room to keep me from straying to the pool if there wasn't proper supervision on the first floor. I do remember one time my cousin rode my bicycle straight into the pool and the gardener had to fish her out of the deep end. That created quite a sensation.

"I keep coming back to Christmas, but so much of my early life was centered around that time of year. I mentioned the way my parents shopped. Nothing was too grand for the kids, and there were lots of gifts for the leeches. They would go out and buy a cashmere sweater and then ask the clerk to give them twenty more like it. Or maybe a gold bracelet—my father would ask for fifty of those. Then there would be the big Christmas Eve party where people from the studios and personal friends and family would gather at our home and everybody was given a gift. Always the leeches would show up and hang around, and it was embarrassing to hear them talking about the spoils. I would hear things like, 'What did he give you?' or 'What do you think you're going to get from him this year?'

"One Christmas at the ranch I let slip to my father that I'd told Paddy's oldest boy that there was no Santa Claus. We were walking around and he stopped dead in his tracks and looked at me as if he were going to break down sobbing any minute. If he had hit me or done anything at

13. *Chris Costello* and *Vickie Abbott Wheeler*

all, I would have appreciated it, but his total silence just crushed me. I never saw much of Abbott's kids, although many people think our families were close on a private level. Others think my father and Abbott hated each other. Neither was true. Both men really had their own personal lives.

"I grew up, graduated, and have gone on with my music and acting. It has been something I've had to do—I had to do it for me. There has been an analogy in my life to that of my father's. When Lou Jr. drowned my father came home from the studio, took care of business, and went back to work. He had just come back to do his radio show after his first heart seizure and asked Mother to keep the baby up to see if he recognized Dad's voice on the radio. He was already at the studio when they called him home. Everybody was worried sick he might have another heart attack. They started calling for NBC right away with a list of names of people who had volunteered to go on for him, but he wouldn't have it. He said, 'No, no, take me back to the studio.'

"My aunt said, 'Lou, how can you do it?'

"He said, 'Marie, I told Ann to keep that baby up tonight and wherever God has taken my little boy today I want to be sure he can still hear me.'"

In 1978 a television movie was made on the lives and partnership of Bud Abbott and Lou Costello. It was a misconstrued story that devastated Lou's daughter, Chris. She tells of her personal reaction to the movie.

"When I saw *Bud and Lou* on television I was a basket case for two days. I didn't want to work. I didn't want to be part of an industry

A recent shot of Chris Costello, all grown up (courtesy Chris Costello).

that could so badly misconstrue a man's life and totally distort what he was. I didn't want to sing anymore. My Aunt Marie called me and I told her I didn't even want to leave the house. I didn't want to do anything. I said, 'If this is the way the industry treats a man who in more ways than one gave his life to that industry, then I don't even want to be remotely associated with it.'

"She said, 'Christy, your dad went on to do his NBC show the day the baby died—you go to work and if anything, you do it for him.' And that's why I did go on and will continue to—for my dad, Lou Costello, who was one helluva human being. If my father had lived I don't think he would have ever said to me, 'I don't want you to go into the entertainment industry,' but I don't think he would have encouraged it because of his realization of what the industry can do to you. I realize that now."

Today, Chris Costello runs her own public relations company out of Burbank, California, and continues to promote her father's legacy. Her book *Lou's on First*, is still in print after an astonishing twenty-one years. In addition to that, Chris is now back on the lecture circuit, having put together a tribute slide and clip show on her dad. Recently she sailed on the *QEII* from New York to Southhampton. It was so successful she was asked to return again in 2002. She recently brought her show to the Fort Lee Film Commission's salute to Universal Studios and was in Manchester, New Hampshire, at the Gaffstown Middle School, talking to students about Abbott and Costello's radio years.

Like Chris Costello, Vickie Abbott Wheeler is also involved in preserving the memory of her father, Bud Abbott. Just like peanut butter and jelly, one ingredient without the other just isn't the same as that special combination of the two together. It seems that Bud and Lou really belonged together; they always did. That's the reason I've chosen to blend Chris and Vickie's stories together. It seems wrong to separate them now, even one generation on.

Vickie was adopted, along with her brother (now deceased), by two very loving parents, Bud Abbott and Betty Smith. The photo of Vickie as a child that is pictured in this book depicts a very special occasion for her. It was the day of her adoption, the day she officially became an Abbott. She tells the story as she remembers it.

13. *Chris Costello* and *Vickie Abbott Wheeler*

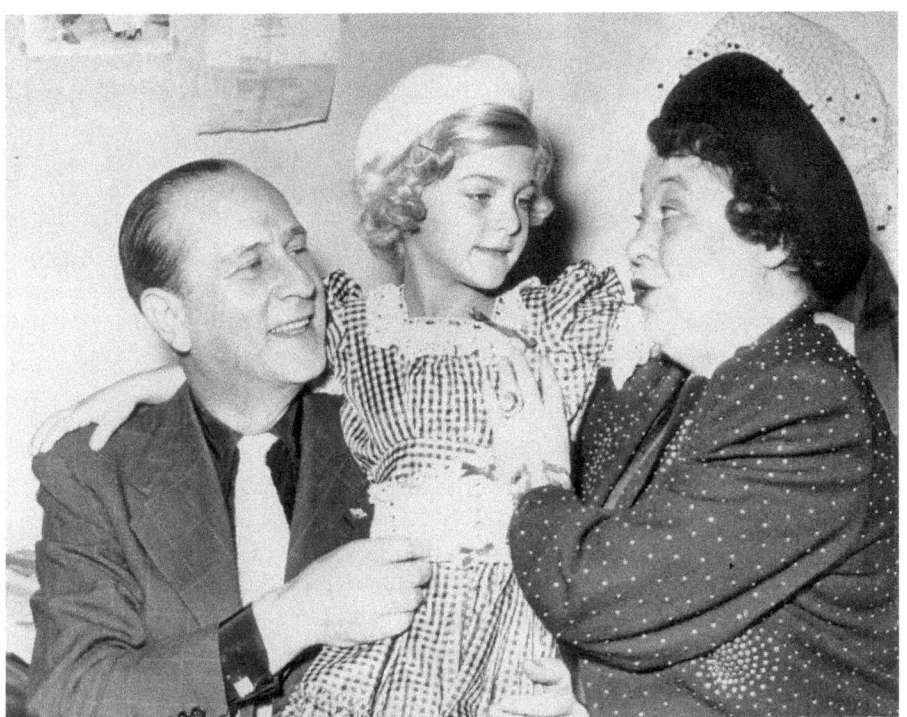

October 25, 1949: This photograph was taken immediately after Vickie Abbott was officially adopted by comedian Bud Abbott and his wife Betty.

"I remember going down to the courthouse with my parents very clearly. They told me a very nice judge would ask me some questions about myself, and then after that I would be an American citizen. Oh, how proud I felt that day. Later on in my life they told me the real reason for our trip down to the courthouse that day and we all had a good laugh about it. You see, in the forties, things were different. Parents kept things from their children; everything was a secret.

"After Mother and Father Abbott died, I did a search and found my birth family. I found that my birth mother was twenty-eight years old and left five children, not knowing who would care for them. However, I ended up being a very lucky little girl from Georgia, chosen by two of the most loving people in the world, and adopted and cared for my entire life.

"I'm married to a wonderful guy, Don [Wheeler]. We've been married more than forty years. Don must have known I was 'the one,' because he asked me to marry him just ten days after meeting me on a blind date, of all things! He moves fast! I of course accepted his proposal but I did tell him he would have to meet my father and ask for my hand in marriage. Don said, 'sure,' but I didn't dare tell him who my father was. I didn't want to scare him off!

"I tried my best to have fun and live a normal life and make it as comfortable and as normal as possible for my dates to be okay with dating a movie star's daughter. It was hard. Well, I took Don home to meet my parents and you should have seen his face when Dad walked into the room! He said to me, '*That's* your father?! Oh my God!!' Poor Don, he almost fainted!

"Dad was gentle and sweet to Don. He was like that with everyone, but poor Don was still in shock after seeing that my father, and his soon to be father-in-law, was none other than Bud Abbott! We sat down and Don eventually got over his initial nerves and speechlessness. He finally got around to asking Dad for my hand in marriage. Dad said, 'Well, if you and Vic love each other and you promise to take care of her, my answer is yes.' More than forty years later Don and I are still together and still going strong.

"You know, I have been thinking about the best way to express what my parents meant to me. I know what my Dad meant to the rest of the world but that was his screen persona, not the way I saw him or remember him. I read a recent newspaper article about the man who wrote the song, 'What Is America to Me.' That song embodies so much of what my parents were all about. Dad and Mom loved America; they loved their country. They helped others who had less than they did, they sold war bonds to fight the war, and they opened their own home to troops and entertained them and took care of them as if they were their own sons. My father was also the caretaker of his family. He supported his mother and father, his brother, his sisters, and anyone who needed help, but family always came first.

"After the tragedy of the September 11th terrorist attacks, I honestly hope that people think more about family. My father loved his family and he truly loved his job, too. He grew up in the world of show business. His mother was in the circus. She was a bareback rider for Ringling Brothers Circus and his father was a booking agent. Dad would joke about being born under a tent. He had to be in show business; it was in his blood. After my parents died, I realized the body of work that Dad and

13. *Chris Costello* and *Vickie Abbott Wheeler*

Lou left to the world and it makes me so proud. Their work is still loved by millions of fans all over the world.

"I've always considered myself a very lucky girl. You see, these two loving, sweet people chose me to be their daughter and in doing so, gave me an unbelievable life. My parents were married for fifty-five wonderful years and I'm pleased to say that Don and I are now well on our way to that milestone ourselves. I have no doubt the love my parents showed me in growing up has made me the person I am today. They were very special people and I miss them every day."

Both Chris and Vickie have devoted a lot of their own lives to preserving the memory of their famous fathers. Their pride and dedication to making their fathers' work known to a whole new generation of fans would make Bud and Lou proud. It certainly seems there's no stopping the ongoing generational fascination of Abbott and Costello. After all, laughter is ageless, and this fabulous twosome left a lot behind for us to laugh about.

14

RON FIELDS

* *Grandson of W. C. Fields* *
and Harriet Hughes

Start every day with a smile and get it over with.
—W. C. Fields

William Claude Dukenfield, better known as W. C. Fields to us film buffs, was the eldest of five children born to a Cockney immigrant, James Dukenfield, and a Philadelphia native, Kate Felton. His schooling lasted all of four years; he then quit to work with his father selling vegetables from a horse cart.

At age eleven, after continuing conflicts and physical fights with his father (who at one time hit him across the head with a shovel), he left home. With nowhere to go, he survived on stolen food and clothing and slept in a self-dug hole in the ground. He would often get into street fights and get beaten. The one consolation about being arrested for such behavior was a warm night in a jail cell. Strangely enough, a cell for the night was more of a luxury than a punishment, so he didn't exactly learn from the experience of a night behind bars!

His first steady job was delivering ice. By age thirteen he was a skilled pool player and juggler. He was soon spotted and recruited as an entertainer at an amusement park in Norristown, Pennsylvania. He developed an act with the technique of pretending to lose the things he was juggling. All of his talents were self-taught, all were unique and he soon realized these very talents had the ability to make him some much-needed money.

In 1893, still age thirteen, he was employed as a juggler at Fortescue's Pier in Atlantic City. When business was slow he pretended to

14. Ron Fields

drown in the ocean. It was the idea of management that this fake drowning and subsequent fake rescue would draw customers. It would have to be one of the strangest marketing schemes ever, but he did exactly as he was told and when business was slow it was time to get wet!

By the age of nineteen he was billed as The Distinguished Comedian and it is widely reported that he began opening bank accounts in every city he played. This commonly reported and too-often-believed story of new bank accounts in every city and in different names is something Ron Fields, his grandson, clears up a little later.

A shot of W. C. Fields, in character, playing cards.

On August 8, 1900, at age twenty, W.C. married his sweetheart, Harriet Hughes. It was a bizarre union of two very complicated people, but they were married until his death forty-six years later. At age twenty-three he was well on his way to stardom; in fact, one might say stardom had already arrived. He opened at the Palace in London. He appeared in a double-bill command performance with Sarah Bernhardt before King Edward VII. He starred at the Folies-Bergere (young Charles Chaplin and Maurice Chevalier were on the program). He was in every Ziegfeld Follies from 1915 through 1921. He starred for a year in the highly praised musical *Poppy*, which opened in New York in 1923. In 1925 D. W. Griffith made a movie of the play, renamed *Sally of the Sawdust* (1925), starring Fields. His first movie *Pool Sharks* was made in 1915 when he was thirty-six. It was the very late start to a very successful film career.

It certainly was a rags-to-riches life, in every sense of the word, from living in a hole in the ground at age eleven to eventually working his way up to his own mansion in Burbank, California. His career spanned thirty-seven movies, most all of them made for Paramount studios.

The most interesting loan of Fields would have been to MGM in 1939. Studio bosses actually considered him for the role of the wizard in *The Wizard of Oz*. Of course, Frank Morgan got the part and the rest is history. Still, the demeanor of Fields made for an appropriate thought on the part of MGM. It was not the silliest of casting ideas to ever be thrown around.

W. C. Fields was a unique comedian and a unique character—that's exactly what he was, a character. His ability to make light of living was the basis of who he was; it was how he entertained. He was often credited under a multitude of false names. Some of the stranger ones were Charles Bogle, Otis Criblecoblis, Mahatma Kane, and even Jeeves. His wit, his one liners, and his attitude often had that "Scrooge-like" feel, but it also made the audience want to believe there was a little bit of good under all of that cynicism. I guess that's what had them coming back time and time again. That and the fact that W. C. Fields would usually always speak the truth. In a situation where most of us would be tactful, Fields would say it exactly how it is. He would say everything the audience would long to say but would never dare to. That's what made him funny; that's what made him unique. Ultimately, *that's* what made him famous!

A recent shot of W. C. Fields' grandson, Ron Fields. Just look at that family resemblance (courtesy Ron Fields).

Although Ron Fields, his grandson, never met "The Great Man," he was always surrounded with his memory. His father, W.

14. Ron Fields

C. Fields, Jr., was compiling information for a book that he never wrote due to his own death. After his father's death, Ron found the information and continued his father's dream. That dream turned into the best selling books, *W. C. Fields: A Life on Film*, *W. C. Fields: By Himself*, and the documentary, *W. C. Fields: Straight Up*.

Ron Fields is an active force in the entertainment industry in his own right. He runs his own production company; he's a sitcom writer for NBC and Paramount Studios, an author, and an executive producer; and he's currently under option with Merv Griffith Entertainment. Here, Ron Fields reflects on what it's like being connected to a branch of the same family tree as W. C. Fields.

"Something not a lot of people know is that my grandfather based a lot of his movies on his own life. Being that he was often miserable it doesn't say much for his 'real life' but it's a fact. For instance, his awful movie-based wife was based on his real wife, Hattie. They never divorced, and my grandfather never asked for one. Instead, he used his personal misery as a motivation to create his character, and it worked. It's the funniest thing—actually it's not really funny, it's a sad situation. They were really very much in love.

"Hattie was part of my grandfather's juggling act. He could always get a laugh by blaming her when he missed. They had been married in 1900, and then in 1904, while they were in Johannesburg, they found out she was pregnant. W.C. wanted the baby born in the United States so it would have a chance to become president. You have to be born in the United States—that's really true. So, he made her go back to Philadelphia, and there she had the baby alone. There was some resentment there that she didn't have her husband with her. She hooked up with him again in England and stayed with him a few months, but then realized, 'Hey, this is ridiculous. I have this little baby, living out of a trunk, going from state to state.' She realized this was no life, and she tried to make W.C. quit. That wasn't a good idea! W.C. was absolutely obsessed with making it to the top—he was like me, or I am like him.

"Hattie of course is getting resentful. He's gone, say, 360 out of 365 days of the year. I think she desperately needed attention, anyway, having been in the entertainment business herself, and Fields wasn't supplying it anymore, so this resentment builds, and when he does finally show up, she'll say, 'Well, it certainly is nice of you to come by and see your son.' She was that type of woman. I hate to say this, but I knew her

> very well because she lived with us until she died in 1963, and I didn't like her very much.
>
> "I thought that what was going on in my childhood because of her was an awful situation. Hattie would much prefer to sit there, long suffering, than to fulfill any emotional or sexual needs. She would rather say, 'There, look at me, I'm a martyr,' and prefer that stance to any other. But she was absolutely devoted to her son.
>
> "She was very prejudiced, domineering, and very overbearing on my father. The relationship between my father and my mother just improved one hundred percent the day she died. As long as Hattie was around—well, she didn't like my mother because she took her son away. There was a definite jealousy there.
>
> Ron's father, W. C. Fields, Jr., would rarely mention his famous father. "He would often speak of him and compare our childhood to his childhood. For instance, he would spank us for one reason or another and after he spanked us he would say something like, 'You're lucky I'm around to discipline you. When I was your age, my father was never around.' He really missed that father figure in his life, even for the discipline."

Oddly enough, Ron didn't even know of his famous heritage until he was twelve years old.

> "I could never understand why we were always allowed to stay up late for a Fields film. I started laughing so hard at that back porch scene in *It's a Gift* that I had to leave the room. My sister was worried about me because I couldn't catch my breath.
>
> "She came out to help me and when I came to, I said, 'I think that guy's the funniest man who ever lived.' And she said she realized right there and then that I didn't have a clue that he was my grandfather. She was surprised because she knew; everyone knew, everyone but me. I guess being the youngest of five, they just forgot to tell me."

After Ron's father's death, he opened the padlocked basement door inside the family's apartment. It was 1971 and Ron found a gold mine of letters and documents, all belonging to his grandfather. It was there he found nine horrible pages of a book about W.C. that his father had begun. In his business correspondence, Fields, however ornery, is frequently tactful—surprising but true. There is a change of tone in his letters to Hattie. He would often write a note home with an accom-

14. Ron Fields

panying check. Below is a sample of his clipped and resentful correspondence.

*****

Pittsburgh, PA
November 23, 1915

Dear Hattie,

The tone of your letter dated November First was more than a surprise to me. For ten years you have inculcated into the boy's mind stories of my atrocities, you used every artifice and cunning employ to turn him from me, and you succeeded. But your success is empty, you have gained nothing.

Last spring I returned to New York anxious to see the boy and buy him everything a boy of his age could desire from a small practical auto down. I felt peeved when he said he preferred a home, and when I offered him one you had changed his mind and wished only a few bits of furniture for a flat, and he argued the home was the thing that had impaired your health. He then showed his hand. "When you did your melodramatic turn on the sofa" by saying when he grew up he would not look at me, he further hurt me by his precocious aggression when you sent him to the theatre....

You have reared your son as your poor dear Mama reared John; you have taught him for ten years what you thought would ultimately prove advantageous to you in later years. He was not capable of thinking in those first ten years, but the next decade is going to be more difficult. He is going to THINK. Right now he does not want my views for they are abysmally separated from yours. I would probably be inclined to bias him in my favor. Let him prospect by himself, and when he gets to be about twenty he might look up some day and want to know what it was all about, or perhaps he will be satisfied with your version. You have put the jinx on anything I wanted to do for him, and incidentally not improved your own case. Now when he asks if I have anything to say about him in my weekly letter, just say no that I have left everything to you.

Claude.

"If you look at these films as W.C., the psychiatrist, he's saying, 'Look, I was a good father. I provided. I tried to do my best; I'm not such a bad guy. But can't you see? My wife's so terrible, my son's a sissy.'"

Children of Hollywood

Ron's father served in the Navy at Long Beach during World War II—W.C. was fond of his daughter-in-law and would visit occasionally.

"When my father wrote letters to W.C. that said, 'Come over to Thanksgiving and we won't talk shop,' that meant, 'I promise we won't be talking about Hattie and the way you've been treating her.' So my father was kind of torn. They got along well later in life, but it was never hugging. You know, it was always, 'Hello father,' 'Hello son.' They had a relationship, but it was very conservative, very restrained.

"But W.C. loved my mother. He gave her a car for the wedding and then picked up my brother Bill when he was born. He would call up my mother on Sundays, because Hattie and my father went to church every Sunday at 10:30. He always attacked religion because Hattie had converted to Catholicism. He said that Hattie was part Jewish; she always tried to deny that her father's name was Levi. And she converted my father, too. W.C. would call at 10:35 every Sunday, and he'd say, 'Listen to this last letter that I just got from Hattie,' and he'd read it in this phony voice. When my brother was born and my mother was so nice, I'm sure W.C. felt, 'Here's another chance to have a family.'

"One thing I'll always remember as being the oddest thing I ever saw was a bunch of photographs of Hattie and W.C. performing together—not because of that but because of what she eventually did to these photographs. As I said, Hattie was a part of his act and there were a number of photographs of them together in costumes onstage. On almost all of them—not all of them, but almost—she kept the photograph but scratched out her face, not *his* face, but her own.

"And what an eerie thing to see, this photograph with its face scratched out. But she kept the photograph. Thank goodness she wasn't so bitter as to throw all of his stuff away. I can't really explain why she'd keep it all and yet harbor such ill will towards him. Maybe she crossed out the face so she could say, 'See, he was with another woman,' when it was in fact her. There's really no way of knowing what she was thinking in doing such a thing, but destroying them completely would have been a much greater tragedy than vandalizing them, as she did. I'm just thankful they survived her wrath.

"While it is true that W.C. was obsessed with his work and traveled almost constantly, the biggest myth must be that he had bank accounts under fictitious names, accounts he even lost track as to their whereabouts. It's commonly reported he had a couple of dozen bank accounts worldwide. In reality, the vaudeville houses would pay their performers'

14. Ron Fields

salaries in cash. W.C. was robbed once and from then on he usually took his salary straight to the local bank. He kept impeccable records and knew by heart where he had his accounts and exactly how much money he held. As for the fictitious names, that on the face of it makes no sense. How would he ever withdraw the money when a teller would ask for proof of identity? He'd also need a slew of fake I.D.s to withdraw cash from each account. It was just too much trouble, even for him.

"Unfortunately, the myth has become the accepted form of truth because his eccentric character made that story believable. In actual fact, he always used his nom-de-art, W. C. Fields. He had his name legally changed (legally shortened) in 1908 from his birth name William Claude Dukenfield."

Always the guy with the sly remark, W. C. Fields has left us a laundry list of famous quotes, far too many to mention here. However, all of them were unmistakably muttered at some time by W. C. Fields. Here's a small sampling of some of his most witty, clever, but not so politically correct statements.

A few weeks before he died some friends visited him in the hospital. They caught the notoriously anti-religious Fields reading the Bible. One of the astonished group asked, "Bill, why are you, of all people, reading the Bible?" W.C. looked up and drawled sagely, "Just looking for loopholes."

Another remark directed within earshot of his co-star Mae West on the set of *My Little Chickadee* was made to a reporter. W.C. pointed her out to him, Mae smiled kindly, but W.C. went on to tell the reporter, "There goes Mae West ... she's the plumber's idea of Cleopatra." Her smile suddenly vanished.

Several other favorite W.C Fields comments are as follows:

"Anyone who hates small dogs and children can't be all bad."
"'Twas a woman drove me to drink. I never had the courtesy to thank her."
"I never drink anything stronger than gin before breakfast."
Asked why he never drank water: "Fish fuck in it."
When asked what he would like his epitaph to read: "On the whole, I'd rather be in Philadelphia"
When asked whether he liked children, he would respond, "Ah yes ... boiled or fried."

"Wouldn't it be terrible if I quoted some reliable statistics which prove that more people are driven insane through religious hysteria than by drinking alcohol?"

"I like, in an audience, the fellow who roars continuously at the troubles of the character I am portraying on the stage, but he probably has a mean streak in him and, if I needed ten dollars, he'd be the last person I'd call upon. I'd go first to the old lady and old gentleman back in Row S who keep wondering what there is to laugh at."

"Horse sense is the thing a horse has which keeps it from betting on people."

Another famous line on one of his favorite subjects, children, was, "Madam, there's no such thing as a tough child—if you parboil them first for seven hours, they always come out tender."

★★★★★

Ron explains further—"I'm often asked if he really hated kids and dogs as much as he claimed. I tell them that I think *hate* may be a tad too strong. Another common question asked of me today is if he really drank as much as they say. I tell them no ... he usually drank more than they say!"

As proud as Ron Fields is to be related to one of the greatest comedians of all time, one part of him confesses with a smile, "You know, I guess I'm pretty lucky that I never met the man." Regardless, W. C. Fields is fortunate to have a grandson he never met carry on a legacy that he worked so hard to create.

The Fields' family resemblance is uncanny. Just take a look at the photo of Ron and W.C. in this chapter. Is there any doubt they're related?

15

GARY CROSBY

* *Eldest son of Bing Crosby* *
and Dixie Lee

That was a great game of golf, fellers.
—Bing Crosby's last words

Bing Crosby is known as the legendary crooner. His trademark big ears gave him the nickname "Bing" from the comic strip *The Bingsville Bugle* because both he and the comic strip's main character had flyaway ears. He was actually born Harry Lillis Crosby on May 2, 1901. He maintained himself as a top star for more than forty years. Whether appearing on film, radio, television or recording an album, his easygoing, laid-back approach made him popular with both sexes all over the world. He won an Academy Award for Best Actor in 1944 for his portrayal of the caring priest in *Going My Way*. He teamed up with friends Bob Hope and Dorothy Lamour in the popular "road movies." *The Road to Singapore* was the first film in that popular series.

He continued his success all the way into the fifties with hits such as *High Society, Country Girl,* and the ever-popular *White Christmas*. The song of the same name, "White Christmas," from the 1942 musical *Holiday Inn* is the biggest selling single of all time, nearing 100 million copies. He still holds the record for the greatest selling recording artist of all time, with sales nearing 500 million. There is no doubt Bing Crosby was a major Hollywood star; his success as an artist was faultless. However, his success as a father is somewhat questionable.

His four sons from his first marriage, Gary, Dennis, Phillip (twins) and Lindsay, were ruled with an iron fist not only by their father but also by their mother, Dixie Lee. Here, Gary Crosby lets us in on life

Children of Hollywood

A family photograph of Bing Crosby and sons. Gary is pictured here on the far left.

behind the front door of the Crosby home. It is a disturbing tale of one Hollywood family who lived a public life of perfection and a private life of pain. In various excerpts taken from Gary's own book, *Going My Own Way,* he explains what it was like to grow up as the son of Bing Crosby.

> "While I was growing up in the late 1930s and early 1940s, the stars and other heavyweights in the business liked to hold elaborate birthday parties for their children, the more extravagant the better. Mom and Dad usually turned the invitations down but every now and then they decided my brothers and I should go. That was about the only exposure I had to the world, and it didn't happen often, which was all right by me.
>
> "I had nothing against the star kids. I simply didn't know them. And by the time I was six years old, I could see we didn't share much in com-

15. Gary Crosby

mon. They always had money jingling in their pockets. They mouthed off at their parents and got away with it. They weren't very physical. They didn't like to play ball or do anything that might work up a sweat. From the way they talked they seemed to spend their afternoons lounging around the house in their nice clothes or going to movies. The parties were really for the parents and the press and were orchestrated with all the efficiency of any other high-budget Hollywood production. The chauffeurs dropped the kids off in their dress-up clothes or costumes, and as soon as they stepped through the front door someone slapped party hats on their heads, stuck noisemakers in their hands and whisked them off into the prescribed routine while the photographer clicked away.

"'Okay, we're going to watch the magician now. Everybody smile. Great. All right now it's time to ride the donkey and the photographer will snap the picture. And here's the cake! No eating the cake yet kids. We have to get the picture of the cake first. Okay, birthday boy, you stand in front of the cake. That's it. And the rest of you make a half circle around him. I said *half* circle. Let's all look like we're having fun now. Good. Thank you very much.'

"The regulars had been through it so often that they went along with the script like the seasoned professionals they were. We never could get the hang of it. The adults led us through wimpy games, like pin the tail on the donkey, calculated to return us back home as clean and well pressed as we left it. Our own birthday parties were different. Mom and Dad let us ask four or five school friends over on Saturday afternoon, and we played ball and ran around the backyard for a couple of hours. Because it was a special occasion, they eased up on the normal rules. As long as we were reasonably well behaved, they allowed us to enjoy ourselves. About three o'clock there was ice cream and cake and we were handed our presents. Mom always made sure we received one or two gifts we wanted along with the usual socks and underwear. At five o'clock the company went home, and that was that for another year.

"There were a few problems in trying to just be an 'ordinary kid.' For one thing, Dad didn't seem to be just an 'ordinary father.' Ordinary fathers didn't make movies and recordings and have their own radio program. Ordinary fathers didn't have their pictures in the newspapers and magazines. I'd find them scattered around the house, and one day, when I was just about old enough to make out the words, I read about what a great singer he was. It said he was the best singer who ever existed; his voice was heard by more people than any other voice in history. I thought that was really something.

"The next morning I told the kids in school that the great Bing Crosby was my dad. By the time I came home that afternoon, word had already gotten back to Mom, and she sat me down for a little talk. 'Listen, Gary, you're no different from anyone else. Just because your father is sort of famous doesn't mean you're anything special. So don't get cocky. Don't get a big head. Don't start thinking you're better than the other kids because you're not.' Once she had said all that to me, I never made that mistake again. Still, it didn't quite fit. Ordinary kids didn't have to go on the radio with their father and be in his movies. Ordinary kids weren't driven to school by a man in a black coat and cap. They walked or their mothers dropped them off. Until we went out of town to high school, my brothers and I tried to con every chauffeur we had into letting us out two blocks away and meeting us back there at the end of the day. They never would do it of course. It would have meant their jobs if Dad found out. And he would be sure to know. He knew everything!

"We wanted to be ordinary. That was our goal. We thought that would please Mom and Dad and make them happy with us. It sounded like it should be simple, but why was it so complicated? They constantly preached we were nobody, yet once we set foot outside the house everyone else insisted we were somebody. We had so many rules to follow, it was hard not to do something wrong. Just about every waking moment was controlled by its own set of regulations. There was a rule about not talking to each other after we went to bed at night and before we got up in the morning. Someone usually checked to make sure we obeyed.

"There were rules about brushing our teeth, showering, making our beds, straightening our room. If the toothbrush wasn't wet or the towel felt too dry, that was good for a punishment. So was not hitting the breakfast table at the right time or not dressing the right way. When one of us left a sneaker or a pair of underpants lying around, he had to tie the offending object on a string and wear it around his neck until he went off to bed that night. Dad called it 'the Crosby lavalier.' At the time, the humor of the name escaped me.

"At breakfast there was a rule about finishing everything that was on our plates. Phil was a picky eater and had his problems with that one. But a rule was a rule. There were no exceptions. The morning he tried to get around it by hiding his bacon and eggs, Mom discovered the bulge

15. Gary Crosby

under the rug and made him scoop the mess back onto his dish, then choke down every bite—dirt, hairs and all.

"In school we were expected to be model students. God help us if the teacher called home with a complaint or made us stay late for misbehaving. That was a certain whipping.

"We were also in big trouble if our grades weren't mostly As and Bs. A D got us a licking. An F meant a licking and having to sit in our room with our books every afternoon for the next month or until the new report card came home. A C, especially in conduct or effort, brought a loss of privileges and intimations of worse things to come if you didn't clean up your act on the spot.

"Dinner was accompanied by a whole slew of rules. It was served formally in the dining room, with the table laid out in a hopelessly confusing array of plates and silverware. Mom studied us closely while we ate to make sure we used them correctly. We sat straight up on the edges of our chairs, with our elbows in at our sides and the forks held in our left hands so we could cut everything in the European fashion. If one of us picked up the wrong spoon or put the butter in the wrong dish, she reached over with the butt of her knife and gave him a whack on the knuckles.

"The meal passed mostly in silence. They didn't have much to say to each other, and unless one of them asked us something, we weren't allowed to speak until we finished eating. Dinner seemed to take forever. It was finally over when Dad cocked back his chair, wiped his mouth, threw his napkin in the middle of his plate and said, 'All right, you boys may be excused.' That was the signal we were free to head upstairs to do our homework and go to bed.

"I tried my best to toe the mark each day and hit all their rules and regulations. Not so much because I hoped to please them and win their approval. That seems too far out of reach to consider a serious possibility. It was more a matter of wanting to steer clear of the lickings and other punishments that followed fast behind their disapproval. When I was due for a licking, Mom sent me outside to pull a switch off a tree in the back yard. I had to be sure to make the right choice. The branch couldn't be dead. It had to be limber with plenty of spring still in it. She examined it carefully when I brought it upstairs to her room. Then she had me roll up my pants and bend over.

"'Okay, don't move and don't cry. And don't reach back with your hands. You just stay there and take it till I'm finished with you.' Then she went to work with the switch, cutting up and down the backs of my legs as fast as she could get her arm to move. It was hard to stay still. My legs felt like they had caught fire or were being jolted by a thousand volts of electricity. But if I jumped out of the way she would turn into a crazy woman and whack me even harder. If Dad wasn't away on location, she would offer me a choice. 'Do you want it from me or do you want it from him?' My answer was always the same. 'I'll take it from you, Mom, I'd rather have it from you.'

"It wasn't that she hurt less, but she was there on the spot and he wouldn't be back until six. I hated the waiting almost as much as the whipping and wanted to get it over with as soon as possible. When it was the old man's turn, I waited in my room listening to the quarter hours go by on the UCLA clock in Westwood. The clock played a tune each time it struck the hour. Every fifteen minutes it performed a different portion of the tune. The closer to six it moved, the longer it seemed to take to get from one part of the melody to the next.

"By five thirty time seemed to have dragged to a standstill and my stomach was coiled as tightly as the main spring. It was practically a relief when the front door slammed closed and he was finally home. A few minutes later I would hear his voice calling from down the end of the hall. 'Gary! Get in here!'

"When I came into his office he would be sitting behind his desk. He would look up with those icy blue agates, then begin the lecture that preceded the whipping. He would be angry, but it was anger from on high, cold and dispassionate and contained, like that of a judge passing sentence on a culprit beneath his contempt.

"'Your mother tells me you shot your mouth off in school again today.'

"'Yes, Dad.'

"'Well, why do you act like that? Why do you do these things?'

"'I don't know, Dad.'

"'What do you mean you don't know? You must have a reason.'

"'I don't know. I just don't know, Dad.'

"It wasn't much of an answer, but that's all I had to say. I learned early that no reason would be good enough to get me out of the licking, so what was the point of trying to explain? Whenever I had, he cut me off before words left my mouth. 'Well, Dad, I think...'

"'Don't think!' he would snap back. 'You can't think anyway.' It didn't pay to argue with him. 'You don't know, huh? Well, then you're either stupid or rebellious or just plain crazy. I don't know what it is with you.

15. Gary Crosby

Your mother and I lay down certain rules very simply. All you have to do is follow them.'

"Then he would launch into three-syllable words and fancy phrases I couldn't understand, though their drift was clear enough. His point seemed to be that the particular outrage I had committed that day was only indicative of all the other things that were wrong with me. So it wasn't just my big mouth; it was also my weight and my temper and the fact that I couldn't get along with people and wasn't smart enough to handle anything but manual labor.

"'...So, if you don't alter your behavior, all you're gonna do is grow up to be a fat, stupid, bad-tempered individual that no one will like or want to have around. If that's what you want to be, just continue the way you're going. Because that's what you're heading for.'

"I usually tuned him out by the middle of the harangue. I had heard it before and was thinking about the beating that would be coming up next. Yet as I stood there in front of him. I would nod in the right places and say yes or no precisely on cue, so that I seemed to be sucking in every word. Eventually, he was ready to get to the main event. 'Okay, take 'em down.'

"I dropped my pants, pulled down my undershorts and bent over. Then he went at it with the belt dotted with the metal studs he kept reserved for the occasion. Quite dispassionately, without the least display of emotion or loss of self-control, he whacked away at me until he drew the first drop of blood, and then he stopped. It normally took between twelve and fifteen strokes. As they came down I counted them off, one by one, and hoped I would bleed early. To keep my mind off the hurt, I would conjure up different schemes to get back at him, ways to murder him. They had to be perfect crimes so I wouldn't get caught. Maybe I could poison his coffee or *accidentally* bump him out his office window. I was forbidden to cry or scream so I had to hold myself together until he cut me loose and sent me back to my room. Then I went berserk! I pummeled my fists against the doors or the walls or anything else I could smack hard without breaking. I did have to be careful of that. If something broke, I'd be in even bigger trouble.

"The twins were a year behind me in school and had a chance to profit from my mistakes. Seeing the grief I brought on myself by shooting off my mouth, they stayed a lot quieter, kept their heads down and did what they could to blend into the crowd. Phil especially didn't want to take any chances. Denny was a bit of a clown in class but never truly offensive. Most of the teachers adored him. He was a naturally likeable, freckle-faced little kid who looked like Andy Hardy. Still, we all lived under the same rules of law at home, and they endured their own share of terror.

"In a way, I did understand why Dad's fans loved him so much. When I saw *Going My Way*, I was as moved as they were by the character he played. Father O'Malley handled that gang of young hooligans in his parish with such kindness and wisdom that I thought he was wonderful, too. Instead of coming down hard on the kids and withdrawing his affection, he forgave them and taught them how to sing. By the last reel the sheer persistence of his goodness had transformed even the worst of them into solid citizens. Then the lights came on and the movie was over. All the way back to the house I thought about the difference between the person up there on the screen and the one I knew at home. When he came back from the studio that night I made a point of telling him I had seen his picture. 'Caught your flick today, Dad. It was great. It was really great.' 'Oh good, glad you liked it.' That was the extent of the discussion.

"A few months later Louella Parsons quoted him saying that he hadn't watched *Going My Way* yet because he wanted to see it with his kids. He hoped we would be as proud of him as he'd like us to be. I remember tossing away the magazine in disgust. The persona wasn't simply an act. That side of him was real, too. Once he left the house and stepped into the world, he became another man—the same nice guy everyone loved in his movies.

"Every now and then he took me along to Paramount, and I would see him change into Bing Crosby the moment he stepped from the car. On the drive over he would still be Dad and I would still be afraid of him. It was a relief when we finally passed through the studio gates and pulled into his space in the parking lot. The first person who saw him would yell, 'Hey, Bing!' and that's who he became. As soon as he made the transition, I felt I was safe. He wouldn't turn on me now, though he did have a way of letting me know when I stepped out of line. He wouldn't make a scene about it in front of the others. He would still be Bing Crosby to them. Nothing more would happen until we got home. But I would surely hear about it then.

"Shooting stopped about five. Back in his dressing room, he took off his costume, makeup and toupee; changed into his street clothes; and with a toss of his head motioned for me to follow him out to the parking lot. The exhilaration of the day kept him in good humor during the drive home. He would be quiet but content. He didn't stop being Bing Crosby

15. Gary Crosby

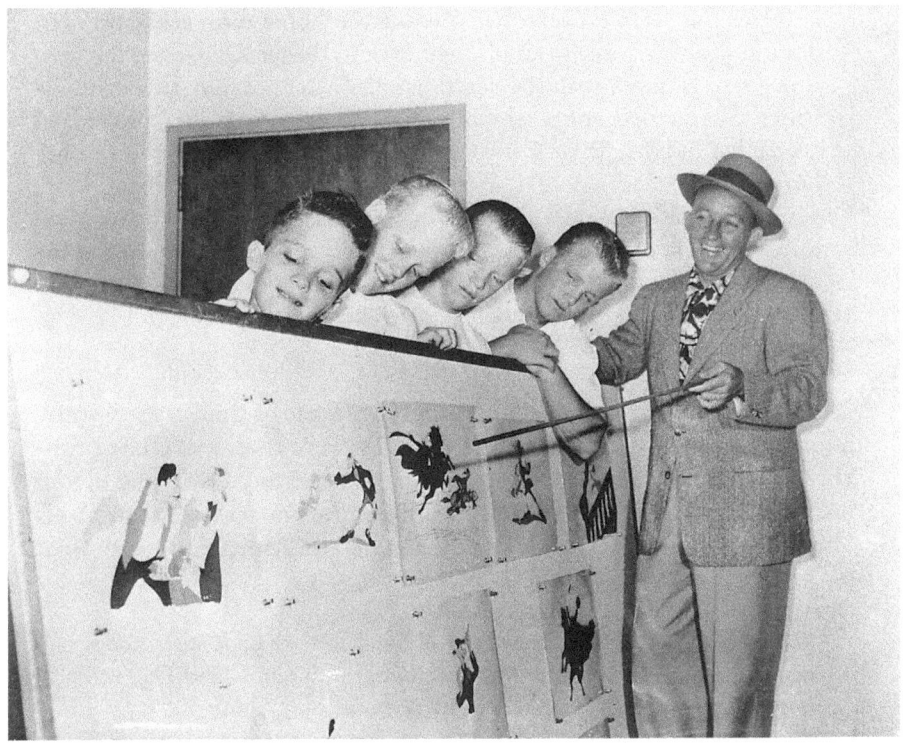

Bing Crosby and sons. Gary is seen pictured closest to his father in this photograph.

until we arrived at the house. The transformation was most extreme when Mom had been drinking. She was easy to read when she was stoned. It was obvious to both of us the moment we stepped through the door. A shadow of disappointment flickered across Dad's face, then he closed off and withdrew. Mom wouldn't or couldn't acknowledge that he knew and would try to engage him in conversation. All through dinner she played out the charade that everything was fine.

"My brothers and I kept our eyes riveted to our plates so we didn't have to look at either of them. Dad ate without saying a word. When he wolfed down the last bite, he left the table. Once he disappeared up the stairs, she let go of the smile she had fixed on her face. The tension and the gloom welling up out of her suffused the entire room. Because then she knew for sure she hadn't been able to bring it off. She hadn't fooled him.

"Over the years I'd seen her stay off the booze for weeks and even months at a time, only to climb right back in the jug again once the pressure got to be more than she could handle." Alcohol wasn't Dixie's only battle. She battled and eventually succumbed to stomach cancer. On November 3, 1952, Dixie Crosby was buried. It was one day prior to her forty-first birthday.

Gary explains those strange days after his mother's death. "Life returned to normal a couple of days later when Dad called my brothers and me into his office for a lecture and pep talk. 'Well, your mother's gone now,' he announced from his customary place behind the desk, 'and now we have to go on with our lives.'"

It did seem mourning was considered a waste of time in the Crosby household, and funnily enough, if the roles were reversed, Dixie probably would have given the boys the exact same speech. Not long before his mother's death, Gary recalls yet another beating at the hands of his father. Only this time, Gary was old enough and strong enough to fight back.

"I was almost eighteen years old, a big galoot, five feet ten inches tall, who tipped the scales at two hundred and ten pounds and Dad was still laying the whippings on like I was a ten year old. About the only difference these days was that he used one of his canes instead of a belt. Once again, I bent over and placed my hands on the couch like he told me, and he went to work, swinging the thing like a baseball bat so that I got it good and hard with the curved handle. At first I resigned myself to the licking like I always did and counted off the strokes myself to keep from feeling the hurt. But then, just after he'd taken his thirteenth swing, I turned my head and saw him leaning into me for the next one, and I suddenly blew. For a split second I went blank. The next thing I knew the cane was in my hands, not his, and I was breaking it across my legs and flinging pieces of it down the hall.

'That's it!' I heard myself scream. 'If you ever hit me again, you motherfucker, I'll kill you! I'll go to jail! They can put me in the fuckin' gas chamber. But lay another hand on me and I swear to God, I'll kill you!'

"I was even more astonished than he was. In all the years he'd been dishing it out, I never once thought to make him stop. I never thought to run. I never thought to fight back. I just took it and took it and took it. He suddenly put his fists up and went into a boxer's crouch. 'Oh,

15. Gary Crosby

you're gonna fight your father now, huh? You'll raise your hand against your old man?'

"'Yeah, give me that fuckin' boxing stance! Come on, I want to see that shit! I ain't gonna box you. I'll take that fuckin' lamp and brain your ass if you touch me again. You don't believe me? You want to try it now? Go ahead, I'll do it right this minute.'

"I would have, too. That's how crazed I was. As I was saying it I looked over at him and saw a kind of small, older man who'd gone about as far as he could go, and I knew I had it in me. Nothing was standing between us. Eventually I simmered down and we stepped around each other, then continued on our separate ways. The next day was as if nothing had ever happened. There were still plenty of other punishments when I failed to live up to his rules, but that was the last time he laid a hand on me.

"The twins and I had covered a lot of ground since the days we were the media darlings, the fair-haired sons of the beloved Bing Crosby. I had dropped out of Stanford and turned into a boozer and a pill head and all-night carouser. Denny and Phil had quit Washington State and knocked around until they were grabbed by the draft. All three of us had gotten into our share of trouble."

There were constant battles with alcoholism. Gary eventually won the battle and got sober. He married and even adopted a son, Steve. His father had also remarried and had a second family with his new wife, Kathryn. Everything seemed to be finally settling down between father and son. Gary felt that his father had mellowed in his old age. He saw it, he felt it, and somehow, he was even starting to understand why he was the way he was. He never thought he had to explain himself to anyone. He always felt he was right. There was no fighting that. Gary explains further:

"It took me a long time to get through my noggin' that the hours we spent together weren't so awful. Eventually, though, I began to notice that he didn't seem to be coming down on me anymore. He wasn't acting so cold and disapproving. He wasn't lecturing me about all the things I was doing wrong. He seemed to be accepting me pretty much for what I was. I suppose to his way of thinking he no longer had that much to bitch about. I had stopped drinking and using. I had married a good Catholic woman he liked. I was raising a son and not doing too bad a job of it. I wasn't carrying on like a maniac when I worked. I looked halfway responsible to him, and now that I was a lot closer to what he wanted he was able to let up. Most likely he was sick and tired of the fight anyhow. Well, if the old man hadn't changed completely, he had still changed a lot.

"After putting one wife in the ground, then turning around to see that his four sons were fuck-ups, he couldn't have been looking forward to too much happiness in the remaining years of his life. But then he was given a second chance, and his whole life brightened up. And he made the most of it. He softened. He was so much better with his second group of kids, Harry and Mary and Nathaniel. Not that he suddenly turned around and became the sweetest, kindest, most sensitive old gentleman in the world. He was still a disciplinarian and could still be rough on them. There was love there and even some leniency. Sometimes, when the kids pressed him too hard, I'd catch an impression on his face that seemed to say, 'Hmmmmm, in the old days you wouldn't have gotten away with this.' But then he'd look over at them and smile and let it slide. And I think he was a happier man for it."

In his 73rd year, it was a game of golf that ended it all for Bing Crosby. Of all the places to depart this world, he died just after leaving the eighteenth hole on a Madrid golf course. Having been an avid golfer all his life, he probably couldn't have scripted his exit any better if he wrote it himself. Gary explains his thoughts after hearing of his father's death:

"I heard he had hit a good shot onto the eighteenth green and sunk the putt. Some people on the verandah gave him a hand. Then he turned around and, without any pain, went straight to God. I thought to myself, well, isn't that just like him? Everything's perfect. He went out doing what he loved most, doing it successfully, taking a bow, knowing he was in good shape with his church and his God and his fellow man. How many guys get to die like that? What an ending.

"When I took my last view of him, the first thing that popped into my head was, 'Jesus Christ, how small he looks in there. How could such a small man strike so much terror in my soul?' Since then, it hardly seems like he's gone. You keep reading about him or hearing stories. Christmas rolls around every year, and here he comes again. They get out the records of 'Silent Night' and 'White Christmas.' They rerun the specials. I don't get to be with him for Christmas dinner, but that's about the only difference.

15. Gary Crosby

Gary and his father, Bing Crosby, in a 1964 ABC-TV promotional photograph.

"I'm happy we made some kind of peace before he went. Neither one of us backed up and neither one of us apologized, yet we made it. We were able to give some love to each other before it was too late. And I'm happy that the last years of his life he was satisfied with me. That's nice. I like that feeling."

Gary and his father, Bing Crosby. With or without matching outfits, the family resemblance is uncanny. Circa 1964.

Gary and his first wife Barbara divorced after eighteen years of marriage. He found happiness and marriage twice more, only to divorce for a second and third time. Just before he was about to marry his fourth wife, Gary was diagnosed with lung cancer. Unfortunately he died in 1995, just two months after the diagnosis was made. He was sixty-two years old. Before Gary's death, his brother Lindsay committed suicide by gunshot in 1989. He was just fifty-one years old. In 1991, Dennis committed suicide, also by gunshot. He was only fifty-six years old. Now Phillip is the only surviving brother of the original Crosby boys.

It is said that Bing Crosby left a clause in his will stating that his sons could not collect his money until they were in their eighties. Well, three of his boys were a long way from making that age when they died, two of them dying by their own hand. When he made that stipulation, he knew only too well that even if his sons did reach that ripe old age, they would be old men, far too old to enjoy the money anyway. It was a hard, brutal, cold-hearted lesson and one that shouldn't really shock anyone. Even from beyond the grave he had one last Bing Crosby rule to dish out to his sons who lived his all too hard, all too tough rules their entire lives. This one simply told them, "I made it myself, now you make it yourself."

15. Gary Crosby

It was a licking that hurt far more than that dreaded studded belt of times past. The Crosby boys battled many demons their entire lives—drugs, alcohol and severe depression. Yet somehow, in some strange way, their biggest demon was the guy that gave them life, their father Bing Crosby.

16

SARA KARLOFF

★ Daughter of Boris Karloff ★
and Dorothy Stine

When I was nine I played the demon king in Cinderella and it launched me on a long and happy life of being a monster.
—Boris Karloff

If ever there was a more opposite person to play a monster, it would have to have been Boris Karloff. In real life he was a quiet, kind and loving English gentleman, but he made a career out of playing menacing monsters and all things spooky on screen. The fact that he was so believable as that hideous monster made him one of the best, if not *the* best, character actors of our time. It was thanks to Bela Lugosi that he was even offered the role of *Frankenstein* (1931) in the first place.

Lugosi, at the time an established actor and best known for his Dracula roles, turned down the part of the scary but lovable monster because he wouldn't be recognized under the heavy makeup and there was no dialogue. Karloff didn't mind being unrecognizable or silent, and so it was he who became the monster. Using only hand gestures and facial expressions, Karloff gave a heartfelt performance. He made the audience care for this hideous creation and he needed no words to do it. With the expertise of makeup artist Jack Pierce and under the direction of James Whale, Boris Karloff stole the show.

At age forty-four and after acting in an impressive seventy-plus films before *Frankenstein*, Boris Karloff was finally known ... or was he? In order to keep the character of *Frankenstein* "real" (for want of a better term), it was decided that Karloff's name not be listed in the credits at all. His name was replaced with a "?" and he even failed to

16. Sara Karloff

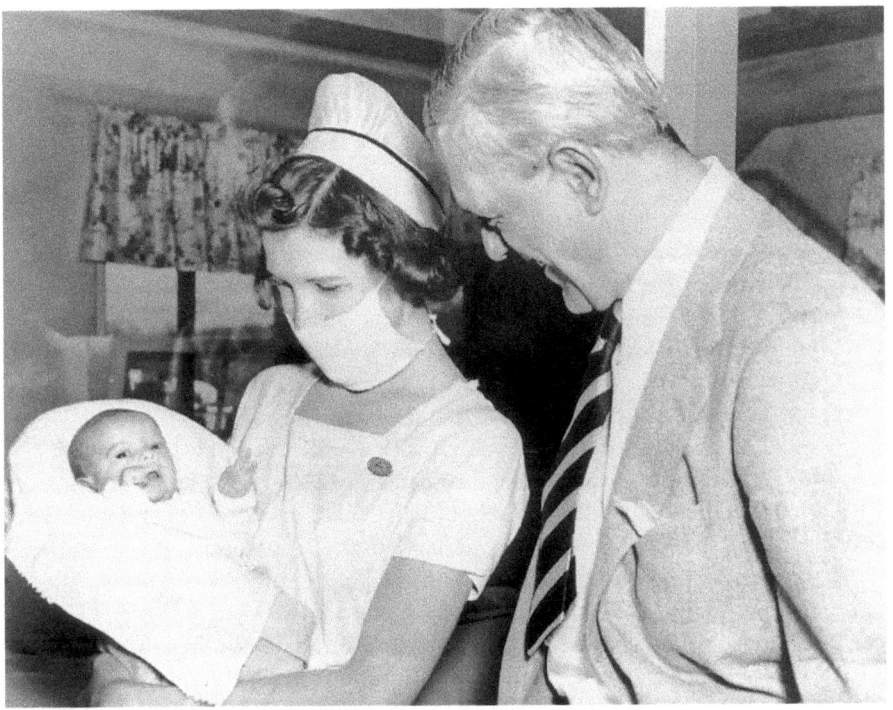

A proud Boris Karloff looks at his newborn daughter Sara for the very first time. Incidentally, they both share the same birthday (courtesy Sara Karloff).

receive an invitation to the film's premiere screening. Well, this studio publicity stunt worked wonders and before too long the studio mailroom was swamped with letters. Thousands of fans were writing and demanding to know who played Frankenstein. Eventually the studio released his name to the public and from that moment on, "Karloff," as he was so often credited, was a star.

Starring in films like *The Mummy* or *Frankenstein*, and being typecast as a horror icon didn't phase him in the slightest. That was his calling and he reveled in it. In fact, *Frankenstein* has now been listed among the American Film Institute's Top 100 American films of all time.

As well as being a late bloomer in the acting field, he followed the same path when it came to fatherhood. His fourth marriage, to Dorothy

Children of Hollywood

Stine, produced a daughter, his only child, Sara. Boris Karloff was a monster to the world and a sweet and loving father to her. It was quite the contrast between fantasy and reality. Here, Sara Karloff shares some of the memories that she holds dear to her heart. I'll let her continue from here.

"My mother's name was Dorothy Stine, and as you all know my father was Boris Karloff. Unfortunately I can't tell you how they first met but my mother was born in Michigan and raised in Oregon. She graduated from Cal Berkely as a librarian. She was never involved in the theater or show business of any kind. She was my father's fourth wife and I was his only child. They were married in 1930, my father was still an unknown at the time, and they were married for fifteen years.

"I was born in Hollywood on my father's 51st birthday, November 23, 1938. We lived in Coldwater Canyon in a wonderful Spanish house on four acres with a pool and a tennis court and a menagerie of animals. We had dogs, mostly Bedlington terriers, and a Scotty and a Welsh terrier named Whiskey and Soda. We had cats, geese, turkeys and a pig called Violet! I went to Miss Buckley's and then to Hawthorne in Beverly Hills. I moved to San Francisco when I was seven years old. That's when my parents were divorced. I relocated with my mother and stepfather and my father and stepmother remained in Beverly Hills. They eventually moved to New York in 1949 and then back to England in 1959, where he died in 1969. He was 81. He commuted to the west coast often during those last twenty years and I saw him as often as possible after the divorce.

"I visited my father on several movie sets. *The Raven* and *A Comedy of Terrors* I remember well, along with several TV shows and stage plays including *Peter Pan* and *The Lark*, with Julie Harris. My father's signature roles as *Frankenstein* and *The Mummy* were made before I was born. He was actually on the set of *Son of Frankenstein* when I was born. An expectant father didn't go into the delivery rooms in those days, not like now.

"I believe he spent four hours being made up and almost as long having the makeup taken off for *Frankenstein*. His makeup for his portrayal of Im-Ho-Tep in *The Mummy* was equally as arduous. Some days he would be on the *Frankenstein* set at three in the morning and work nearly nineteen hours straight. He lost twenty-five pounds during that film. When the makeup for *The Mummy* was finally completed, he patiently pointed out that they had forgotten to include a fly. Going to the bathroom was not an option!

16. Sara Karloff

"He always credited the genius of Jack Pierce for the success of those films. They worked together for weeks perfecting the look of the makeup before the first scenes were even shot. The makeup in those days was very toxic. It was all lead based, but my father was very fortunate and had no skin problems in relation to being exposed to it.

"My father was horrified at the thought of going back to performing on stage. He was cast in the Broadway production of *Arsenic and Old Lace* and was very nervous when he was first approached for that role. He ended up loving the part and desperately wanted to do the film version. Unfortunately, he was still under contract to run in the play and they wouldn't release him to do the film version. Raymond Massey was cast in my father's role in the film version.

"I had many celebrity kids as friends. As a child I played with the Cagney kids and many others

Top: A 1960s shot of Boris Karloff in character with his daughter Sara. *Bottom:* A recent shot of Sara Karloff with a strategically placed background photograph of her father, Boris Karloff, in his most famous role as Frankenstein's monster. (Both photographs courtesy Sara Karloff.)

whose parents were in the business, but they were all just playmates and their parents' 'jobs' made no impression on me or on them, I'm sure. I knew the Jimmy Stewarts and the Ray Millands and the Greg Pecks and the Henry Fondas; they were all good friends as was Sir Aubrey Smith and his wife and many others who worked on the other side of the camera. Christmas in our home was a magical blend of English tradition and American tradition—lots of decorations and lots of parties and lots of presents!

"There's one particular story I remember vividly about my father and me. We had some family friends, Gertie and Sydney Brown, who raised rabbits. I, of course, as a child *had* to have one! My father made it very clear that if I got a bunny the responsibility for its care would be mine and mine only. Of course I said, 'of course,' anything to get the bunny. He took me to select my pet and after looking them all over, including one with a droopy ear, I selected my bunny, not the one with the droopy ear. On the trip home my father asked me why I had selected the one I had, and I gave him whatever reason. He then said that he would have selected the one with the droopy ear because obviously it was the one that needed the most love....

"As often happens, I neglected my promised duties. After a fair amount of time, one day I went out to see my bunny and it was gone! My father said I had not met my part of the bargain and the bunny had gone to a better home ... full of lessons, hopefully learned at some point by a very disappointed child. Keep your end of the bargain and never be less than attentive to one's pets and promises.

"Now, I'm all grown up and married to a wonderful man I've known for forty years, but we have been married for ten years. We both had other happy lives previous to the one we share now. He has three sons and I have two sons: Michael, who is dark like my father and I are, and David, who was a towhead as a child. I have three grandchildren: Kacey, Kyle and Mackenzie Cotten. None of my family seems interested in 'the business.' I am a real estate broker but no longer use my license actively. I have a business, Karloff Enterprises, which handles the licensing of my father's name and likeness, and through that we have been able to meet a lot of my father's fans and learn even more about the impact he and his work made on their lives.

"My father was a soft-spoken English gentleman who felt he was the most lucky fellow to be able to spend his life doing something he dearly loved and then be 'jolly well paid for it.' He lived his life with quiet dig-

16. Sara Karloff

nity and respected the opinions and privacy of others. He was regarded by his co-workers as the consummate professional and by those who knew him personally as 'Dear Boris.' He was indeed, a lovely human being. He was my father."

17

SUZANNE LLOYD

Granddaughter of Harold Lloyd and Mildred Davis

I do not believe the public will want spoken comedy. Motion pictures and the spoken arts are two distinct arts.
—Harold Lloyd

Ten days after Harold Lloyd was born in 1893, moving pictures were introduced to the world at the Colombian Exposition in Chicago. Harold grew up with the new art form. He was a filmmaker who was a product of the movies. His comedy wasn't imported from Broadway or the British Music Hall. He didn't recreate old vaudeville acts. Making silent films, he learned to use the camera the way other comics used a bowler hat or a funny walk. He was the first comedian to put an average guy up on the screen, a guy with faults and fears—the boy next door. His signature horn-rimmed glasses made him recognizable around the world.

Of all the silent film comedians, Harold Lloyd was the most profitable. His films outgrossed Chaplin and Keaton put together. He pioneered new camera techniques and was the first filmmaker to preview his films to a test audience. In the 1920s, he was the number one box office star two years in a row. His movies were adored. He was a world-famous star. Even today, at film festivals around the world, the response to his comedy attests to Lloyd's comic genius.

But it almost wasn't to be. Early in his career, long before he began making features, Harold was almost killed at a photo shoot to promote his "million dollar" two reelers. On a Sunday in August of 1919, Harold posed with a prop bomb—round, black, with a long fuse attached. The bomb wasn't a prop; it exploded in his hand. It ripped open the six-

17. Suzanne Lloyd

A young Suzanne with her grandfather, Harold Lloyd, by a fountain on the grounds of the lavish Lloyd estate, Greenacres (courtesy Suzanne Lloyd).

teen-foot ceiling above and left Harold blind, bleeding, and with most of his right hand missing. Doctors told him he would never see again. His career was over. But the doctors were wrong. Eventually, his sight did return. The scars healed. A glove was crafted to hide his handicap from his public. The comedian known for doing all his own daredevil stunts felt his audience would be concerned for his safety and not laugh at the picture, so they never knew. He wore the glove in every movie he would make.

In one of his most famous films, *Safety Last!*, Harold hung from the face of a clock twelve stories above city traffic. He performed the hair-raising comedic bit all by himself. There was no trick photography back in 1923. Harold was a brilliant physical comedian, and he did it all with only one complete hand.

After he made *Safety Last!*, Harold married his leading lady, Mildred Davis. Together they constructed the most elaborate movie star home of its time, Greenacres. At a cost of two million dollars, it had forty-four rooms, not including the twenty-six bathrooms. In the days before home theaters, the living room featured a 35mm projection booth and a 30-rank Aeolian Duo-Art pipe organ. The lush sixteen acres had seven formal gardens, twelve fountains, a golf course and the largest swimming pool in Beverly Hills. The year after she was born, Harold's granddaughter Suzanne arrived at Greenacres to be raised by Harold and Mildred. This is Suzanne's story.

"In 1953, Harold Lloyd received an honorary Academy Award for being a 'Master Comedian and Good Citizen.' A few months after he brought home the Oscar, I arrived on Harold's doorstep. For over eighteen years they raised me in their home, Greenacres. I called my grandfather 'Daddy' and my grandmother 'Mimi.' I had a wonderful childhood.

"I had no idea growing up that my grandparents had been film stars. Because Harold devoted so much of his later life to the Shriners and raising money for their children's hospitals, I thought my grandfather worked in the medical profession. My grandparents loved life and we traveled a great deal. Once a year we sailed to Europe. We traveled all around the United States for my grandfather's work with the Shriners. I had as much fun in Cannes as I did at the New York World's Fair.

"The house was always filled with music and laughter and very good family friends. There were old acquaintances of my grandparents like Mary Pickford, Edith Head, King Vidor, and my godmother Colleen Moore. There were newer stars like handsome Robert Wagner, heartthrob Tab Hunter, Roddy McDowall, Debbie Reynolds and good friend of the family, Jack Lemmon. No wonder we laughed so much. Cary Grant and my grandfather were old friends and Cary would often confer with Harold on the movie business.

"It's no secret that Cary consulted with Harold on his character in the

17. Suzanne Lloyd

movie *Bringing Up Baby*. He even wore a pair of Harold's signature horn-rimmed glasses. I remember the day when the phone rang and it was Cary on the other end of the line. I had such a crush on Cary Grant and here he was talking to me on the phone asking to speak to Harold. I had seen *An Affair to Remember* five times on the Million Dollar Movie the previous week—I could barely speak. I argued through the bathroom door with my grandfather that he had to come to the phone. To this day, I can't imagine telling Cary Grant you'll call him back. A few years later, I got a chance to spend more time with Cary. He lived next door to our house in Palm Springs. He was funny and charming. I'll never forget the summer I spent on the French Riviera while Cary was there. He was not only charming—he was tan!

"As a little girl, I walked the red carpets of movie premieres and flipped through picture books with Marilyn Monroe. I had no idea that other little girls my age weren't also dining with presidents and meeting the Pope. I didn't realize how fortunate I really was until the Beatles arrived on their first trip to America. Not only did we have tickets to see them at the Hollywood Bowl, I was lucky enough to meet them backstage. Many years later, I attended the gala party at Greenacres for Wings' final tour. I reminded Paul of the little girl in the pink chiffon dress who got his autograph. He didn't remember me, but he sure remembered Harold. He said the Beatles were such fans of Harold Lloyd, they couldn't speak when they met him—obviously, how I felt meeting the Beatles.

"The memories I cherish the most from my childhood are not too different from most kids: swimming in the pool underwater on my grandfather's back, my grandparents happily listening to me practice my violin—badly. They attended all my ballet recitals. When friends would come over to play football on the lawn, my grandfather always brought us potato chips and popcorn and cheered us on. Most of all, I remember Christmas.

"It started sometime around Thanksgiving. My grandparents would take me downtown to the train yards where the annual shipment of trees would arrive for the holiday season. We would pick out three large Douglas firs and they would be wired together to make one enormous, fantastic Christmas tree. It sat at one end of the garden room rising twenty feet in the air. It was nine feet wide and almost thirty feet around. Imagine the number of presents that can fit under a tree that is thirty feet around!

"It took from Thanksgiving until Christmas to decorate the tree. Over the years, my grandfather had collected thousands of ornaments from all

Harold Lloyd poses with his granddaughter, Suzanne, in front of the huge Christmas tree mentioned in Suzanne's story (courtesy Suzanne Lloyd).

over the world. The tree held one-of-a-kind rare ornaments valued in the hundreds of dollars when they were first purchased in the 1930s and 1940s. The tree also held homemade ones that Harold received from his charity work.

I remember a jewel-encrusted ostrich egg and a sequined football, a ref-

17. Suzanne Lloyd

erence to the college football hero Harold Lloyd played in his most popular film, *The Freshman*. I particularly loved a Christmas ball given to him by his friend, makeup artist Wally Westmore, that was a miniature diorama depicting a bespectacled Harold in a red bathrobe trimming the tree. One year we counted more than five thousand ornaments hanging from the tree and we still had enough left over to decorate three more trees just as big! Every year the tree grew larger to hold more ornaments; then one year it became a permanent fixture in our home. It was simply too large, too decorated and too engineered to disassemble. So we had it fireproofed and celebrated Christmas every day of the year!

A recent shot of Suzanne Lloyd, all grown up (courtesy Suzanne Lloyd).

"Recently, Christopher Radko recreated two of Harold's most beautiful ornaments: The Rose, originally given to Harold by silent film siren Gloria Swanson and Holiday Bounty, a colorful ornament from friend and fellow silent film comedian Charlie Chaplin. I was thrilled to have these ornaments added to the Radko collection. Now everyone can have one of Harold's ornaments on their own holiday tree.

"One Christmas, I was with Daddy shopping for more ornaments in Saks Fifth Avenue. He plucked more and more ornaments off the store's white-flocked display tree unable to decide which ones to purchase. Finally, he realized that every ornament on the tree would look nice at Greenacres and quickly decided right then and there to buy them all. Since there was no room on the tree at home, his impulse purchase had to include Saks' white-flocked display tree as well! So the twelve-foot, completely decorated tree was shipped off to Greenacres and found a home in our front entrance hall. I have no idea where Saks put their presents that year after Harold left a gaping hole in their Christmas display.

Children of Hollywood

Harold Lloyd hangs from the hands of a clock in his most famous on-screen image in *Safety Last!* (1923). Trick photography gives the illusion of Harold being in a potentially life-threatening position; in actual fact, the building on which he climbs was a fake wall set up on the roof of a skyscraper. At the time of its release, audiences screamed as they watched this stunt on film.

> "My memories of growing up at Greenacres continue to remind me that I was truly loved and cherished. I knew from the first moment of my recollection to the day that I laid my grandparents to rest that they supported me and loved me unconditionally. Both Harold and Mildred gave me everything a child needed—most importantly, laughter and joy that filled our house and instilled in me an optimism that is perhaps the greatest gift in life."

18

ERIC LAMOND

★ *Grandson of Larry Fine and Mabel Haney* ★

> *For $100, I'll forget everything!*
> —Larry Fine to Ted Healy, after Ted offered
> Larry $100 to join the act,
> but to "forget the violin."

Larry Fine was a born performer. He did it all, and he started young. A violinist as a child, a singer and boxer (a strange but true combination) in his teenage years, and a vaudeville entertainer by 18, it wasn't until 1925 that he truly came into his own. Ted Healy and Moe Howard took on the wild-haired performer and they formed the first stages of a comedy threesome that would eventually be known all over the world as The Three Stooges.

Playing the most slapped upon Stooge for more than forty years, Larry used to complain that one side of his face was all but numb from the years of being slapped by his comic partners. It was a small price to play for doing what he loved best. He was born to make people laugh and laugh they did. They're still laughing, and thanks to the preservation of their extensive film and television work, The Three Stooges will be forever remembered.

Through the magic of television, it's a fact that The Three Stooges are more popular today than in their heyday. They *are* slapstick comedy; they represent that little piece of silliness in all of us; and their lifetime of hard work entertains millions of children, one generation after the other. They do a pretty good job of making us adults feel like children again, too, and for that we honor them with our continued laughter. What child, what adult, wouldn't want to just play around with The Three Stooges?

Children of Hollywood

Eric was lucky enough to have Larry Fine as a grandfather. He was even luckier to have The Three Stooges put on a private show here and there, just for him. Here, Eric Lamond lovingly remembers his grandfather, Larry Fine. These are his memories.

"All of us remember our grandfathers. All of us recall cherished moments from our childhood when our grandfather took us to a movie or the park or a ball game. We show pictures to our children of us as a child with our grandfather and with a twinge of nostalgia relate what wonderful times those were all those many years ago. Of course, if your grandfather was Larry Fine of The Three Stooges, you don't have to show your children pictures; you just have to turn on the TV to catch one of their shorts or pop a tape into the VCR!

"Larry's influence on my life was, and is, quite profound. As you will see, his presence touched most aspects of my childhood and continued into my adult years and even my professional life. He worked very hard to perfect his craft, loved his work, doted on his family and was a real gentleman. He was also the quintessential Stooge. Here's a story that shows how Larry was able to be a family man, a Stooge, and a true professional and fun-loving granddad all at once.

"I was recently asked if I had a favorite bit the Stooges performed in their shorts or movies. The thought that struck me first was that my favorite bits were something Moe and Larry did 'live' at Larry's home in the Los Feliz Hills area of Los Angeles, an encounter with Joe DeRita on the set when the boys were filming the wraparounds for their cartoon series in the mid–1960s and a live guest shot they did on my father's television show.

"My next thought was a moving, mental montage of so many bits and shticks from their shorts and movies that I couldn't really focus on just one or two because they had so many, many funny moments. I kept coming back to the memories of watching Larry live. So let me relate what I got to see Moe and Larry do away from the cameras that for me was one of the funniest pieces of business I ever saw them perform.

"When I was growing up my family visited Larry and Mabel (my grandparents) quite a lot, since we lived close by. On one of these occasions Moe was there and he and Larry were practicing their routines, which they did all the time since timing was so important to the physical side of their humor.

"While I was watching them, Larry had to stop and take a phone call.

18. Eric Lamond

When he was done he told Moe that he needed to take a break, go to his den, get some papers and call the fellow who had called back. He said it was the contractor he was talking to about doing some remodeling in the bathroom of his den. Larry had a very large den upstairs at his home with its own—also large—bathroom. It was done all in black tile with black wallpaper with a sea-theme motif pattern in pastels. It was quite elegant.

"Back then many bathrooms had walls that were tiled part-way up, and the rest were wallpapered and topped with cap molding. The wallpaper at Larry's needed replacing because the water and steam had caused it to fade. Larry also wanted to change some of the cabinetry and fixtures so some of the tile would need to be redone.

"Moe asked Larry what it would cost and Larry told him what the contractor had quoted. Moe said they—Larry and Moe—could do it themselves for a lot less. Yes, the boys all were actually very handy around the house. Larry said that sounded like a good idea so they set up a day for this home improvement project. When the day came, Moe arrived and the Boys changed into white overalls, completing the work outfits with painter caps. Again, my family was visiting because I had told my Mom that I was going to help. Actually, I was just going to watch but Larry told me that I would be helping. So as I settled in, they started to work. Larry already had all the materials neatly stacked—the tile, wallpaper, wood, solvents and wallpaper glue—and all the tools (Yes ... they got the tools!) ready and at hand.

"They set out some wooden sawhorses and large planking to lay out all the wallpaper. At that point in time wallpaper was much more difficult to handle than today. It was quite a chore. It had to be rolled out and smoothed and treated with an adhesive agent and a settling liquid that was brushed on both sides. Once on the wall, it was brushed again to remove the front coating and to smooth it out. The liquid evaporated as the wallpaper glue dried and you got a nice tight fit and a very smooth look.

"Larry had already prepped the first wall for the paper. Well, they're standing side by side and begin brushing on the goo. Larry brushes right over Moe's hand and without missing a beat Moe—still looking down at the wallpaper—just goes Whap! right across Larry's face with his brush. Larry, without looking, does the same. Both then turned towards each other and the real fun started! Whap! Whap! Boink! Splat! Moe and Larry are laughing as they bring more 'props' (the tools and the other materials) into play and they just slide right into their on-screen personas and start up a masterful Three Stooges routine.

After a few minutes they stop, look around, survey the damage, put down the brushes and exit the bathroom. To say the least, it's a mess. I was laughing the whole time as they did what they did so well, and it looked like so many of the wonderful scenes from their shorts. There were even sound effects with the Whaps! from the brushes and the clanging from the scattering tools and various boinks as the wood clattered to the floor! Eventually the bathroom was finished ... and the contractor only charged Larry a little more to clean up the mess.

"That was the last time I saw Larry and Moe tackle a home improvement job together but I can still see it in my mind vividly all these years later. They just winged it and started with the snappy patter and the slapstick and I was the only audience. That's a moment from my youth that I will also treasure. I sure wish we had video recorders then because it was as good a routine as they ever did.

"Another great memory was working with my grandfather and his partners when they made their cartoon series in the mid-1960s. Working on the production crew and appearing in some of the filmed wraparounds filled up my summer that year in a way that is difficult to describe. There were days when I would go to the set; work with Larry, Moe and Curly Joe; and still get home early enough to turn on the TV and watch my father's TV show, *The Don Lamond Show*, which included showing Three Stooges shorts with Larry, Moe and Curly or Shemp. My dad's TV show ran for many, many years in Los Angeles and The Three Stooges made many, many live appearances on the show. For me, it was family but it was also a lot of fun to watch, especially when I would be at the TV studio to watch my dad's show from the set.

"By the time Larry had his stroke I was almost through college and married. Fortunately, Larry recovered enough that he had the chance to hold my sons—his great grandchildren—on his knee. My sons Don and Kurt remember Larry. My older son Don, named after my father, appeared as a baby a few times on my dad's TV show. Kurt, my younger son, was born just early enough in the day to enable my dad to announce his birth on his TV show. We still have the audio tape and I still sometimes just shake my head in wonder how The Three Stooges were such an integral part of my life growing up—what with Larry and my dad, who also appeared in most of the Stooges' feature films, so involved on daily basis.

"Fast forwarding somewhat, that involvement still exists. During the holidays in 2001, my wife and I spent some time with my son Don and his family in Seattle. It was a little odd the first time I sat in his living

18. Eric Lamond

A candid snapshot of Larry Fine on the golf course (courtesy Eric Lamond and C3 Entertainment).

room watching my son and my grandchildren watching my grandfather on television!

"Working at C3 Entertainment, Inc., the home of *The Three Stooges*, as the Director of Marketing keeps my grandfather alive for me since I can watch him and listen to him every day. It also keeps the memories of all the times I spent with Larry and with my grandmother Mabel very fresh in my memory. Larry was devoted to his family and when not working he spent his time with the family.

"One aspect of Larry's life I always get asked about was his appearance when not in character. Larry was a very sharp dresser and was always well groomed and well dressed. Walking past him on the street you would take him for a successful businessman. In fact, all of the Stooges—and I remember them all—were just the same—devoted to their families, sharp dressers, and true gentlemen. Of course, it wouldn't take much prompting to get Larry to frizz out his hair and slip into his Stooge persona, especially if one of the other guys was around.

"In October 2002 (on the 5th) we celebrated what would have been Larry's 100th birthday. His legacy as a comedian is still very much alive. Besides television stations around the world showing daily *The Three Stooges* shorts, cartoon series and the features they made in the 1960s, C3 Entertainment produced *The Three Stooges 75th Year Anniversary Special* that aired on NBC April 1, 2003. Then there is the upcoming *Three Stooges* major motion picture that we are working on in connection with Warner Bros. Pictures and the Farrelly Brothers.

"So even though Larry left us in 1975 and all the other Stooges are also gone from us, we do have their incredible body of work to enjoy and with the new movie, there is more to come from the best comedy team ever. At the personal level, Larry's legacy is strong and growing. Although Larry's sister Lila passed on in 2002 and his children have left us—son John in 1961 and daughter Phyllis, my mother, in 1989—Larry's family continues to through his grandchildren. Here's a bit about each of Larry's progeny:

"Kris Cutler: Daughter of Phyllis (Fine) and Don Lamond. Kris lives with her husband Ben in Burbank, California. Don Lamond was not only Larry's son-in-law but also appeared in most of their feature films and hosted *The Three Stooges* on television for many years on KTTV in Los Angeles.

"Christy Lynn Clark: Eldest daughter of John Fine and Christy (Clark). Christy Lynn and her husband Jan live in Ramona, California, and have owned and operated a home furnishing store, the Victoria Supply Company, for 22 years. Christy Lynn has a section in the store with pictures and memorabilia of Larry and The Three Stooges and constantly entertains customers and fans with stories about Larry.

"John Fine, Jr.: Son of John and Christy. John Jr. was actually born after his father passed away as a result of a tragic auto accident in Novem-

18. Eric Lamond

Larry Fine, his wife Mabel, and grandchildren Eric and his sister Kris. This is the last photograph of the four of them together, taken shortly before Mabel's death (courtesy Eric Lamond and C3 Entertainment).

ber of 1961 while Christy was pregnant. John and his wife Gloria live in San Antonio, Texas, where John is approaching 20 years of service with the United States Air Force. Gloria also serves in the Air Force.

"Phyllis Miller: Daughter of John and Christy. Phyllis and her husband Kevin reside in Orem, Utah, where Phyllis juggles the various activities of their six children who range in age from grade schoolers to college students.

"As for me, I am Larry's eldest grandchild, born to Don Lamond and Phyllis (Fine) Lamond. I live with my wife in Huntington Beach, California. You've already met my two sons (from my first marriage to Mary Aruta with whom I share our grandchildren and friendship). My older son Don lives in Kent, Washington. He's engaged to Stacey Jorgenson and both serve in law enforcement. My grandchildren (from Don's previous marriage) Megan and Drew are Larry's great-great-grandchildren and represent another generation of Larry's family and fans. My younger son Kurt resides in Burbank, California, and works in the entertainment business. He's engaged to his college sweetheart, Joan May, a model and

Top: The trademark opening credits logo leading to a Three Stooges film. *Bottom:* Eric Lamond as he looks today. Look at that strategically placed Larry doll behind him. (Both photographs courtesy Eric Lamond and C3 Entertainment.)

actress. My wife June has a son, Joseph, and a recently married daughter, Madeline, who live in Colorado.

"Larry's late sister Lila was survived by her daughters Barbara Cantor, Phyllis Goldbloom and Joan Sandler; grandchildren Michael and Faith Hollander, Barry Cantor, Scott Sandler, Brett Sandler and Josh Goldbloom; and great grandchildren Lauren and Alan. There are cousins, like Mary Schwartz in Las Vegas and other relations around the country, all with their special memories of Larry Fine of The Three Stooges and Larry Fine, my grandfather.

"So, as I said, Larry's legacy is very well and growing ... and whenever I pass a display of wallpaper or bathroom tile I get a smile on my face and utter a little chuckle as I silently say, 'Thanks, Larry, for all the love and laughter.'"

19

JOHN LONGENECKER

★ *Son of Ruth Hussey and Robert Longenecker* ★

> *We all go haywire at times, and if we don't, maybe we ought to.*
> —Elizabeth Imbrie (Ruth Hussey)
> in *The Philadelphia Story*

Ruth Hussey is perhaps best known for her role as the cynical photographer Elizabeth Imbrie in one of Hollywood's most sophisticated comedies, *The Philadelphia Story* (1940). Directed by the legendary George Cukor and starring Katharine Hepburn, James Stewart and Cary Grant, Ruth's stand-out performance won her critical acclaim and an Oscar nomination for Best Supporting Actress. The film received six nominations, with two wins. Screenwriter Donald Ogden Stewart won for Best Screenplay and James Stewart won for Best Actor.

Before being signed to MGM in 1937, Ruth attended Pembroke College at Brown University and took postgraduate courses at the University of Michigan, where she continued her drama studies. She played two seasons of summer stock in Michigan.

Her parents, George R. Hussey and Julia Agnes Corbett Hussey, had two other children, Robert and Betty. The family tree goes way back. Christopher Hussey arrived in America in 1632 and promptly bought Nantucket Island in New England. Ruth was proud of her heritage. Unlike many stars who changed their names once they hit Hollywood, Ruth Hussey stayed Ruth Hussey.

Her show business beginnings began in her hometown of Providence, Rhode Island, when she worked as a fashion commentator on radio. Still longing for the stage, she sought work in local theater. She was turned down after being told that all roles were cast out of New

19. John Longenecker

Ruth Hussey, center, with Katharine Hepburn and James Stewart in a scene from Ruth's Oscar-nominated role in *The Philadelphia Story*.

York City. With only one thing to do, a determined Ruth packed her bags, headed to the Big Apple and was signed by a theatrical agent on her first day in the city. He immediately got her a role in a play opening at the same Providence theater she had visited a week before.

Ruth soon moved to New York City permanently. She was signed to the exclusive Powers Modeling Agency and continued to look for acting jobs on her days off. After a number of small roles in New York and after touring with several stock companies, Ruth was cast in the touring company for the smash hit play *Dead End*. She traveled with the play across the country, city to city, until the cast finally ended their run at the grand Biltmore Hotel in Los Angeles, California.

MGM talent scout Billy Grady liked what he saw and wasted no time letting Ruth know it. He sent a note backstage after the opening

Children of Hollywood

act, asking if she would be willing to submit herself to a screen test at the studio. Ruth agreed. She was successful. The most notable movie studio in the world offered her a five-year contract and that offer was later extended to eight years. Ruth Hussey, small-town girl, was now a contracted player at MGM. This was the only studio that touted itself as having "more stars than there are in heaven," and suddenly Ruth Hussey was one of those stars.

As Ruth's son, John, tells it, luck and a second chance got Ruth to Hollywood and subsequently onto the MGM payroll. It was her alarm clock that almost robbed her of the Hollywood career she so enjoyed. John explains further:

> "When *Dead End* was playing in Newark, New Jersey, my mom was living in New York City. She was to appear in a matinee performance and she set her alarm clock to make the show in more than enough time. The only problem was, she slept in! Mom called the theater, then rushed to New Jersey in a taxi and the production was held up until a stage manager saw her arrive in front of the theater. The moment he spotted her, the stage manager gave the signal for the play to start. My mom ran in, got into her wardrobe and walked on stage in just enough time for her first entrance. The production *had* to know she was at the theater before they could start the play. Although she made it, with little interruption to the show, the producer fired her when the curtain fell. One of the lead actors talked the producer into giving Mom a break. He soon had a change of heart and agreed to let her stay on. Since that was the play that brought Mom to Hollywood, it was just swell that the producer gave her that second chance."

Ruth's first role as a contracted studio player was a bit part in a Spencer Tracy drama, *The Big City* (1937). The same year she was given the role of the adult abandoned daughter in the remake of *Madame X* (1937). She followed that with another small role in one of the popular Andy Hardy series of films, *Judge Hardy's Children* (1938). Ruth appeared in seven films in 1939, including *Honolulu*, *The Women* and *Another Thin Man*.

Her frequent appearances in 1939 undoubtedly lead her to more prominent roles the following year. Starring alongside Spencer Tracy and Robert Young in the action-adventure *Northwest Passage* (1940),

19. John Longenecker

Ruth played Elizabeth Browne. It was a role initially offered to Greer Garson, but a scheduling conflict forced her to back out, leaving the role open for Ruth to take over. In *Susan and God* (1940) she played Charlotte, one of her son John's favorite characters. The wartime drama *Flight Command* (1940), starring Robert Taylor and Walter Pidgeon, was next. For Ruth, it was an important film, personally and professionally. Robert Longenecker walked into a movie theater in 1940 after buying a ticket to see *Flight Command*. He had no idea he was about to fall in love. As soon as Ruth Hussey appeared on the screen, he decided right there and then that he wanted to marry her. Two years later, he did! John elaborates on his parents' first in-person meeting:

> "My dad went to lunch at the Brown Derby in Hollywood. Mom was at a booth with two of her girlfriends. They already knew Dad and invited him over to join them. A short time later the two girls left and Mom and Dad started getting acquainted. They poked around a bookstore after lunch, and Mom offered Dad a ride back to work. He happily took her up on the offer. Not missing out on chance to get to know Ruth Hussey better, he left his own car parked at the Brown Derby and rode with Mom."

John asked his mom what she remembers most about their first meeting.

> "She told me that she could picture it as if it were yesterday. He drove her car and she was in the passenger seat. She remembers looking over at my dad and thinking, 'Now why can't I find a man like that?!' Well, she *had* found her man and Dad *had* found his woman. Later that day Dad went back to the bookstore and bought Mom two books of poetry by Emily Dickinson. She still has those books today. It was a whirlwind romance, and they were married just seven weeks after their first 'accidental date' at the Brown Derby. They happily celebrated their 60th wedding anniversary in 2002."

The Philadelphia Story, along with an Oscar nomination for Best Supporting Actress, rounded out Ruth's 1940. It was the most successful year of her career. These stand-out performances led other studios to feature Ruth Hussey in their films, too. MGM was more than happy to loan its stars to other studios for a fee, and Ruth was no exception. The early forties saw Ruth work on various productions for Paramount, Columbia and RKO Radio Pictures. She also took on the role of first-time mother. Her son Robert was born on July 19, 1944.

On their wedding day, August 9, 1942, Ruth Hussey and Robert Longenecker are all smiles.

19. John Longenecker

Ruth's most popular role away from MGM was the lead opposite Ray Milland in the classic Paramount horror film *The Uninvited* (1944). Without the modern wonder of special effects, this film still manages to give the viewer goose bumps through fear of what's *not* there rather than what is.

Despite her on-screen successes, Ruth returned to her Broadway roots to star in the Pulitzer Prize–winning play *State of the Union* (1946) at the Hudson Theater in New York City. It was her son John's first taste of show business. "In 1946, Mom was in the play *State of the Union* in New York," John said with a smile. "I was on stage, too. I was born in February 1947 and was the reason she left the show." Motherhood didn't stop Ruth from working, but working didn't stop her from being a mother either.

A glamour portrait of Ruth Hussey in her prime.

"My mom was as awesome at being a mom as she was working as an actress. She drove my brother and me to little league baseball practice, made tasty sandwiches for our school lunches, and we all remember her delectable lamb dinners. Our family was pretty down to earth. My pop worked as a talent agent and formed the Robert Longenecker Agency. He'd make dinner at our family weekend cabin in the mountains near Lake Arrowhead. He had his own special recipe for hobo steaks—grilled hamburger with great spices on open-face rye toast.

"Our house in Lake Arrowhead was designed by my mother. It was a unique design based on clock-face mathematics, a twelve-sided polygon that was three stories high. The house slept up to twelve people and was just 28 feet in diameter. It was practical, yet different. It had a good-sized deck and picture windows overlooking the lake in the distance through the pine trees. My mom enjoyed sketching floor plans for years, and we

The house of her dreams: Ruth designed the family's vacation house at Lake Arrowhead. It was a twelve-sided polygon, three stories high. It looked different on the outside, yet was extremely practical on the inside.

were all thrilled when she was able to make her architectural talent a reality. My dad wanted to build a round cabin, and he got what he wanted. He loved to spend weekends with the family there—summer and winter. The locals all know the house. It's so unique, it was inevitable that it would become a local landmark.

"Our main residence was on the neighborhood street North Carmelina Avenue in Los Angeles, California. Next door was Greta Garbo's house, then film director's H. C. Potter's house, then athlete and broadcaster

19. John Longenecker

Tom Harmon's house. He and his wife, actress Elyse Knox, had three children, Kristin, Kelly and Mark Harmon. Kristin Harmon, a renowned fine artist, married singer/songwriter, Rick Nelson. A Spanish style house two doors up was the bachelor pad of James Stewart and Henry Fonda before I was born. The neighborhood was a revolving door of who's who in Hollywood."

Ruth returned to the screen as strong as ever, taking the lead role in *I, Jane Doe* (1948), a film noir classic. Ruth played Eve Meredith Curtis, an attorney defending a woman accused of murdering her husband. Her career continued to flourish in the late forties and early fifties with roles in the classic *The Great Gatsby* (1949), the Martin and Lewis comedy *That's My Boy* (1951) and the musical *Stars and Stripes Forever* (1952). Ruth was now an MGM star player. She had a thriving career and the Hollywood friends that went along with it.

I asked most of the star children during the course of this book if they idolized their parents' famous friends. Their answers were all similar: "Not really, they were just the people who Mom or Dad worked with," they'd say flippantly. John is the first Hollywood child who thought otherwise. He explains further:

"To me, accomplished motion picture actors, directors and producers are larger than life, they are not at all typical folks. I worked with George Roy Hill, Paul Newman, Robert Redford and Robert Shaw on *The Sting* (1973). I met John Ford, William Wellman, Clint Eastwood, Katharine Hepburn and George Cukor. All of them were larger than life. These folks are NOT typical everyday people. That's why they do what they do. That's why they are who they are. They're motion picture stars, accomplished actors, icons, *because* they aren't just regular folks. They take over a room, a concert hall, a movie theater with their presence and their powerful personalities. Folks who don't get that just don't have their eyes open, that's all. Ask yourself: Was James Dean or Marlon Brando just a typical everyday guy?"

By 1950, Ruth was making the transition from the silver screen to the small screen. Television was the new medium, and Ruth was making her mark. Throughout the next decade she was a frequent guest star on many well-known television programs, including *Pulitzer Prize Playhouse, Shower of Stars, Alfred Hitchcock Presents, Climax!, Lux Video Theater, General Electric Theater* and *Science Fiction Theater*.

Children of Hollywood

On June 17, 1954, Ruth gave birth to her third and last child, daughter Mary. With a husband and three children to take care of, Ruth did scattered work throughout the 1960s. For now, she was content to play the role of wife and mother.

It was Robert Young, Ruth's old MGM co-star, who lured Ruth back to television as a guest star on a 1972 episode of his ABC series *Marcus Welby M.D.*, and again as his love interest in the made-for-TV movie *My Darling Daughter's Anniversary* (ABC, 1973). Ruth's acting career spanned close to five decades. Her marriage to her beloved husband Robert lasted six decades. Robert Longenecker passed away at age ninety-three on December 10, 2002. He and Ruth had celebrated their sixtieth wedding anniversary a few months before.

John tells me his mother is still "as sharp as a tack at 93 years of age." She lives in Thousand Oaks, California. Mary lives nearby in Oak Park, California, with her husband, Bob, a real estate developer. She is a talented watercolor artist. They have three children. Carol, a teacher, Holly, a college student and Daniel, a high school student and talented baseball player. Rob is a former Navy jet fighter pilot. He and his wife, Beth, live in Houston, Texas. Their son, Todd, and grandson Corban live nearby. Rob established the RL Company there and sells business products to corporate clients.

As for John, he is a member of the Directors Guild of America, often works as a cinematographer and is an Academy Award–winning filmmaker. At twenty-three, as producer, he won an Oscar for Best Live Action Short Film. *The Resurrection of Broncho Billy* (1970) starred Johnny Crawford, and John's next-door neighbor, Kristin (Harmon) Nelson. *Broncho Billy* was released theatrically by Universal Studios and has been released on DVD. Ordering information can be found at Ruth Hussey's official website—RuthHussey.com.

John was born into a Hollywood family, but he did have a choice of careers and chose to make his own path in the entertainment industry. "After applying to the American Film Institute internship program, I had specifically selected *The Sting* (1973) to work on as an assistant to legendary director George Roy Hill. He approved, and I was delighted. It was the first feature motion picture I worked on after winning an Oscar. We shot on the back lot of Universal Studios and at the historic Green Hotel in Pasadena, California. We had a one-week location shoot in Chicago, mostly for the art deco LaSalle Street train sta-

19. John Longenecker

Robert and Ruth with their children, Mary (on swing), Robert Jr. (standing), and John (kneeling), and Pala, their cocker spaniel.

Children of Hollywood

tion sequences where the story takes us to the poker game on a train ride from Chicago to New York City.

"Robert Redford's performance was terrific on set. Paul Newman seemed less so somehow, but in the dailies, he jumped off the screen. He knew how to do it for the camera. Amazing! I am honored to have been a part of making that picture. *The Sting* went on to win multiple Academy Awards for Art Direction, Cinematography, Costumes, Music, Screenplay, Director and of course, Best Picture. I learned a lot about how to get it done right working on that picture.

"As we were finishing up production on *The Sting*, Robert Redford was about to start work on the remake of *The Great Gatsby* [1974]. He was eager to meet my mother because she had worked on an earlier version of *The Great Gatsby* [1949]. George Roy Hill, the director, invited my mom to the Universal Studios set. She was treated wonderfully. My mom was over sixty years old at the time yet she navigated herself around the lighting and sound cables, the light stands and sound stage fixtures as if she were a dancer. She didn't miss a step. She was in a familiar landscape. It was as if she never left it.

"She was introduced to Robert Surtees, the director of photography, Henry Bumstead, the production designer and Edith Head, the costume designer. They were all delighted to meet Ruth Hussey. She and Robert Redford talked together for a while about *The Great Gatsby*. They were equally impressed with each other. It was a nice moment.

"There is no controversy or dramatics in the Ruth Hussey story. Just a good family with parents the kids look up to with admiration and respect. To this day, my sister Mary and her whole family and I continue to enjoy simple outdoor family get-togethers, like barbecues in the back yard and fly-fishing for trout on the streams of the Eastern Sierra in California.

"As I see it, Ruth Hussey is an accomplished actress and a great mom to her kids. She married the right guy—my dad, Bob Longenecker. He was a gentleman, a great guy, a great dad who grew up in Litiz, a small rural Pennsylvania town, and accomplished his own dreams in Hollywood with grace and integrity. He always treated his wife, my mother, wonderfully and was completely devoted to his family."

Ruth Hussey had it all. She was blessed with a happy marriage, children who felt loved, and a steady career as an actress. It was a

19. John Longenecker

combination that few Hollywood actors could juggle successfully. With the help of a dedicated husband, Ruth did it just fine. A good old fashioned American family—in Hollywood. What a refreshing change.

MOTHERHOOD MISSED

I only wish I'd had some children. They would be good company for me and give me a little something more to do around the house. As you know, I had plenty of kids as Ma Kettle.
—Marjorie Main,
in The Slapstick Queens
by James Robert Parish

In conclusion, I felt it necessary to touch upon those Hollywood stars who *didn't* have children. Whether it be out of personal choice, circumstances beyond their control, or even premature death, there were many actresses who missed the opportunity of becoming a mother.

As Marjorie Main commented above, her biggest regret was not having children of her own. The fact that she had married a man twenty-five years her senior may have played a part in that decision; however, it's ironic that a woman who is best known for playing one of the most lovable mothers in Hollywood history, Ma Kettle, didn't have the chance to become a mother in real life. Despite her fame, wealth and successful career, she felt something was missing in her old age—the company of children.

Lupe Velez, known as "The Mexican Spitfire," had a long list of lovers and broken romances, but it was the father of her unborn child, Harold Raymonds, who refused to believe the child was his and finally pushed her over the edge.

On December 13, 1944, Lupe Velez took an overdose of Seconal. She was thirty-six years old. Lupe decided her own fate, but if she was going to die, she was going to die with class, or so she thought. Dressed in a silk nightgown, in full makeup, and with perfect hair, Lupe envisioned her lifeless yet still glamorous body splashed across the morning papers. However, the pills reacted violently with her system. She had rushed to the bathroom to vomit and it was in that tiny room that Lupe Velez was found dead, with her head in the toilet bowl. Her suicide note read, "To Harold, may God forgive you and forgive me too but I prefer to take my life away and our baby's before I bring him with shame or killing him, Lupe."

Ava Gardner, undoubtedly one of the most beautiful actresses ever to emerge from the Hollywood production line, married three times, but none of those marriages produced any children. With three famous ex-husbands, Mickey Rooney, Artie Shaw and Frank Sinatra behind her, Ava chose to live out her final days in seclusion in an apartment in London. Her long-time housekeeper and her beloved Welsh Corgi, Morgan, were her constant companions.

Following Gardner's debilitating stroke in 1989, Frank Sinatra covered all of her medical bills until her death on January 25, 1990. Her housekeeper flew her body back to her native North Carolina for burial. Ava's former co-star and friend Gregory Peck took in her dog Morgan and employed her housekeeper at his main residence.

Despite Ava Gardner's beauty and fame she never really found true love or the right man to give her the family that she longed for. She once publicly stated, "I would give it all up for one good man I could love and marry and cook for and make a home for, someone who would stick around for the rest of my life. I never found him." Ironically, she reportedly confessed to becoming pregnant not once but twice while married to Sinatra; however, she chose to abort both pregnancies.

Much has been written about the fascinating life and equally fascinating, if not suspicious, death of Marilyn Monroe. A child bride at sixteen, she eventually divorced Jim Dougherty to pursue her love of acting. Her subsequent marriages to baseball legend Joe DiMaggio and playwright Arthur Miller ended in divorce and she had at least three known miscarriages. It has been rumored that Marilyn gave birth to a daughter when she was barely out of her teens. It is said that she carried the baby to term and the baby was taken away at birth without Marilyn's knowledge of her whereabouts. None of these rumors were ever proven as factual, but the story rears its head from time to time and it's lingered around long enough to suspect there may actually be some truth to the rumor.

Marilyn Monroe's premature death at age thirty-six was officially ruled as a suicide. The cause? An overdose of sleeping pills. Marilyn was found dead on her bed, naked and with the phone receiver in her hand. Was she trying to call for help? No one really knows the truth. The years of innuendoes and rumors of foul play have surrounded her life and her death for more than forty years. The conspiracy theories are still being discussed to this day. It is somewhat sad to think that Marilyn will never truly rest in peace, simply because she is buried with too many secrets.

Marion Davies, despite her fifty films, is best remembered as the mistress of media tycoon William Randolph Hearst. Their relationship started when she was a budding twenty-year-old starlet and he was fifty-four years old and married with five children. Their love affair lasted for thirty years until his death. It is unclear whether Hearst's wife, Phoebe, refused to grant him a divorce or even if Hearst ever asked her for one. On the other hand, Marion's devoutly religious upbringing may have played a part in her not wanting Hearst to divorce his wife in order to marry her.

They were one of the most openly adulterous couples in Hollywood history; however, Marion's devotion to Hearst and their inability to marry prevented her from having children ... or did it? Here's the mystery. Marion's niece Patricia, the supposed daughter of Marion's sister Rose, claimed toward the end of her life that she wasn't Marion's niece after all. She was in fact the secret love child of Marion and William Randolph Hearst.

Patricia's family backed up this claim after her death, but it's never been officially proven as fact. In a slight twist that points to her story being somewhat valid, Patricia and her husband, Arthur Lake, are both buried in the same crypt as Marion at the star-scattered Hollywood Forever Cemetery, located in Hollywood, California.

In light of this information, Patricia is in most of the home movies with Marion and Hearst, she accompanied them on trips, and they even jointly gave her away at her wedding. In the days where little things like babies out of wedlock were frowned upon, it is entirely possible that Patricia was the product of one of the greatest love stories in history. She was their little secret.

Hearst passed away in 1951 at Marion's home, and it was believed that the Hearst family sedated Marion so that she was unable to attend his funeral and say her final farewell to the man she truly considered to be her husband. Marion got the last laugh when the will was read and the entire Hearst corporation was left to her. The Hearst family

Motherhood Missed

was forced to deal with Marion for the rest of her life. However, she dealt with the empire with responsibility and generosity.

Dying at age sixty-four of cancer of the jaw, Marion left most of her estate to children's charities. The biggest bequest of $1.5 million was left to the UCLA Medical Center and the Marion Davies Children's Clinic is one of the most influential organizations that still bears her name.

Jean Harlow was another Hollywood tragedy and a woman who wanted nothing more than to be a mother. Like Marilyn Monroe, she also married at the tender age of sixteen. Her new husband was Charles McGrew, and the newlyweds moved to Southern California to escape the overbearing ways of Jean's mother, known to all as "Mama Jean." Jean was happily married and happily working as a Hollywood extra when she discovered she was pregnant. Thrilled at the prospect of becoming a mother, her hopes were soon dashed when "Mama Jean" stepped in and pressured her to either have an abortion or lose her budding career. Jean relented and reluctantly aborted the pregnancy. Not surprisingly, her marriage ended two months later.

During her short life, Jean endured another divorce after a troubled two year marriage to Harold Rosson. That, combined with the suspicious death of her second husband Paul Bern, threatened Jean's career, and it was now time for the studio to step in and bail out their troubled star. Despite the police investigation that pointed to Jean as the main suspect in Bern's death, he was eventually ruled a suicide. A studio cover up? Who knows ... Jean took the truth to her grave with her own premature death at age twenty-six of nephritis (otherwise known as kidney disease). Her early demise not only halted her prospering career but it prevented her from ever finding true love and realizing her dream of becoming a mother.

Charlie Chaplin's most glamorous wife, Paulette Goddard, married four times without bearing a child of her own. The closest she came to being a mother was to Chaplin's two young sons, Charlie Jr. and Sydney (their mother was Lita Grey, Chaplin's second wife). During Paulette's six-year marriage to Chaplin, she filled the parental void when Chaplin was working or overworking as he so often did. As an adult, Sydney still remembers her fondly. "We adored her," he said.

Incidentally, between 1919 and 1962, Chaplin fathered twelve children with three of his wives; eleven of them were healthy. Norman

Children of Hollywood

Spencer Chaplin was born prematurely to Chaplin's first wife, the sixteen-year-old starlet Mildred Harris. He was too small to survive. His three days of life and subsequent death were the beginning of the end of their brief marriage. In a touching tribute, he is buried with the simple inscription "The Little Mouse—July 7—July 10, 1919" etched into his headstone. Chaplin's eventual brood of children did nothing to ease the pain or fill the void of his infant son's death.

Myrna Loy married four times and remained childless. Ginger Rogers married five times, and had no children with any of her husbands, either. Despite two marriages, her first to William Powell and her second to Clark Gable, Carole Lombard's tragic death in a plane crash at age thirty-six prevented her from becoming a mother, too. The list goes on. Lillian Gish never married and never had children. Her sister Dorothy married and divorced and no children came from her one and only marriage. The closest Greta Garbo got to marriage was standing up a devastated John Gilbert at the altar; she "got cold feet" she said. She never married or had children. Greer Garson, Pola Negri, Carole Landis, Alexis Smith, Louise Brooks, Claudette Colbert, Mabel Normand, Mae West, Theda Bara, Tallulah Bankhead, and Carmen Miranda remained childless, despite the fact that they all married at least once.

The most famous female soprano and on-screen partner of Nelson Eddy, Jeanette MacDonald, married fellow screen star Gene Raymond in June of 1937. An elaborate ceremony that saw thousands of fans line the streets behind police barricades in order to catch a glimpse of the newlyweds was a Hollywood press agent's dream. Their love endured the often-fickle unions that Hollywood creates. Gene Raymond was at his wife's side when she died, age fifty-seven, of a heart attack on January 15, 1965. They had no children.

Ann Sheridan had two brief marriages, both of them childless. Her first marriage to S. Edward Norris lasted just three hundred seventy-five days. Her second marriage to George Brent broke that record, lasting just two hundred sixty-three days. After those two failed attempts, she never attempted to tie the knot for a third time; however, she was romantically linked to Steve Hannagan, a well-known publicity agent, for many years. There were persistent rumors that they had indeed married; however, Hannagan officially died a bachelor in 1953. Proof of the seriousness of their romance was finally evident in his will. Ann received a lump sum of $250,000 from his estate. There were no children from their relationship.

Ann Miller came closer than most of these women to realizing the joys of motherhood, but her tragic story is perhaps worse than never having a child at all. Her marriage to steel heir Reese Milner was violent and abusive and subsequently ended in divorce. The divorce was instigated from Ann's hospital bed after she lost her baby daughter as a result of one of Milner's drunken rages. During an argument with Milner, Ann fell down a flight of stairs, sending her into premature labor. Her baby lived for three hours but she was too small to survive. Ann never really got over the tragedy. She later remarried, but that marriage also ended in divorce. She had no other children.

On a lighter note, Katharine Hepburn once commented on why she specifically chose *not* to have children. Despite never being married, her long-standing affair with Spencer Tracy is common knowledge, even to non-movie buffs. Again, it was religious beliefs that prevented Tracy from divorcing his wife to marry Katharine, but despite that, their affair lasted some twenty-six years, until his death on June 10, 1967.

Katharine Hepburn was so ahead of her time, had she wanted a child, I cannot see a little thing like a marriage certificate getting in her way. Remaining childless was her choice, and in *Kate Remembered* by A. Scott Berg, she explains why she made such a decision.

"Let's say I have a little child," she explained, "and it's seven o'clock at night and Baby Johnny or Baby Janey suddenly comes down with a one-hundred-and-three-degree fever. And I've got twelve hundred people waiting to see me that night at the St. James Theatre. Now some of those people, I'm thinking, have waited months for their tickets, and some of them have scraped together money they can't really afford and arranged baby-sitters so that they can have their special night that year. And now little Johnny or little Janey is in pain and screaming and yelling. And there's no question what I have to do. I would walk into that baby's room and take a pillow and smother that adorable child."

Katharine Hepburn just didn't have that motherly instinct in her. Her career was her baby and she nurtured that. For that devotion she became a legend and that was enough for her. Despite the fact that she could have easily adopted children so as not to interrupt her career with a pregnancy or two, and despite the fact that she had more than enough money to hire all the help she needed to raise those children, she knew she'd be a bad mother and she wasn't afraid to admit it. For that admission, she did more for her unborn child or a child in need of adoption than raising kids that she really didn't want simply because she felt society or publicity pressures to do so. It was a decision that took guts to make, but it was the best decision for her and it was an even better decision for her children that never were.

★★★★★

There are many instances of celebrity mothers and fathers who, despite the gift of money, failed to give their children the greatest gift of all, their time. So next time you feel guilty about not being able to afford to buy your children the latest toy they crave, know that in the long run, it's not the presents you buy them, it's your *presence* in body that will stay with them long after that toy is forgotten.

BIBLIOGRAPHY

Books

Berg, Scott A. *Kate Remembered*. New York: Putnam, 2003.
Burk, Margaret, and Gary Hudson. *Final Curtain: Eternal Resting Places of Hundreds of Stars, Celebrities, Moguls, Misers and Misfits*. Santa Ana, CA: Seven Locks Press, 1996.
Chaplin, Michael. *I Couldn't Smoke the Grass on My Father's Lawn*. London: Leslie Frewin, 1966.
Crane, Cheryl, with Cliff Jahr. *Detour: A Hollywood Tragedy*. London: Michael Joseph, 1988.
Cronkite, Kathy. *On the Edge of the Spotlight: Celebrities Children Speak Out About Their Lives*. New York: William Morrow, 1981.
Crosby, Gary, and Ross Firestone. *Going My Own Way*. New York: Used with permission of Doubleday, a division of Random House, 1983. Reprinted by the permission of Russell & Volkening as agents for the author.
Fairbanks, Douglas, Jr. *The Salad Days*. New York: Bantam Dell, 1988.
Farber, Stephen, and Marc Green. *Hollywood Dynasties*. New York: Delilah, 1984.
Fonda, Peter. *Don't Tell Dad: A Memoir*. New York: Hyperion, 1998.
Hutchinson, Thomas. *Niven's Hollywood*. London: Macmillan, 1984.
Keylin, Arleen, and Suri Fleischer. *Hollywood Album: Lives and Deaths of Hollywood Stars from the Pages of The New York Times*. New York: Arno Press, 1977.
Marx, Arthur. *Life with Groucho*. New York: Published by arrangement with Barricade Books, 1992.
_____. *Son of Groucho*. New York: David McKay, 1972.
Marx, Harpo. *Harpo Speaks!* New York: Used by permission of Limelight Editions and Chrysalis Books, 1988.
Olivier, Tarquin. *My Father: Laurence Olivier*. London: Headline, 1992.
Parish, James Robert. *The Slapstick Queens*. New York: A.S. Barnes, 1973.
Robertson, Patrick. *Film Facts*. New York: Billboard Books, 2001.
Sinatra, Tina, with Jeff Coplon. *My Father's Daughter*. London: Simon and Schuster, 2001.
Stinchcum, Sheryl. *Leatrice Gilbert Fountain: Daughter of Hollywood Legends*.
Strait, Raymond. *Hollywood's Children*. New York: St Martin's Press, 1982.
Strait, Raymond. *Star Babies*. New York: St Martin's Press, 1980.
Wagner, Walter. *You Must Remember This*. New York: Used by permission of G. P. Putnam's, a division of Penguin Group (USA), 1975.

Bibliography

Magazines

Copner, Michael. "Harry Langdon Jr. Speaks!" *Cult Movies Magazine,* Issue # 35.

Internet Resources

Amusing Quotes: www.amusingquotes.com
Bangley, Jimmy. "An Interview with Leatrice Gilbert Fountain." *Classic Images,* 1999.
Brainy Quote: www.brainyquote.com
Dlugos, Jenn. "Chris Costello Meets Classic-Horror: An Interview." *Classic Images Online,* www.classicimages.com.
Hawkins, Geraldine. "Douglas Fairbanks, Jr.: A Part I Am Playing." *Classic Images Online,* www.classicimages.com.
Internet Movie Database: www.imdb.com
Lybarger, Dan. "The Fairbanks Legacy: An Interview with Douglas Fairbanks, Jr." February 26, 1996, www.tipjar.com/dan/douglasfairbanks.htm.
Marlowe, Sam. "Kate Burton: Daddy's Girl." March 27, 2003, www.enjoyment.independent.co.uk
May, Steve. "Lois Laurel Hawes Interview." www.homecinemachoice.com.
Simon, Tom. "Gary Lewis and the Playboys Article." www.tsimon.com/lewis.htm.
UMP Collection: www.UMPCollection.de

Television

Scheinfeld, John. "The Unknown Marx Brothers" LSL Productions, Documentary, 1993.

Although the author has made every effort to offer attribution for all quotes and extracts, that has not been possible in some few cases.

Index

Page numbers in *italics* indicate photographs

Abandon Ship 73
Abbott and Costello 131–132, 135, 147
Abbott and Costello Meet Frankenstein 132
Abbott and Costello Meet the Mummy 135
Abbott, Betty (Mrs. Bud) *see* Smith, Betty
Abbott, Bud 131–132, *134*, 137, 144–147, *145*
Abbott, Vickie *see* Wheeler, Vickie Abbott
abortion 207, 209
abuse *see* parental neglect, victims of; physical abuse, victims of
Academy Awards 15, 79, 100, 157, 194, 202, 204
Academy of Motion Picture Arts and Sciences 100
acting careers, first generation: Bing Crosby 157, 164; Boris Karloff 172–175; Douglas Fairbanks, Sr. 99–100; Eleanor Powell 88, 90, 93; Glenn Ford 88, 93; John Gilbert 116–118, 127–128; Leatrice Joy 116–118; Ruth Hussey 194–199, 201–202
acting careers, second generation 14–16; Chris Costello 137; Diana Barrymore 13; Don Lamond 190; Douglas Fairbanks, Jr. 102–104, 106–107; Jamie Lee Curtis 5, 7; Janet Cantor Gari 84; Kate Burton 21; Leatrice Gilbert Fountain 115–116, 128; Michael Douglas 7, 8; Peter Ford 93–96; Romina Power 74
acting careers, third generation 130
adopted Hollywood children: Billy, Alex, Jimmy and Minnie Marx 39–43; Joan Benny 50–53, 58–59; Mario Lanza's children 69; Sandy and Ronnie Burns 53; Steve Crosby 167; Suzanne Lloyd 180; Vickie Abbott 144–147
adoptions, Hollywood style 16–18
Adoree, Renee 117
advantages of being a Hollywood child: Arthur Marx 29–30, 31–32; Chris Costello 133; Douglas Fairbanks, Jr. 103, 104; Harry Langdon, Jr. 110–112, 114; Jamie Lee Curtis 7; Jeff Bridges 14; Joan Benny 57–58; Michael Douglas 7; Peter Ford 89–90; Suzanne Lloyd 181
An Affair to Remember 181
alcoholism in Hollywood: Ann Battlers Costello 139–141; Diana Barrymore 13; Dixie Lee Crosby 165–166; Edward G. Robinson,

Index

Jr. 13–14; Gary Crosby 167; John Gilbert 120, 122; Reese Milner 211; Scott Newman 14
Allen, Gracie 6, 53, 57, 85; *see also* Burns, Gracie
American Bandstand (television show) 94
American Film Institute 173, 202
The Americano 93
Andrews, Dana 14
Arnaz, Desi *19*, 56
Arnaz, Desi, Jr. *19*
Arnaz, Lucy *19*
Arsenic and Old Lace (stage play) 175
Ashley, Lady Sylvia 100
autobiographical writings: *Detour: A Hollywood Tragedy* (Crane) 20–21; "Gilbert Writes His Own Story" (Gilbert) 119; *A Hell of a War* (Fairbanks) 104; *Life with Groucho* (Marx) 26; *My Father: My Son* (Robinson) 13; *Salad Days* (Fairbanks) 104; *Son of Groucho* (Marx) 26; *Sunday Nights at Seven* (Benny) 50–59; *Too Much, Too Soon* (Barrymore) 13
awards 85, 91; *see also* Academy Awards

Ball, Lucille *19*, 56
Banjo Eyes (stage show) 85
Bankhead, Talluluah 105, 210
Bano, Al 73–74
Barnaby Jones (television show) 96
Barrymore, Diana: *Too Much, Too Soon* 13
Barrymore, Drew 3
Barrymore, Ethel 3
Barrymore, John 3, 13, 119
Barrymore, Lionel 3, 13
Battlers, Ann 131, 133, *136*, 137–138, 139–141
"Be My Love " (song) 65
Be My Love: A Celebration of Mario Lanza (Lanza and Dolfi) 70

Beatles 181
Benny, Jack 50–59, *51*, 85, 112
Benny, Joan 50–59, 51, 59; *Sunday Nights at Seven* 50–59
Benny, Mary (Mrs. Jack) *see* Livingstone, Mary
Bensen, Signe 53
Berg, Scott A.: *Kate Remembered* 211
Bern, Paul 209
The Big Parade 117
The Bingsville Bugle (comic strip) 157
biographies of the stars: *Be My Love* (Lanza and Dolfi), 69–70; *Dark Star* (Fountain) 115–120; *Glenn Ford: A Life in Film* (Ford and Nickeus) 98; *My Father: Laurence Olivier* (Olivier) 12; *Niven's Hollywood* (Hutchinson) 12; *Sunday Nights at Seven* (Benny) 50; *W. C. Fields: A Life on Film* (Fields) 151; *W. C. Fields: By Himself* (Fields) 151; *see also* autobiographical writings
birthday parties, Hollywood style 1, 7; Damon Lanza 66–67; Gary Crosby 158–159; Leatrice Gilbert Fountain 126; Lucille Ball and Desi Arnaz 19; Michael Chaplin 9
boarding school days: Chris Costello 141; Leatrice Gilbert Fountain 126; Peter Fonda 11; Romina Power 72–73, 74; *see also* school days
Bogle, Charles 150
Bolger, Ray 79
Boyer, Charles, Jr. 14
Brent, George 210
Bridges, Jeff 14
Bridges, Lloyd 14
Bringing Up Baby 181
Bruce, Virginia 122–123
Bud and Lou (television movie) 143–144
Bunty Pulls the Strings 117

216

Index

Burns, George 6, 53, 57, 85
Burns, Gracie 41, 57; *see also* Allen, Gracie
Burns, Ronnie 6, 53
Burns, Sandy 53
Burton, Kate 21
Burton, Richard 21
business acumen: Bing Crosby 170; Bud Abbott 135; Chico Marx 44–46; Douglas Fairbanks, Jr. 104; Douglas Fairbanks, Sr. 99–100, 103; Groucho Marx 25, 30, 33; Harry Langdon 108–110; Lou Costello 135, 138, 142; Mary Pickford 99–100, 103; W. C. Fields 149, 154–155; *see also* financial struggles; wills and estates

C3 Entertainment Company 189, 190
Cade's County (television show) 95
Cantor, Eddie 2, 56, 78–83, *79*, *81*, 85–87, 90; *Caught Short* 82; *Yoo Hoo, Prosperity* 82
Cantor, Ida (Mrs. Eddie) *see* Tobias, Ida
Cantor, Janet *see* Gari, Janet Cantor
Cantor, Margie 80, 87
Capra, Frank 96, 108–110
The Captain Hates the Sea 118
carpentry and woodworking: Harry Langdon, Jr. 112–114; Peter Ford 91, 95, 96–97
Caruso, Enrico 65
Casablanca 91
Caught Short (Cantor) 82
celebrity clients: Harry Langdon, Jr. 110; Peter Ford 97
celebrity friends, memories of: Harry Langdon, Jr. 110–111; Janet Cantor Gari 85; Joan Benny 56–57; John Longenecker 201; Leatrice Gilbert Fountain 119, 126–127; Peter Ford 90; Romina Power 73; Sara Karloff 176; Suzanne Lloyd 180–181
Chaplin, Charles, Jr. 209
Chaplin, Charlie 9, 90, 99, 103, 105, 108, 149, 178, 183, 209–210
Chaplin, Michael: *I Couldn't Smoke Grass on My Father's Lawn* 9, 22–23
Chaplin, Norman Spencer 209–210
Chaplin, Sydney 209
charitable causes: Bud and Betty Abbott 146; Eddie Cantor 85, 87; Harold Lloyd 180; Marion Davies 209; Peter Ford 97–98
childless actresses 206–212
Christian, Linda 68, 71–73, *72*
Christmas celebrations, Hollywood style: Boris Karloff 176; Gary Crosby 168; Harold and Mildred Lloyd 181–183; Jack and Mary Benny 53–55; Lou and Anne Costello 133–135, 139–140, 142–143; Mario and Betty Lanza 67
Clark, Christy 190–191
Clark, Christy Lynn 190
Classic Images Online 105, 120, 132, 135
The Clinging Vine 117
Cocozza, Maria and Tony 69
Cohn, Harry 90
Cole, Nat King 94
Columbia Pictures 111, 118
comedy careers: Abbott and Costello 131–132, 144, 147; Harold Langdon 108–110; Harold Lloyd 178–180; Jerry Lewis 60; Larry Fine 185–186; The Marx Brothers 25, 28, 31, 37, 44–49; W. C. Fields 148–152
A Comedy of Terrors 174
competition between parent and child: Charlie and Michael Chaplin 22–23; Douglas Fairbanks, Sr. and Jr. 102–104; Judy Garland and Liza Minnelli 10–11

217

Index

Costello, Anne (Mrs. Lou) see Battlers, Anne
Costello, Carol 135, 137, 141
Costello, Chris 132–144, *134*, *136*, *143*, 147; *Lou's on First* 144
Costello, Lou 131–144, *134*, *136*
Costello, Lou, Jr. 133, 143
Costello, Paddy 137, 139, 141
Country Girl 157
Crane, Cheryl: *Detour: A Hollywood Tragedy* 20–21
Crawford, Christina: *Mommie Dearest* 1
Crawford, Joan 1, 104–105, 106, 117
The Creations 94
Criblecoblis, Otis 150
Crosby, Barbara 170
Crosby, Bing 14, 157–171, *158*, *165*, *169*, *170*
Crosby, Dennis 157, *158*, 163–164, *165*, 167, 170
Crosby, Dixie (Mrs. Bing) see Lee, Dixie
Crosby, Gary 157–171, *158*, *165*, *169*, *170*; *Going My Own Way* 158–170
Crosby, Harry 168
Crosby, Kathryn 167
Crosby, Lindsay 157, *158*, *165*, 170
Crosby, Mary 168
Crosby, Nathaniel 168
Crosby, Phillip 157, *158*, 160–161, 163, *165*, 167, 170
Crosby, Steve 167
Cukor, George 194, 201
Cult Movies Magazine 110–114
Curtis, Jamie Lee 5, 7, 16
Curtis, Kelly 6
Curtis, Tony 5
Cutler, Kris 190

Dance with Me Henry 132
Dark Star: The Untold Story of the Meteoric Rise and Fall of the Legendary John Gilbert (Gilbert) 115, 119–120
Davies, Marion 208–209
Davis, Bette 90
Davis, Mildred 178, 180, 184
The Dawn Patrol 104, 107
Dead End (stage play) 195–196
death of a child: Anne Miller and Reese Milner 211; Charlie and Mildred Chaplin 210; Lou and Anne Costello 133, 143–144; *see also* suicides, children of Hollywood
death of a parent 2; Arthur Marx 35–36; Chris Costello 133, 139, 140, 141; Damon Lanza 65, 68–70; David Niven, Jr. 12; Douglas Fairbanks, Jr. 104; Gary Crosby 166, 168; Harold Langdon, Jr. 110, 112; Joan Benny 58–59; John Clark Gable 72; Leatrice Gilbert Fountain 119, 123, 130; Maxine Marx 48; Peter Ford 98; Romina, Taryn and Tyrone Power, Jr. 71–73, 77; Ron Fields 152; Vickie Abbott 145; W. C. Fields, Jr. 152
deaths: Bud Abbott 132; Carole Lombard 210; Eddie Cantor 87; Harpo Marx 39; Ida Cantor 87; Irving Thalberg 31; Jean Harlow 209; Jeanette MacDonald 210; Lou Costello 132; Marilyn Monroe 207–208; Marion Davies 209; Mary Lee Fairbanks 106; Mary Pickford 100; Spencer Tracy 211; W. C. Fields 149; William Randolph Hearst 208–209; Winnie (Janet Cantor's nanny) 82
deaths of adult children 13–14, 66; Eddie Cantor 87; *see also* suicides, children of Hollywood
DeMille, Cecil B. 116, 128
Detour: A Hollywood Tragedy (Crane) 20–21
Dietrich, Marlene 16, 17, 105, 119, 123, *124*
DiMaggio, Joe 207
directing careers 15, 95; Harry

218

Index

Langdon 110; John Longenecker 202–204
disadvantages of being a Hollywood child: Cheryl Crane 21; Chris Costello 135; Gary Crosby 160; Michael Chaplin 22–23; Michael Douglas 7; Vickie Abbott 146
discipline 12, 17; Bing Crosby 157, 160–163, 166–167, 168; Boris Karloff 176; Eddie Cantor 82–83; Glenn Ford 91–92; Groucho Marx 32; Jack Benny 52, 54; Lou and Anne Costello 135, 137–138; W. C. Fields 152
divorce, effects on Hollywood children 2; Arthur Marx 31, 32–33; Douglas Fairbanks, Jr. 102; Leatrice Gilbert Fountain 118–119, 125; Peter Ford 91–92; Romina Power 73; Sara Karloff 174; Tarquin Olivier 12; see also stepparents
divorces, multiple: Ava Gardner 207; Charlie Chaplin 209; Douglas Fairbanks, Jr. 104–106; Gary Crosby 170; Ginger Rogers 207; Groucho Marx 33; John Gilbert 119; Marilyn Monroe 207; Myrna Loy 210
documentaries *see* biographical films
Dolfi, Bob 69–70; *Be My Love: A Celebration of Mario Lanza* 70
The Don Lamond Show (television show) 188
Don't Tell Dad: A Memoir (Fonda) 11
Dougherty, Jim 207
Douglas, Kirk 7, *8*, 16, 110
Douglas, Michael 7, *8*
Douglas Fairbanks, Jr. Presents (television show) 107
drug addictions: Diana Barrymore 13; Gary Lewis 62; Scott Newman 14
Duck Soup 27

Dukenfeld, William Claude *see* Fields, W. C.
Durante, Jimmy 48

Eagle Squadron 13
Eastwood, Clint 201
The Ed Sullivan Show (television show) 62
The Eddie Duchin Story 73
Edwards, Harry 108–110
entertaining at home: Boris Karloff 175; Douglas Fairbanks and Mary Pickford 100; Eddie Cantor 82; Eleanor Powell and Glenn Ford 90; Groucho Marx 25; Harold Lloyd 180–181; Harry Langdon 110–111; Jack Benny 56–57; Jamie Lee Curtis 16; John Gilbert and Leatrice Joy 126–127; Lou and Anne Costello 139; Mario Lanza 66; Ruth Hussey and Robert Longenecker 199, 200–201, 204; Tyrone Power 73; *see also* birthday parties, Hollywood style; Christmas celebrations, Hollywood style

Fairbanks, Anna Beth (Mrs. Douglas, Sr.) *see* Sully, Anna Beth
Fairbanks, Daphne 106
Fairbanks, Douglas, Jr. 99, 100–106, *101*, *106*; *A Hell of a War* 104; *The Salad Days* 104
Fairbanks, Douglas, Sr. 99–106, *101*
Fairbanks, Melissa 106
Fairbanks, Vera (Mrs. Douglas, Jr.) *see* Shelton, Vera
Fairbanks, Victoria 106
Faith of Our Children (television show) 91
family traditions: Eddie Cantor 81, 82–83; Groucho Marx 29; Harpo Marx 39–43; Mario Lanza 67–68; Ruth Hussey and Robert Longenecker 199–200; *see also* birthday parties, Hollywood style;

Index

Christmas celebrations, Hollywood style; Christmas celebrations in Hollywood
fans of the stars: Bing Crosby 164; Boris Karloff 173, 176; Eddie Cantor 87; Jack Benny 55–56; Leatrice Gilbert Fountain 127; Lou Costello 135; Mario Lanza 70
Farber, Stephen: *Hollywood Dynasties* 7, 14, 16
Farrelly Brothers 190
Fields, Harriet (Mrs. W. C., Sr.) *see* Hughes, Harriet
Fields, Ron 150, 150–155, 152, 156; *W. C. Fields: A Life on Film* 151; *W. C. Fields: By Himself* 151
Fields, W. C. 2, 148–156, *149*
Fields, W. C., Jr. 151–154
film lists: David Britten Prior 130; Douglas Fairbanks, Jr. 106–107; Jamie Lee Curtis 5; John Gilbert 116–119; Leatrice Gilbert Fountain 128; Leatrice Joy 116–117; Ruth Hussey 195–197
film set visits: Arthur Marx 27; Chris Costello 135, 137; Damon Lanza 66; Douglas Fairbanks, Jr. 102; Gary Crosby 164–165; Harry Langdon, Jr. 111; Joan Benny 57; Maxine Marx *45*; Romina Power 73, *74*; Sara Karloff 174, *175*; *see also* studio visits
financial struggles: Douglas Fairbanks, Jr. 102; Eddie Cantor 82; Eleanor Powell 92–93; *see also* poverty; wills and estates
Fine, John 190–191
Fine, John, Jr. 190–191
Fine, Larry 2, 185–193, *189, 191*
Fine, Mabel (Mrs. Larry) *see* Haney, Mabel
Fisher, Carrie 15
Fisher, Eddie 15
Fleming, Erin 33–36
Fleming, Susan 37–43
Flesh and the Devil 117

Folies-Bergere (stage show) 149
Fonda, Henry 11, 57, 110, 176, 201
Fonda, Peter: *Don't Tell Dad: A Memoir* 11
Fontaine, Joan 127
For the First Time 68, 69
Ford, Eleanor (Mrs. Glenn) *see* Powell, Eleanor
Ford, Glenn 88–93, *89*, 98
Ford, John 201
Ford, Peter 88–98, 89, 95; *Glenn Ford: A Life in Film* 98
Fountain, Christopher 129
Fountain, Gideon 129
Fountain, John Gilbert 129
Fountain, Leatrice Gilbert 115–116, 118–129, 124, *129*; *Dark Star: The Untold Story of the Meteoric Rise and Fall of the Legendary John Gilbert* 115, 119–120
Frankenstein 172–173, 174
The Freshman 183
funerals: Bing Crosby 168; Groucho Marx 35; Harpo Marx 48; John Gilbert 119; Mario Lanza 68; William Randolph Hearst 209; Winnie, Janet Cantor's nanny 82

Gable, Clark 72, 90, 127, 210
Gable, John Clark 72
gambling: Chico Marx 46; Lou Costello 139
Garbo, Greta 117–118, 122–123, 200, 210
Gardner, Ava 127, 128, 207
Gari, Amanda 84
Gari, Brian 79, 84–87, *86*
Gari, Janet Cantor 78, 79, *81, 86*
Garland, Judy 9–11, *10*, 84, 127
Garson, Greer 126, 197, 210
Gary Lewis and the Playboys 61–64, *63*
The Gazebo 93
Gilbert, John 115–123, 125, 127–128, 130, 210
Gilbert, Leatrice (daughter of

220

Index

John) *see* Fountain, Leatrice Gilbert
Gilbert, Leatrice (Mrs. John) *see* Joy, Leatrice
Gilda 88, 90
Gish, Dorothy 210
Gish, Lillian 117, 210
Glenn Ford: A Life in Film (Ford and Nickeus) 98
Glenn Ford and Eleanor Powell Library and Archives 97
Gobel, George 133
Goddard, Paulette 209
Going My Own Way (Crosby) 158–170
Going My Way 157, 164
Goldwyn, Samuel 78, 119
Gone with the Wind 91, 116, 117
Grady, Billy 195
grandchildren of Hollywood: Barrymore family 3; Boris Karloff 176; Douglas Fairbanks 106; Eddie Cantor 79, 84–87, *86*; Eleanor Powell and Glenn Ford 96–97; Harold Lloyd 2, *179*, 179–184, *182*, *183*; John Gilbert and Leatrice Joy 129; Larry Fine 2–3, 186–193, *192*; Ruth Hussey 202; Tyrone Power 75–76; W. C. Fields *150*, 150–152, 154, 156
Grant, Cary 61, 180–181, 194
Grayson, Kathryn 68, 70
The Great Caruso 65
The Great Gatsby 201, 204
Green, Marc: *Hollywood Dynasties* 7, 14, 16
Grey, Lita 209
Griffith, D. W. 99, 103, 149
"Guardian Angels" (song) 68
Gumm, Ethel 10–11
Gundersen, Lynda 94–98

Hal Roach Studios 111
Halloween 141
Haney, Mabel 185, 186, 189
Hannagan, Steve 210

Hargitay, Mariska 16
Harlow, Jean 126, 209
Harmon, Kelly 201
Harmon, Kristin 201, 202
Harmon, Mark 201
Harmon, Tom 201
Harpo Speaks! (Marx) 39–43
Harris, Mildred 210
Hart, Lorin 129
Hartford, Mary Lee Epling 106
Have Rocket Will Travel 86
Hayworth, Rita 88, 95
Healy, Ted 185; *see also* The Three Stooges
Hearst, William Randolph 208
A Hell of a War (Fairbanks) 104
Hepburn, Katharine 110, 117, 194, *195*, 201, 211–212
High Society 157
higher education: Gary Crosby 167; Peter Ford 92–94; Ruth Hussey 194
Hill, George Roy 201, 202–204
His Hour 119
hit songs: Bing Crosby 157; "Blue Ribbons" 93; Eddie Cantor 78; Gary Lewis 62, 64; Mario Lanza 65, 68; Romina Power and Al Bano 74
Hitchcock, Alfred 5–7, 132
Hogan, Ben 89
Holiday Inn 157
Hollywood Dynasties (Farber and Green) 7, 14, 16
"Hollywood mothers": Ethel Gumm 10–11; Judy Garland 11; "Mama Jean" Harlow 209
Hollywood neighbors: Eleanor Powell and Glenn Ford 90; Jack Benny 56; Ruth Hussey and Robert Longenecker 200–201
Hollywood or Bust 60
Hollywood "royalty": Clark Gable 72; Douglas Fairbanks and Mary Pickford 99–100; the Fondas 11; Harold Lloyd 180
home improvements: Glenn Ford

Index

91–92; Larry Fine 187–188; Peter Ford 96
homes: Boris Karloff 174; Chris Costello 137–139; Eddie Cantor 83–84; Eleanor Powell and Glenn Ford 89–93, 98; Groucho Marx 27, 29–31; Harold and Mildred Lloyd *179*, 180; Jamie Lee Curtis 16; Mario Lanza 66; Mary Pickford 99, 100, 105; Peter Ford 89–93, 95, 96, 98; Ruth Hussey 199–201, *200*
Hope, Bob 57, 157
Howard, Moe 185–188; *see also* The Three Stooges
Hughes, Harriet (Hattie) 149, 151–154
Hullabaloo (television show) 94
Hunter, Gladys 126
Hussey, Betty 194
Hussey, George R. 194
Hussey, Julia Agnes Corbett 194
Hussey, Robert 194
Hussey, Ruth 194–205, *195*, *198*, *203*
Huston, Angelica 16
Huston, John 15
Hutchinson, Thomas: *Niven's Hollywood* 12

I Couldn't Smoke the Grass on My Father's Lawn (Chaplin) 9, 22–23
"Ida, Sweet as Apple Cider" (song) 78
"If You Knew Susie" (song) 78
illnesses: Ava Gardner 207; Chico Marx 48; Dixie Lee Crosby 166; Eddie Cantor 87; Gary Crosby 170; Groucho Marx 33–35; Jean Harlow 209; Lou Costello 143; Mario Lanza 68, 69–70; Mary Pickford 105; Peter Ford 94–96; *see also* alcoholism in Hollywood; drug addictions
It's a Gift 152
The Jack Benny Show (radio and television) 50, 57, 110–114, 111–112
Jeeves 150
Johnson, Ruth 25–26, 28, 30–31, 32–33
Jolie, Angelina 16
Jolson, Al *20*, 57, 90
Jolson, Al, Jr. *20*
Jones, Jennifer 14
Jourdan, Louis 14
Joy, Leatrice 115, 116–117, 118, 120–128, *121*

Kane, Mahatma 150
Karloff, Boris 172–177, *173*, *175*
Karloff, Dorothy (Mrs. Boris) *see* Stine, Dorothy
Karloff, Sara *173*, 174–177, *175*
Karloff Enterprises 176
Karp, Betty 46
Kate Remembered (Berg) 211
Kaye, Danny 57, 58, 85
Keaton, Buster 108, 111, 112, 178
Keeler, Ruby *20*
Kid Boots 78
Kid Millions 78
Knox, Elyse 201

Ladd, Alan, Jr. 15
Lake, Arthur 208
Lake, Patricia 208
Lamond, Don (Eric's father) 188, 190, 191
Lamond, Don (Eric's son) 188, 191
Lamond, Eric 2–3, 186–193, *192*
Lamond, June 193
Lamond, Kurt 188, 191
Lamond, Phyllis Fine 190, 191
Lamour, Dorothy 157
Lancaster, Bill 15
Lancaster, Burt 15
Langdon, Harry, Jr. *109*, 109–114, *112*, *113*
Langdon, Harry, Sr. 108–113, *109*, *112*

Index

Langdon, Mabel (Mrs. Harry, Sr.) *see* Watts, Mabel
Lanza, Betty (Mrs. Mario) *see* Lyhan, Betty
Lanza, Colleen 66
Lanza, Damon 65–70, 67, 69; *Be My Love: A Celebration of Mario Lanza* 70
Lanza, Marc 66
Lanza, Mario 65–70, 67
The Lanza Legend 70
The Lark (stage play) 174
Laughton, Charles 73, 126
Law and Order: SVU (television show) 16
Lee, Dixie 157–162, 165–166
Lee, Rowland V. 120
legacies: Abbott and Costello 131–132, 144, 146–147; Bing Crosby 170; Boris Karloff 176–177; Harold Lloyd 178, 184; Harry Langdon 114; John Gilbert 116, 130; Larry Fine 185, 188, 190–193; Ruth Hussey 204–205; W. C. Fields 150, 155–156
Leigh, Janet 5–7
Leigh, Vivien 12, 73
Lewis, Gary 60–64, *61*, *63*
Lewis, Jerry 60–63, *61*; *see also* Martin and Lewis
Lewis, Patti (Mrs. Jerry) *see* Palmer, Patti
Life with Groucho (Marx) 26–33, 35
Livingstone, Mary 50–52, 54, 55, 57, 58
Lloyd, Harold 2, 108, 178–184, *179*, *182*, *184*
Lloyd, Mildred (Mrs. Harold) *see* Davis, Mildred
Lloyd, Suzanne 2, *179*, 179–184, *182*, *183*
Lombard, Carole 210
Long Pants 110
Longenecker, John 196, 197, 199–204, *203*
Longenecker, Mary 202, *203*, 204

Longenecker, Robert 197–200, *198*, 202–204, *203*
Longenecker, Robert, Jr. (Rob) 202, *203*
Lou's on First (Costello) 144
Loy, Myrna 119, 210
Luft, Joey *10*
Luft, Lorna *10*, 10–11
Lugosi, Bela 132, 172
Lyhan, Betty 65–69

MacDonald, Jeanette 210
Main, Marjorie 206
manners 16, 17; Bing Crosby's sons 161; Leatrice Gilbert Fountain 126; Peter Ford 92
Mansfield, Jayne 16
Manslaughter 116
Marcus Welby, M.D. (television show) 202
The Mark of Zorro 100
Markle, John Fifield 14
marriages, successful: Bud and Betty Abbott 145–147; Harold and Mildred Lloyd 184; Jeanette MacDonald and Gene Raymond 210; Lou and Anne Costello 139; Ruth Hussey and Robert Longenecker 202, 204–205
marriages, unsuccessful: Ann Miller and Reese Milner 211; Spencer Tracy 211; W. C. and Harriet Fields 149, 151–154; William Randolph Hearst 208; *see also* divorce, effects on children; divorces, multiple
Martin, Dean 11, 60
Martin, Dean, Jr. 11
Martin and Lewis 60, 201
Marx, Alex 39–43, *42*
Marx, Arthur 11, 15, 26–35, *27*, *34*; *Life with Groucho* 26–33, 35; *Son of Groucho* 11, 26–33, 35
Marx, Betty (Mrs. Chico) *see* Karp, Betty
Marx, Billy 39–40, *42*
Marx, Chico 25, 26, 28, 30, 44–

223

Index

49, 45; *see also* The Marx Brothers
Marx, Groucho 11, 15, 25–36, *26, 27, 34,* 46–47, 86; *see also* The Marx Brothers
Marx, Gummo 25, 30, 35; *see also* The Marx Brothers
Marx, Harpo 25, *26,* 30, 37–43, *38,* 46, 48, 68; *Harpo Speaks!* 39–43; *see also* The Marx Brothers
Marx, Jimmy 39–43, *42*
Marx, Julius H. *see* Marx, Groucho
Marx, Maxine 44, *45, 48*
Marx, Melinda 27, 33
Marx, Minnie (daughter of Groucho Marx) 39–43, *42*
Marx, Minnie (mother of The Marx Brothers) 44
Marx, Miriam 26–27, 31–33
Marx, Ruth (Mrs. Groucho) *see* Johnson, Ruth
Marx, Steve 33
Marx, Susan (Mrs. Harpo) *see* Fleming, Susan
Marx, Zeppo 25, 30, 35; *see also* The Marx Brothers
The Marx Brothers 35, 37, 44–49; as family men 25–26, *27,* 30–31, *34,* 37–43, *45,* 48; as performers 11, *26,* 28, 35, 37, *38,* 44–49
Mason, James 90
Massey, Raymond 175
Mayer, Louis B. 31, 117–118
McCambridge, Mercedes 14
McCartney, Paul 181
McGrew, Charles 209
Member of the Wedding (stage play) 96
Menage all'italiana 74
The Mephisto Waltz 95
Merman, Ethel 14
The Merry Widow 117, 119
Merv Griffin Entertainment 151
Metro Goldwyn Mayer (MGM): Eleanor Powell 88; John Gilbert 117–118; Leatrice Gilbert Fountain 115–116, 127, 128; Leatrice Joy 117; Mario Lanza 65; Marx Brothers 31, 44; Ruth Hussey 194–197; *Wizard of Oz* 78–79, 150
military service: Arthur Marx 33; Douglas Fairbanks, Jr. 104; Gary Lewis 62; John Fine, Jr. 191; Leatrice Gilbert Fountain 128; W. C. Fields, Jr. 154
Milland, Ray 57, 176, 199
Miller, Ann 211
Miller, Arthur 207
Miller, Phyllis 191
Milner, Reese 211
Minardos, Debbie Ann 72
Minnelli, Liza *9,* 9–11, *10*
Miranda, Carmen 58, 210
Mommie Dearest (Crawford) 1
Monroe, Marilyn 181, 207; death of 35, 207–208
Montgomery, Elizabeth 16
Montgomery, George 57, 94
Montgomery, Robert 16, 57
Moore, Colleen 180
Morgan, Frank 150
The Mummy 173, 174
museums 70, 97
musical careers, first generation: Bing Crosby 157, 159–160; Chico Marx 46; Eddie Cantor 78–79; Eleanor Powell 92; Harpo Marx 37; Mario Lanza 65–70
musical careers, second generation: Chris Costello 138, 143; Gary Lewis 61–64; Janet Cantor Gari 83–84, *84;* Leatrice Gilbert Fountain 129; Peter Ford 93–94; Romina Power 73–74
musical careers, third generation 85, 87
My Darling Daughter's Anniversary (television movie) 202
My Father: Laurence Olivier (Olivier) 12
My Father: My Son (Robinson) 13

Index

My Friend Irma 60
My Little Chickadee 155
Mysteries and Scandals (television show) 70
mystery children: daughter of Marilyn Monroe 207; daughter of Marion Davies 208–209; daughters of Lionel Barrymore and Doris Rankin 3–4

names: Bing Crosby 157; Chico Marx 44; Gary Lewis 61; Harpo Marx 37; Leatrice Gilbert Fountain 115; Romina Power 72; Ruth Hussey 194; W. C. Fields 148, 150
National Velvet 116
neglect *see* parental neglect
neighbors *see* Hollywood neighbors
Nelson, Kristin Harmon 201, 202
Nelson, Rick 201
The New Perry Mason (television show) 95
Newman, Paul 14, 15, 201, 204
Newman, Scott 14
Newman, Susan 15
Nickens, Christopher: *Glenn Ford: A Life in Film* 98
Ninth Street West (television show) 94
Niven, David 12
Niven, David, Jr. 12, 15
Niven, Primula 12
Niven's Hollywood (Hutchinson) 12
"normalcy" in Hollywood 1–2, 11, 16, 158–160
Norris, S. Edward 210
Nutty Professor 60

Of Human Hearts 116, 128
Olivier, Laurence 12, 73
Olivier, Tarquin: *My Father: Laurence Olivier* 12
Oscars *see* Academy Awards
Our Gang Comedy troupe 126
Out of the Frying Pan (stage show) 111

Palmer, Patti 61
Paramount Studios 57; Bing Crosby 164; Leatrice Joy 116; Ron Fields 151; Ruth Hussey 197, 199; W. C. Fields 150
parental discipline *see* discipline; physical abuse, victims of
parental neglect, victims of: Cheryl Crane 20–21; Diana Barrymore 13; Leatrice Gilbert Fountain 118, 125; Peter Fonda 11
Parish, James Robert: *The Slapstick Queens* 206
Parkinson, Robert 70
Parsons, Louella 164
parties *see* entertaining at home
Peck, Gregory 14, *15*, 176
Peck, Greta *15*
Peck, Jonathon *15*
Peck, Stephen *15*
Peter and Gordon 94
Peter Pan (stage play) 174
The Philadelphia Story 194, 195, 197
photographs and photography 110, 114, 127
physical abuse, victims of: Ann Miller 211; Christina Crawford 1; Gary Crosby 160–163, 166–167; W. C. Fields 148
Pickford, Mary 90, 99–100, 102, 103, 105, 116, 180
Pierce, Jack 172, 175
Pocketful of Miracles 96
Pool Sharks 149
Poppy (stage show) 149
Potter, H. C. 200
poverty: Eddie Cantor 80; John Gilbert 120; W. C. Fields 148–149; *see also* financial struggles
Powell, Eleanor 88–93, *89*, 98
Power, Debbie Ann *see* Minardos, Debbie Ann
Power, Linda (Mrs. Tyrone) *see* Christian, Linda
Power, Romina 71–77, *72*, *74*, *75*, *76*

225

Index

Power, Taryn 71, 73, *75*
Power, Tyrone 12, 68, 71–73, *72, 74, 75,* 76–77
Power, Tyrone, Jr. 71, 72, 77
Presley, Elvis, death of 35
Princess of the Dark 116
Prior, David Britten 130
privileges *see* advantages of being a Hollywood child
production careers 15, 16, 26, 70, 87, 202; Douglas Fairbanks, Jr. 104; Eric Lamond 188; John Longenecker 202; Ron Fields 151
The Proud and the Damned 94, 95
Psycho 5–7
publicity, use of children for 16–17, 159; Judy Garland 9–10; Lana Turner 21; Peter Ford 90, 91

quips and quotes: Ava Gardner 207; Bing Crosby 157; Boris Karloff 172; Bud Abbot 131; Chico Marx 44; Douglas Fairbanks, Jr. 99, 103, 105; Eddie Cantor 78, 85; George Gobel 133; Glenn Ford 88; Groucho Marx 25, 33, 44; Harold Lloyd 178; Harpo Marx 37; Harry Langdon 108; Jack Benny 50, 52; Jerry Lewis 60, 62; John Gilbert 115; Katharine Hepburn 211; Larry Fine 185; Lou Costello 131, 139, 143; Mario Lanza 65; Marjorie Main 206; Ruth Hussey as Elizabeth Imbrie 194; Tyrone Power 71; W. C. Fields 148, 155–156

radio programs: Fred Allen 111–112; *Jack Benny Show* 50, 111–112; Lou Costello 143, 144; Peter Ford 97
Radko, Christopher 183
Rankin, Doris 3
The Raven 174
Raymond, Gene 210
Raymonds, Harold 206–207

Redford, Robert 201, 204
religion: Chris Costello 142; Eleanor Powell 91, 96; Jack Benny 54–55; Leatrice Joy 122, 126; Marion Davies 208; Spencer Tracy 211; Tyrone Power 73; W. C. Fields 154, 155
The Resurrection of Broncho Billy 202
Reynolds, Debbie 15, 93
Ringling Brothers Circus 146
Riva, J. Michael 16
Riva, Maria *17*, 123, *124*
The Road to Singapore 157
Robert Longenecker Talent Agency 199
Robin Hood 100, 102
Robinson, Edward G. 13
Robinson, Edward G., Jr.: *My Father: My Son* 13
Rogers, Charles "Buddy" 100, 110
Rogers, Ginger 210
Romero, Cesar 73, 94
Rooney, Mickey 127, 207
Rose, David 133
Rosson, Harold 209
rumors 69–70
Russell, Leon 62

Safety Last! 180
The Salad Days (Fairbanks) 104
Sally of the Sawdust 149
school days: Chris Costello 135, 138, 140; Gary Crosby 160–164; Janet Cantor Gari 83; Leatrice Gilbert Fountain 126; Peter Ford 93; *see also* boarding school days
Segura, Pancho 89
Selznick, David 14, 118
servants in Hollywood families: Anne Costello 138; Bing Crosby's chauffeurs 159, 160; Eleanor Powell's "Frank" the gardener 92; Hollywood norms 9, 13, 17, 27; Janet Cantor's "Winnie" 81–82;

Index

Joan Benny's "Bens" 53; Leatrice Gilbert Fountain's "Miss Gladys" 126; Leatrice Gilbert Fountain's rotating nurses 125; Mario Lanza's household 66; Mary Livingstone 57
The Seven Hills of Rome 66
Shaw, Artie 207
Shaw, Robert 201
Sheridan, Ann 57, 210
shopping: Anne Costello 139–140; Harold Lloyd 183; Leatrice Gilbert Fountain *124*; Lou Costello 142
Shore, Dinah 57, 86
silent films: Douglas Fairbanks, Jr. 102; Douglas Fairbanks, Sr. 99, 103; Eddie Cantor 78, 82; Harold Lloyd 178–180; John Gilbert and Leatrice Joy 116–117, 127
"Silent Night" (song) 168
Sinatra, Frank 57, 207
Skelton, Red 110
The Slapstick Queens (Parish) 206
Smith, Sir Aubrey 176
Smith, Betty 144–147, *145*
Solomon and Sheba 71
Some Like It Hot 141
Son of Frankenstein 174
Son of Groucho (Marx) 11, 26–33, 35
songs *see* hit songs
stage plays: *Arsenic and Old Lace* 175; *Banjo Eyes* 85; *Dead End* 195–196; *The Lark* 174; *Let's Face It!* 58; *Out of the Frying Pan* 111; *Peter Pan* 174; *State of the Union* 199; Tyrone Power 76
Stanwyck, Barbara 57, 90
Star Babies (Strait) 132
State of the Union (stage play) 199
Steiner, Max 91
Stella Dallas 102, 106
stepparents: Elizabeth Taylor 21; Marlene Dietrich 123; Mary Pickford 105; Paulette Goddard 209; Vivien Leigh 12
Stewart, Donald Ogden 194
Stewart, Jimmy 56, 57, 116, 128, 176, 194, *195*, 201
Stine, Dorothy 173–174
The Sting 202, 204
"Storia di Due Innamorati" (song) 74
"Story of Two Lovers" (song) 74
storytelling: Groucho Marx 29; Harpo and Susan Marx 39–43; Mario Lanza 68
Strait, Raymond: *Star Babies* 132
The Strong Man 110
studio visits 57, 188; *see also* film set visits
suicides 206–207, 207–208
suicides, children of Hollywood 14–15, 170
Sullivan, Ed 62
Sully, Anna Beth 102
Sunday Nights at Seven (Benny) 50–59
Swanson, Gloria 116, 183
swimming: Chris Costello 133, 142; Groucho Marx 31; Janet Cantor Gari 86; Joan Benny 55; Peter Ford 89

Taylor, Elizabeth 21, *22*
television 62, 83, 96, 112, 201–202; Bud and Lou 143–144; *Faith of Our Children* 91; Peter Ford 93–94; Ruth Hussey 201–202; The Three Stooges 185, 188–190
Television Corporation of America 142
The Ten Commandments 117, 128
Texaco Star Theater (radio show) 111
Thalberg, Irving 31, 44
That Midnight Kiss 65
The Thief of Baghdad 100, 102
Three Men on a Horse (stage show) 85

Index

The Three Musketeers 100
The Three Stooges: as family men 3, 186–190, *192*, 193; as performers 86, 185, 186, 190, *192*
The Three Stooges 75th Year Anniversary Special (television show) 190
Tierney, Gene 73
Tobias, Ida 78, 80–82, 87
Too Much, Too Soon (Barrymore) 13
Tracy, Spencer 127, 196, 211
Trading Places 16
Tramp, Tramp, Tramp 110
travel: Eddie Cantor 80, 83; Groucho Marx 30–31; Harold Lloyd 180; Jack Benny 58
The Treasure of the Sierra Madre 15, 91
Trevor, Claire 73
Tripplehorn, Jean 63
Tripplehorn, Tom 62, 63
Tucker, Sophie 90
Turner, Lana 20, 21
20th Century–Fox Studios 58, 71, 95

The Uninvited 199
United Artists 99–100, 103
Universal Studios 84, 135, 144, 202, 204
"The Unknown Marx Brothers," 44–48

vaudeville: Eddie Cantor 78–80; Harry Langdon 108, 113; Larry Fine 185; W. C. Fields 149
Velez, Lupe 206–207
Voight, Jon 16

W. C. Fields: A Life on Film (Fields) 151
W. C. Fields: By Himself (Fields) 151
W. C. Fields: Straight Up (documentary film) 151
Wagner, Natasha Gregson *18*
Wagner, Robert *18*

Wagner, Walter 102–103, 105; *You Must Remember This* 102–105
Warner Bros. Studios 57, 108, 110, 190
Watts, Mabel *109*, 112–114
Wayne, John 15
Wayne, Michael 15
websites: Mario Lanza 70; Ruth Hussey 202
weddings: Greta Garbo and Tyrone Power 118; Ida Tobias and Eddie Cantor 80; Jeanette MacDonald and Gene Raymond 210; Linda Christian and Tyrone Power 72; Linda Gunderson and Peter Ford 95; Patricia and Arthur Lake 208; Ruth Hussey and Robert Longenecker 197, *198*
Weissmuller, Johnny 89
Welles, Orson 73
Wellman, William 201
West, Mae 155, 210
Westmore, Wally 183
Wheeler, Don 145–147
Wheeler, Vickie Abbott 144–147, *145*
White Christmas 157
"White Christmas" (song) 157, 168
Whoopee 82
Whoopee (stage show) 80, 82
Wilber and the Baby Factory 96
Wilding, Christopher *22*
Wilding, Michael, Jr. *22*
Williams, Sybil 21
wills and estates: Bing Crosby 170–171; Gladys Lloyd Robinson 13; Groucho Marx 36; John Gilbert 123; Lou Costello 142; William Randolph Hearst 208–209
Wings 181
Winnie (nanny) 81–82
Witness for the Prosecution 71
The Wizard of Oz 78–79, 150
Wood, Natalie *18*
writing careers 15, 26; Chris

Index

Costello 144; David Britten Prior 130; Douglas Fairbanks, Jr. 104, 115; Leatrice Gilbert Fountain 115, 129; Peter Ford 97; Ron Fields 151
Wynn, Keenan 15, 57
Wynn, Tracy 15

Yoo Hoo, Prosperity (Cantor) 82
You Must Remember This (Wagner) 102–105
Young, Robert 196, 202

Ziegfeld Follies (stage show) 78, 80, 149

www.ingramcontent.com/pod-product-compliance
Ingram Content Group UK Ltd.
Pitfield, Milton Keynes, MK11 3LW, UK
UKHW041945140426
5217IPUK00014B/657